Apocalypse Later
Books by Hal C F Astell

<u>Cinematic Hell</u>
Huh? An A-Z of Why Classic American Bad Movies Were Made

<u>Filmography Series</u>
Velvet Glove Cast in Iron: The Films of Tura Satana

<u>Festival Series</u>
The International Horror & Sci-Fi Film Festival 2012

Apocalypse Later
Cinematic Hell

Huh?

An A-Z of Why Classic American Bad Movies Were Made

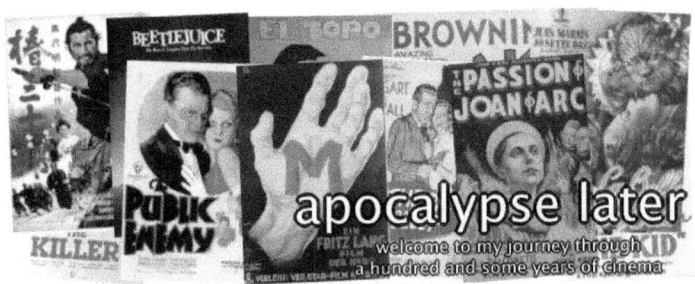

Apocalypse Later Press
Phoenix, AZ

Apocalypse Later Cinematic Hell Series
Huh? An A-Z of Why Classic American Bad Movies Were Made

ISBN-10: 0989461300
ISBN-13: 978-0-9894613-0-6
Apocalypse Later Press catalogue number: ALP001

Reviews by Hal C F Astell

These reviews originally appeared, albeit
in evolutionary form, at Apocalypse Later
http://www.apocalypselaterfilm.com

They evolved out of a series of reviews
I wrote for Cinema Head Cheese
http://cinemaheadcheese.blogspot.com

Front cover art by Eric Schock
http://www.evilrobo.com

Published through CreateSpace
https://www.createspace.com

Typeset in Gentium
http://scripts.sil.org/FontDownloadsGentium

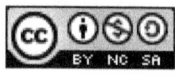

Dedication

This book is dedicated to three ladies and three gentlemen, all of whom had a hand in its evolution, however inadvertently.

Pam Astell, you've put up with me longer than anyone else and, in doing so, taught me to read, to write and to think.

Tracy Barnett, you showed me films that I had no excuse for not having seen before and, in doing so, started me on the road to what would become Apocalypse Later and, now, this book.

Dee Astell, if there was anything worse than suffering through each of these pictures (and more besides) with me, sometimes more than once, it was surely suffering through me figuring out what to do with this project as well.

That heartfelt dedication of yours deserves a heartfelt dedication of mine. This first book has been a long time in the making and it isn't the title with which I expected to start out, but it really doesn't matter which it turned out to be; it's book number one and it was always going to be for the three of you.

And because it turned out to be this one, it's also dedicated to the folk at Cinema Head Cheese. David C Hayes, Jeff Dolniak and Kevin Moyers, you graciously allowed me to pollute your site with reviews of many of the worst movies ever made and never once complained that they didn't star yourselves. Maybe in the sequels...

Acknowledgements

No book is ever created by one person, regardless of whose name is on the cover. Many other people deserve credit, along with my undying gratitude and appreciation for their part in bringing this one to print. Thank you, one and all!

Most obviously, thanks to Dee Astell, my long suffering better half. She watched everything reviewed here with me, sometimes more than once. Reread the contents page and shiver at that thought! Think about all the other films that didn't make into the eventual A-Z! And it gets worse; after managing to put them out of her mind, I then forced her through them once again by reading my reviews aloud to her. That helped me to find odd errors and her to point out where I got the wrong end of the stick. She even got to endure this particular project in a growing number of incarnations until I finally figured out how to do it right. You are a saint.

I write in OpenOffice because I like free software (free as in both beer and speech), so naturally I laid out this book in OpenOffice too. I found that I didn't know as much as I thought I did on that front, so thanks to Alexandra Rowland, who doesn't know me from Adam but who wrote a thoroughly informative blog entry on the subject that you should read too if you find yourself in the same situation. She taught me a lot and saved me a lot of time. That blog entry is:

```
http://alexandrarowland.wordpress.com/2012/06/21/
formatting-pod-novels-with-openoffice-in-linux/
```

Thanks to Bob Nelson, emperor extraordinary of the Brick Cave Publishing empire who talked me through every other technical aspect of expanding Apocalypse Later from blog to print.

Thanks to Eric Schock of Evil Robo Productions for his awesome cover, especially on such short notice.

Finally, special thanks to the titans of terror, the sultans of sleaze, the unholy trinity of Admiral Jeff Dolniakbar, demonic teddy bear David C (for Cuddly) Hayes and Kevin Moyers (who honestly doesn't hate everything), for allowing, even encouraging, my scribbles to help build Cinema Head Cheese. It's good to know that far below your gleaming spires lies a dank dungeon with my name scrawled on its wall in blood.

Contents

Introduction

Like many of the films reviewed in this book, *Huh?* encountered a fundamental reevaluation partway through. It wasn't as emphatic as the reevaluation Ray Dennis Steckler gave *Rat Pfink a Boo Boo* at the halfway mark, but it was important nonetheless.

Originally this was an online review project that aimed at tearing apart the sort of classic bad movies which are frequently ranked amongst the worst of all time. I was doing my part to build a website called Cinema Head Cheese by contributing a new review every week throughout 2010 for a series I called Cinematic Hell, as an obvious balance to the Cinematic Heaven project I was also working through at the time, for which I aimed to watch and review every movie in the IMDb Top 250 list. Cinematic Hell and its choice of material seemed appropriate for the venue.

I set few boundaries outside the inherent lack of quality these films have, covering a wide variety of films across multiple decades and from multiple countries. I hadn't planned out the list of films entirely to begin with, but I knew that I wanted the end product to be a representative guide to bad pictures.

For instance, while American cinema has given us many awful movies, I knew that I had to include *The Crippled Masters*, which is a Taiwanese martial arts movie starring a man with no arms and a man with no legs; the surreal Mexican Christmas story, *Santa Claus*, and the German exploitation flick called *The Horrors of Spider Island*, which, for some reason that still escapes me, remains the most visited review of all time at Apocalypse Later by a factor of two.

I also knew that I wanted to span the decades. I had to include the 1934 Dwain Esper picture, *Maniac*, because it was so far ahead of its time as a movie that's "so bad, it's good". I also had to include the Brucesploitation movie, *Fist of Fear, Touch of Death*, because it's a definitively awful work containing so much that's fundamentally wrong that I could easily ride through a long review. These two became my bookends in time at Cinema Head Cheese; I conjured everything else up from the years in between.

That effective cut-off date of 1980 to ensure a focus on classic material was spawned from another idea: for me to stop after fifty reviews and then follow up in 2011 with a similar project that covered the modern equivalent to these classic awful pictures. Maybe that will still happen one day, but I cringe at the thought of having to watch films like *From Justin to Kelly*, *Gigli* or *Norbit*. I may have seen *The Room* at least half a dozen times on the big screen, but I don't ever want to see *Twilight* again. If this sequel series ever happens, it'll be confirmation that I'm a masochist.

At least classic bad movies often have a fun element. However bad *Plan 9 from Outer Space* is, and it really is as bad as it's been made out, it's also a great deal of fun. I'd rather watch it twice than sit through a *Transformers* film once and that's the truth. I have a soft spot for movies like *Jesse James Meets Frankenstein's Daughter*, *The Wild World of Batwoman* or *The Terror of Tiny Town*. I have difficulty believing that there's anyone who can't raise a chuckle from an all midget western.

I deliberately kicked off the project with three particular movies, to provide a solid grounding before I delved deeper into the world of Cinematic Hell.

First up was *The Beast of Yucca Flats*, partly because it was the worst film I'd ever seen at that point and partly because my hosts at Cinema Head Cheese had made a long overdue sequel, *Return to Yucca Flats: Desert Man Beast*, with a glorious tagline: "30 Corpses... 1 Man Beast... 0 Plot."

I followed that with *Plan 9 from Outer Space*, because it was the original "worst movie of all time," awarded that title by Michael and Harry Medved in their iconic book, *The Golden Turkey Awards*. I knew the film well and knew that I could both tear it apart and talk it up, because it deserves better than it's been given.

That became especially apparent with week three's review, of *Manos: The Hands of Fate*, an obscure young pretender to the throne that *Plan 9 from Outer Space* had held so long. After being discovered by the folks behind *Mystery Science Theater 3000*, it has slowly grown in influence to become the new king of bad movies. When I asked Elvira, Mistress of the Dark at Phoenix Comicon which she felt was the worst movie of all time, this is the one she chose.

It really wasn't much of a stretch to tear these films apart, but I had fun developing a humorous writing voice in the process. I read all my reviews aloud to my better half anyway as a sort of sadistic version of proofreading, so I knew that they were funny from the reactions I got and I feel that they got better over time.

However, they also got more serious. I always tried to include some serious historical value along with the riffing, but gradually the jokes fell away and the serious side took over. Perhaps this was the point at which I ceased to tear these films apart and began to ask myself why anyone ever thought it was a good idea to make the things in the first place. As the weeks and the reviews ran on and a variety of quirky reasons why started to trickle out, they gradually provided the reason why this project needed to change, to become what you're holding in your hands right now.

It took three years to get from that growing realisation that there was a story in the why of it all to finishing up this book. In between, I went back and watched many of these films again. I researched a lot more diligently, not only the titles I knew would make it into the finished book, like *The Creeping Terror* and *They Saved Hitler's Brain*, but also other films that would fit the scope. I ended up writing 43 Cinematic Hell reviews for Cinema Head Cheese but 18 of them ended up in this book, often in vastly revised form. The other 8 were entirely new, brought in during the research phase.

I'm sure that many of you, when watching films like these, had the same reaction I did. "Huh?" you exclaimed at something you'd seen, as your brain asked why. Why were these films made? Why did someone start them and, perhaps even more importantly, why did someone finish them?

I discovered a lot of answers to these questions as I wrote this book. Hopefully, by the time you've made it through my carefully selected alphabet of why classic American bad movies were made, traumatised but intact, you'll have discovered some of them too.

And when you hear someone else exclaim, "Huh?" you'll know to give them a copy of this book, so that they can join in the discovery.

Hal C F Astell
Apocalypse Later
2013

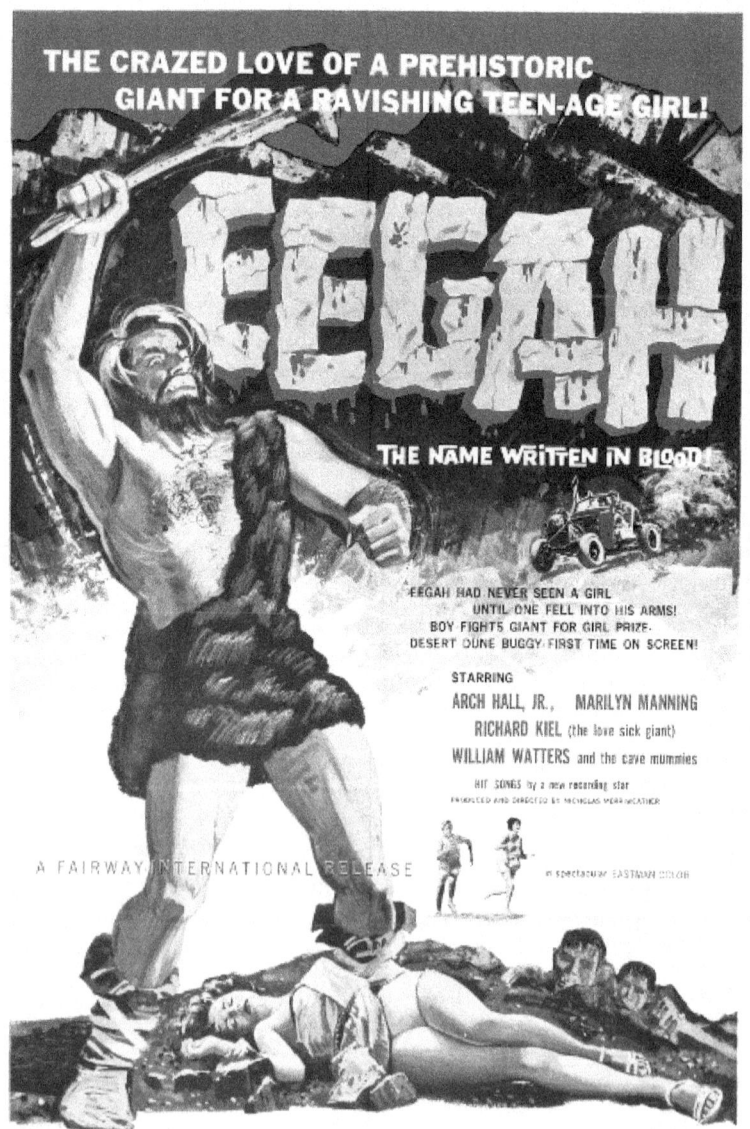

A is for Ambition
Eegah (1962)

Director: Nicholas Merriwether
Writer: Bob Wehling
Stars: Arch Hall Jr, Marilyn Manning and Richard Kiel

There are films that live on in legend because whatever else they might be, they're also prominent embarrassments in the career of someone eminently recognisable. Usually they're either at the very beginning or the very end of careers, because it's at those points when actors tend to be willing to take whatever roles they can get.

Fifteen years before he put on steel teeth to tussle with James Bond in *The Spy Who Loves Me*, Richard Kiel was working as a night club bouncer, with a sprinkling of scattered rôles behind him. He'd played a small part in a small sci-fi movie, *The Phantom Planet*, a bigger one in *The Phantom*, the unrelated pilot for a television series that didn't happen, and a few odd roles on a few odd TV shows. So, when Arch Hall Sr met this 7'2" giant and immediately thought of shooting a picture with him as an 'ageless prehistoric caveman', he was hardly going to say no? Robert Vaughn had just gone from *Teen Age Caveman* to *The Magnificent Seven* in a mere two years, after all.

While this is a Richard Kiel movie today, back in 1962 it was all about Arch Hall Sr and his son, Arch Hall Jr, whom he was dead set on making a star. Junior had turned eighteen in 1961 and he showed talent as a singer and guitarist. Senior had experience in the movie industry, having been a stuntman in the thirties and a bit part actor in westerns in the forties, so it seemed like a natural step to form his own production company, Fairway Productions, and use it as a means to thrust his son into superstardom. If it worked for Elvis Presley, it would work for Arch Hall Jr, right? I won't fault the logic but, six pictures later, Junior gave it all up as a bad job and became an airline pilot.

The Choppers, Arch Hall Jr vehicle number one, was a juvenile delinquency movie which tasked him with leading a gang, which in 1961 meant that he sang rock 'n' roll and stripped cars. It must have had promise as only a year later, Senior put *Eegah* into production with what seems like everyone he knew.

How's this for keeping it in the family? The leading man was his son and the leading lady was his secretary, Marilyn Manning. The title character was 7'2" of nobody that he discovered bouncing at a nightclub. He played the leading lady's father himself, under the pseudonym of William Watters, not the only one he used here as he also wrote, produced and directed as Nicholas Merriwether. Near the end of the film, Addalyn Pollitt shows up to play the wife of a drunkard; off set, she was Senior's wife and Junior's mother.

As his family obviously wasn't big enough to fill every role, he also gave Ray Dennis Steckler an early shot at being an assistant cameraman. Steckler had worked on Timothy Carey's cult hit, *The World's Greatest Sinner*, so Hall put him to work here and elevated him to director later in 1962 for Arch Hall Jr vehicle number three, the surprisingly decent *Wild Guitar*.

The story is a little bizarre. For a while we follow Roxy Miller, who does all the everyday stuff that teenage girls did in 1962: Roxy walks out of a fashion store, Roxy gets into her sports car, Roxy stops at the gas station. We're supposed to feel the magnetism of the leading lady but we don't, so the attendant, Tommy Nelson, has to point out to his customer, "That's my girl; her father's Robert I Miller." You know, because the most important thing about your cute sixteen year old girlfriend is who her father is.

I never managed to figure out just where Tommy fits into the social scale, given that he works as a gas station attendant but is able to take the entire film off from work on a whim. Also, if this is a part time job to get him through college, he's doing pretty well at it, given that he's saved up enough to buy a pretty cool car and a neat dune buggy by act three. Anyway, the story kicks in when Roxy drives her car into that 7'2" caveman.

No, I'm not kidding. You weren't expecting subtlety from a movie called *Eegah*, were you? You should have realised what you were getting into when you saw the opening credits: the title of the film is etched on a rock with blood dripping from the last two letters, as this film is apparently so painful it makes rocks bleed. The rest are painted on wizened corpses stuck into the ground like scarecrows for the camera to fail to focus on. Rocks would have been cheaper.

Anyway, Bob Wehling, who turned Hall's story into a screenplay, obviously couldn't figure out how to build a back story from the material provided, so he chose instead to have the plot stand right there in the middle of the road, complete with loincloth, huge club and beard, not to mention the dead deer draped over its shoulder, just waiting for our heroine to drive into it. This prehistoric giant threatens and mutters but does little else, while poor Roxy faints dead away.

He does get to look longingly on her delectable form, but he's interrupted by Tommy driving up. "Roxy, it's me, Carl," he says. "Oh Tommy!" she replies, waking up. Perhaps Carl is a name he adopts when he hangs out with Roxy's dad because it's more appropriate for the Ocotillo Lodge than plain old Tommy, but we're never given an explanation. We just get explanations for why there was a giant caveman on the road. "There were giants," says Roxy. "The Bible says so."

This odd introduction of Biblical quotation into a giant caveman movie, right down to the chapter and verse, may be what forces everyone to become a stereotype. Tommy wants to head out into the desert with a flashlight because he's a big man happy to take on a prehistoric giant with a club. Roxy goes mushy and doe eyed as she has the funniest feeling he wouldn't hurt her; she thought he was kinda cute. I hope this was just to rile up Tommy. And so does he. Oh boy, so does he.

Mr Miller leads the way. When he finds a huge footprint in the desert the next day, he pulls his safari suit out of mothballs and has himself flown up to Shadow Mountain by helicopter. Sorry, Tommy, helicopters trump dune buggies, and you'll have to work a lot more weeks at the gas station for one of those. At least Daddy doesn't have a rifle like the trigger happy cop in *The Beast of Yucca Flats*, but he probably couldn't use one anyway because he can't even use a camera. Just as he tries to focus his box brownie on the remnants of a fire, Eegah the caveman looms up in front of him, and he proves that the clothes don't make the man by promptly backing up a step, falling over his bag and breaking his collarbone. Tommy and Roxy have to head out in the dune buggy to save him, whizzing around the sand dunes for a while having a great time until they remember why they're there. That sort of thing happens a lot in this picture.

You may be excused at this point for forgetting that this film is here to showcase the talents of Arch Hall Jr. He did have surprising ability as an actor, as you'll discover with 1964's *The Sadist*, Arch Hall Jr vehicle number four, a tight thriller based on the spree killings of Charles Starkweather. In that movie he gives a searing performance which to hindsight is unfortunately overshadowed by utter dreck like this. Here, he's annoyingly chipper and whiny as a character and painfully soporific as a performer, as we find out when he hauls his electric guitar over to the poolside to serenade his girlfriend, singing, "I love you, Vicky," even though her name's Roxy. When his next song, out in the desert, is about a girl named Valerie, even she calls him on it. Surely Roxy music wasn't already copyrighted in 1962? It's more surprising that she doesn't ask about his magic guitar, which doesn't just play music but generates whistles and backing vocals and everything.

Of course, Eegah is within earshot, so he wanders over to ogle Roxy again while she sleeps, but he's promptly scared off again. The longer this film runs the more you feel sorry for Richard Kiel as this can't have been what he signed up for. Arch Hall Sr understandably wrote this story for him because he's a 7'2" giant resonating with power who screams out to be the title character in a movie. Yet somehow he's emasculated in every way possible. Some things can be discounted as dumb things in a dumb movie, like the loincloth and boots, the huge flowing beard but inexplicably well trimmed moustache or the mummified relatives he talks to in one sided caveman gibberish. We expect things like that. The problems tie to the fact that he's a politically correct caveman who carries a huge club with no willingness to use it. And yeah, if you want to get Freudian, as I'm sure drive-in audiences in 1962 were happy to be, that applies too.

He doesn't kill anyone, he doesn't rape anyone, he doesn't even crap in his cave. He's rather civilised for a caveman. He does throw Ray Dennis Steckler into a swimming pool, but that's about it. He's even the perfect gentleman when carrying Roxy away to his cave, eventually going so moonfaced that he brings her flowers and carries her purse. Sadly, I'm not kidding. He runs from a poodle at one point, which is truly surreal. He even sits still for Roxy as she shaves him, though he does rudely slurp up the foam. And, get this, the polite prehistoric lounge lizard even shows her his etchings, scrawled sparingly on his cave wall in Bronson Canyon, the very same cave that served as Ro-Man's headquarters in *Robot Monster*. How's that for a Z movie pilgrimage site? Watch enough bad movies and you'll learn this place by heart. The only thing Kiel really accomplishes is to make Arch Hall Jr, who was over six feet tall, look like a ten year old schoolboy, hardly what his father was aiming at.

In fact, I'm really not sure what Senior could have been aiming at here. *Wild Guitar* makes a lot of sense, because it showcases his son's musical ability. *The Sadist* makes sense too, because it showcases his acting chops. I have no idea at all what this showcases. He's given inane dialogue to speak like, "Wow. Wow de wow wow." That's when Roxy's skirt has become so short that it can no longer go without comment, so we don't care about Junior at that point anyway. He's given lyrics to sing like, "If I had a thousand paintings in a marble gallery, every single picture would be of Valerie." He's supposed to be awesome because he's the singer and guitarist in a rock 'n' roll band, but we only see him play with them once; then we find that they can cope without him as there's a spare rock 'n' roll star at the next table to fill in whenever needed. He just hands over his guitar to someone else and wanders off to dance with his girl and nobody cares. Somehow I don't think that would have worked for Elvis.

The six Arch Hall Jr pictures are an amazing testament to one father's ambition to turn his son into a superstar. Of course, that's hardly a rare or inappropriate attribute in a father but, fortunately for us, most fathers don't have the ability to make half a dozen movies in five years, changing the genre every time just in case that made a difference. *The Choppers* was a gang picture, while *Eegah* was a caveman flick. *Wild Guitar* was the only one that really made sense, as it's a rock 'n' roll movie, while *The Sadist* was the best, a thriller. That leaves *The Nasty Rabbit*, a spy film, and *Deadwood '76*, a western, as well as a picture Junior wrote but didn't star in, a teen comedy called *Magic Spectacles*.

Given that his son was a singer and guitarist, playing Sunset Strip clubs like the Whisky a Go Go, you might have thought he'd have aimed at recording an album instead, but as it turned out, it was Junior's bandmate Alan O'Day who ended up making the big time, hitting number one in 1977 with *Undercover Angel*. Junior went on to fly planes for FedEx instead.

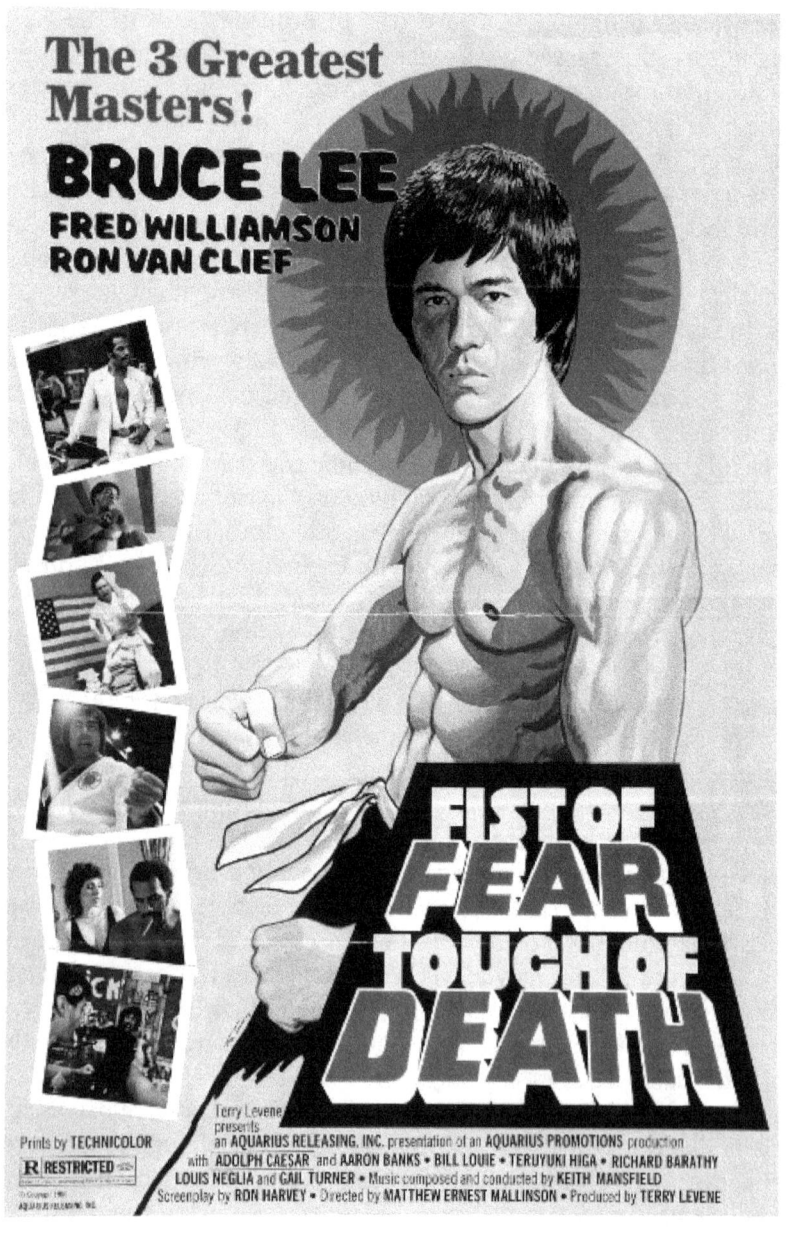

B is for Bruce:
Fist of Fear, Touch of Death (1980)

Director: Matthew Mallinson
Writer: Ron Harvey
Stars: Bruce Lee, Fred Williamson and Ron Van Clief

Bruceploitation is a wild and rather crazy world, one conjured into existence by exploitation filmmakers in Hong Kong, China and Taiwan after the untimely death of Bruce Lee in 1973.

Lee had been a godsend to them, a breakthrough to entirely new markets, after he had become the first international superstar from China. He was an iconic figure around the globe, initially through the television series *The Green Hornet*, then through Chinese martial arts films and eventually with *Enter the Dragon*, an iconic Hollywood production shot mostly in English. Suddenly everyone knew who Bruce Lee was in the same way everyone knew who Charlie Chaplin was. Yet now he was dead and thus unable to make another movie, so naturally they conjured up a successor. Actually they conjured up a lot of successors. What seemed like every martial artist in Asian cinema suddenly changed their name to either Bruce or Lee and they suddenly starred in films with portmanteau titles of other Bruce Lee movies.

There was Bronson Lee and Conan Lee and Dragon Lee. There was Bruce Chen and Bruce Liang and Bruce Thai. The really extravagant took both names, merely changing the spelling, such as Bruce Le, Bruce Li and Bruce Ly. When two letter surnames weren't enough, they went for Bruce Lai, Bruce Lei and Bruce Lie. There may even have a Lee Bruce and a Bluce Ree, though I can't swear to those. They made films like *Enter the Game of Death*, *Return of the Fists of Fury* or *Re-enter the Dragon*. Even a pre-fame Jackie Chan, who was a stuntman in *Enter the Dragon*, got stuck inheriting the throne with *New Fists of Fury* but his attempt to wave his arms in the iconic way Bruce did was entirely ludicrous. Some films had Bruce Lee's name in the title but otherwise had nothing to do with him at all, like *Bruce Lee Fights Back from the Grave* or, ultimately, the Brazilian *Bruce Lee vs Gay Power*, which has precisely nothing to do with either element of the title.

The most unlikely were titles like *The Dragon Lives Again* and *The Clones of Bruce Lee*. The latter has been described as "the Mount Rushmore of Bruceploitation films" for its use of a whole slew of these Bruce Lee imitators in the same picture, including Bruce Le, Bruce Thai, Bruce Lai, Bruce Liang and Dragon Lee, all trained by Bolo Yeung, who was beaten by the real Bruce in *Enter the Dragon*. If that wasn't enough, it also has men made of bronze, poisonous plants and a beach full of naked women. *The Dragon Lives Again* is even more surreal. It has the soul of Bruce Lee travel down to the Underworld where he teams up with Kwai Chang Caine from *Kung Fu* and Popeye the Sailor Man to prevent Dracula, Clint Eastwood and James Bond from mounting a coup and deposing the King of the Underworld. Oh, and there's the Godfather, the Exorcist and even Emmanuelle added into the mix for good measure too. At least it has the benefit of being insane.

By comparison, *Fist of Fear, Touch of Death* has no such gleeful insanity, it's just really awful. It's also notably more exploitative than any of the films mentioned above, leaving a notably bad taste in the mouth.

It supposedly takes us to the 1979 World Karate Championships held at Madison Square Garden, which are apparently being fought to find a successor to the title of Bruce Lee. It's so deadly serious that we're shown footage of the previous year's tournament, when black belt champion Bill Louis plucked out his opponent's eyes and threw them into the crowd to the magical accompaniment of laser sound effects. And you thought UFC was for tough guys? Well, you ain't seen nothin' yet. Then again, we're told this by TV presenter Adolph Caesar, who's standing under a marquee that reads "The Oriental World of Self Defense", so it would surely take someone who's gullible enough to believe in spaghetti trees to buy into anything whatsoever that unfolds here.

Caesar has the pivotal role here in this "new Bruce Lee movie", but then the filmmakers had the slight problem that the real Bruce Lee had been dead for seven years, making it a continual stretch to conjure up new ways to fit him into the story. Beyond turning a karate tournament into the fight for his title, Caesar is given every chance to rattle on about anything remotely connected to the Little

Dragon.

Nobody explains why we're supposed to listen to Caesar, given that at this point he was perhaps best known for having narrated the trailer to *Dawn of the Dead*. He did garner an Oscar nomination for his next role, playing an abusive black sergeant in Norman Jewison's *A Soldier's Story*, but that was four years away. At this point he was precisely nobody so perhaps we're just supposed to believe he's a hitherto unnoticed TV journalist. Certainly he determinedly plays it straight enough but he was clearly onto a lost cause from moment one.

To kick it off, he interviews fight promoter Aaron Banks about whether he thinks Lee died of natural causes, because naturally that's the first question that leaps to mind when discussing a karate tournament. Banks is apparently convinced that Lee was murdered through use of the touch of death, also known as the vibrating palm. Apparently the technique is simple, but he can't tell us what it is because it's a martial arts secret and all martial artists have to sign a vow of secrecy when they start out in the business, just like conjurers. So instead of telling us what it is, he... well, he tells us what it is, even demonstrating it in video footage. You just hold your fist really close to the target and punch really hard, using all the chi you can muster. Quite what this has to do with a vibrating palm and how it would leave no trace when it can snap inch thick boards, we have no idea, but that's the secret of martial arts right there, ladies and gentlemen. Three weeks later you're dead. I can kill you by looking at you.

Then we get to see a series of interviews Caesar apparently conducted with Bruce Lee himself. How could that be, you ask? Well, given that Caesar is shown in black and white but Lee in sepia, they're never shown on screen at the same time and Lee has clearly been badly redubbed to say whatever fits remotely after Caesar's questions, I'd dare to suggest that he didn't interview him at all, but perhaps that's just me being cynical. Of course he discovered Bruce Lee's talents! How could I doubt him? He's an important man! He even drives a Rolls Royce and we get no less than two lingering close ups of the Spirit of Ecstasy on the front to ram that point home.

You might ask why a Rolls Royce has suddenly entered the story.

It's because Caesar is tasked with randomly driving it over to the Hotel Mayflower twenty minutes before the beginning of the match so he can give a lift to Fred Williamson after he gets cheated out of a cab. You're following all this, right?

What is American football player and blaxploitation legend Fred Williamson doing in this film? Well, he's still wondering about that too. He plays himself, in a sort of spoof of early reality television, as the camera is there at his bedside when Harry Belafonte's 10.00am wake up call comes in from the desk. Mistaking the Hammer for Harry Belafonte is a running gag in this film and you can just tell we're all splitting our sides at how hilarious that is. Can you tell? Anyway, good old Fred has spent the night with some cheap ass ugly hooker acting like Marilyn Monroe in pancake makeup and he gets to satisfy her again before he heads out. Man, he must be quick! "Whoever heard of fighting for a Bruce Lee title that doesn't even exist!" he suggests to Caesar and while he's got a valid point, we can't help but wonder why someone would actually poke holes in this movie when they're in this movie.

Everyone is being talked about as the next Bruce Lee, of course. Bill Louie is the next Bruce Lee because he looks like him. You know, because he's Asian and has two arms. Later we'll watch him save a girl from being raped while dressed up as Kato from *The Green Hornet*. Having Kato be played by Louie instead of the rape victim is a lost opportunity. "Please, somebody!" cries a jogger, so Kato saunters over to kick ass and save the day, all while failing dismally at some of Bruce's animal noises. "Who was that masked man?" her friend asks. Ron Van Clief is also the next Bruce Lee as he works out for five hours a day and is a three time world champion. He demonstrates a crucial martial arts move over videolink, the ability to use a blunt sword to cut carrots held over his students' throats. He's had a lot of practice, and given the scars on one throat, he needs it. He can save a girl in the park too. "How can I ever repay you?" she asks, after he proves victorious. He merely looks at the camera and smiles.

Most bizarrely of all, we get a "dramatisation" of Lee's life story. We're told that his great-grandfather was Chan Li, a 19th century master swordsman, the greatest samurai warrior of his era. Bruce was apparently born on the very same day, so he romanticises his great-grandfather's achievements and practices karate all the time, even though his parents disapprove. I'm not sure how that works, given that samurai and karate are both Japanese, while Lee was of Chinese heritage, but hey. The footage really is of Lee, taken from a dramatic film which he made when he was seventeen, 1957's *The Thunderstorm*, merely redubbed so as to appear to be about his life. Apparently his mother thinks he should grow up. "I can kill with my bare hands," he tells her politely. "You don't understand me." She suggests, "All boys go through this stage." I don't think I went through the being able to kill with my bare hands stage, but then I'm not Japanese. Or Chinese. Anyway, wasn't Bruce Lee born in San Francisco?

What's most hilarious about these scenes is that they're all shot in black and white because the footage is stolen from a 1957 movie, but when the characters go into flashbacks, as they often do, they find that they're in colour because that footage is all stolen from a 1971 movie called *Invincible Super Chan*. The only good thing about *Invincible Super Chan* is that it looks so insane that I need to watch it outside of this ridiculous framework, especially as it seems to be banned in West Germany for some reason. Invincible Super Chan, I mean Bruce Lee's great-grandfather, Chan Li, takes on characters with bizarre weapons, throws others into trees and sideswipes still more into huge rocks. Those characters have iron heads to boot. He's so insanely tough that he can withstand a midget poking at him with a stick, while a couple of other guys hit him with an abacus and a sword that's kept in its scabbard. All at once. What a guy! No wonder Bruce was inspired.

Anyway, where this is getting us is that Bruce runs away from home "to pursue his dream, never to return again." He gets into films because it's "the quickest way to become a samurai soldier of fortune," and sure enough, a promoter explains that if he doesn't get seriously injured by hitting people, one film could be enough to get him into a supporting role in *The Green Hornet*. And so we return to Madison Square Garden having learned precisely nothing except that we shouldn't have watched this film, only to find that we have a bunch more crap to watch.

There's Fred the Hammer complaining yet again about how the upcoming title fight is pointless because nobody can follow Bruce

Lee. Oh, and, just so you know, Fred is fantastic. He tells us so. There's Teruyuki Higa and his Okinawa Kenpo students in the ring strutting their stuff, most of which involves breaking boards. Didn't they watch *Enter the Dragon?* I did. "Boards don't hit back," Bruce taught us. Remember?

Oh, and eventually there's also the World Welterweight Karate Championship, a full contact bout of twelve rounds between Louis Neglia and John 'Cyclone' Flood to determine who will inherit the title of Bruce Lee but frankly, I don't care any more. Someone won. You want to find out who, you watch this piece of trash. I'd watch *Manos: The Hands of Fate* a dozen times without a bathroom break before I'd watch this again. It's that painful.

Bizarrely though, for a film that frames itself as a documentary but probably doesn't contain even a single word of truth, in a very twisted way it may be the most honest of the many pictures that attempted to follow in the wake of Bruce Lee's passing. It's certainly that rarest of all of the many Brucesploitation movies, namely a Brucesploitation movie that really does feature Bruce Lee, and in footage that most of his fans haven't seen too. Unfortunately, that's not any excuse to watch this. Watch anything starring Bruce Le instead.

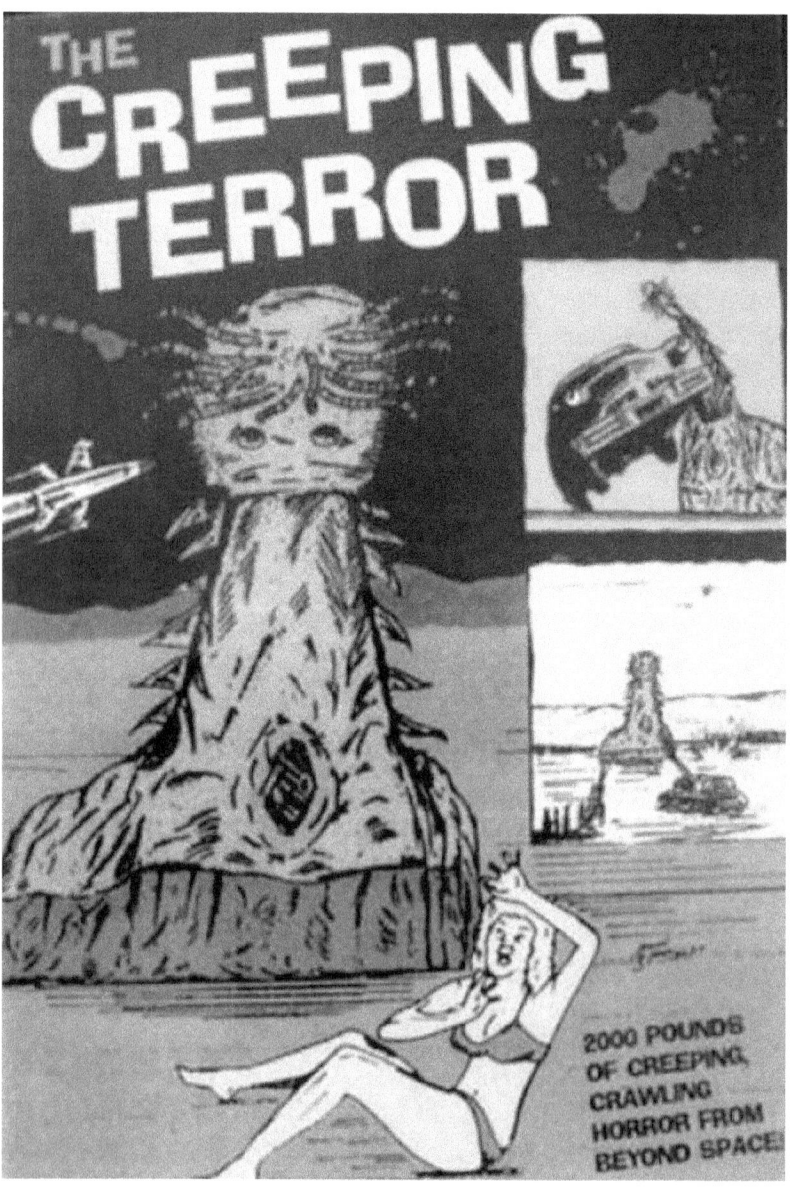

C is for Con:
The Creeping Terror (1964)

Director: A J Nelson
Writer: Robert Silliphant
Stars: Vic Savage and Shannon O'Neil

Of all the many atrocities low budget cinema has thrust upon us thus far, *The Creeping Terror* is perhaps the most honest because its title describes the film itself far better than it does its monster.

Unfortunately, that's a particularly cruel irony because there's nothing honest about the film at all, as its back story highlights, though hilariously the back story is also more interesting than the picture itself. It was made by a man named Arthur N White, who had previously shot *Street-Fighter* in 1959. He was a small scale con artist from Connecticut who came up with a new name and a new gimmick every time the wind changed, creating this picture under a pair of different pseudonyms. As A J Nelson, he produced it, edited it and directed it. As Vic Savage, he played the lead role of Martin Gordon. His real role was as conman though, because the movie itself was the gimmick and during a break in filming he simply packed up and left town with the money, never to be heard of again.

Fortunately (or perhaps unfortunately) for us, the primary financial backer of the film managed to salvage the footage from White's house, under the noses of the men repossessing his furniture, and he had the dedication to finish the job too.

He's William Thourlby, a small time model, actor and writer whose biggest claim to fame was being the first Marlboro Man, and it isn't known how much money he sank into this film. Given that Frederick Kopp, composer and college music professor, ponied up $6,000, that suggests that Thourlby may have been in for a tidy sum. Certainly not much of it made it to the screen though, as production quality is cheap throughout, albeit a notch above *Manos: The Hands of Fate* as we can actually see things. Whether that's a benefit or not we can argue about once you've made it through the 75 minute running time intact. So while White made most of it, it's

Thourlby we can thank for finishing it. The bastard.

There is a story, though only just. It has to do with an alien spaceship bringing a couple of huge slug like creatures to Earth to eat people, then analyse their biological and chemical make up and beam the results back to their home planet. That's it. While the credited writer is Robert Silliphant, it was in fact written by his younger brother, Allan, who owned the studio White had rented to shoot the indoor scenes. Allan was probably chosen because he was the half brother of noted Hollywood scriptwriter Stirling Silliphant. Stirling, who wrote *The Poseidon Adventure* and *In the Heat of the Night*, but had nothing to do with this film at all, though he was indirectly responsible for *Manos: The Hands of Fate*. Of course, conmen really don't care about such picky details when creative fabrications bring in money. Allan's nine page treatment was tongue in cheek, supposedly "intended to be a spoof on sci-fi/flying saucer movies," but that didn't show. White certainly didn't get the joke and the funniest thing is that people still watch the result.

We're in Angel County, California, where our hero, Martin Gordon, gets a prompt promotion to temporary sheriff because his uncle Ben is an idiot. It's late August and Martin has been away on honeymoon with Brett, his wife of two weeks. He gets back into town just in time to hear that a plane has crashed out by Willow Creek so the pair follow Uncle Ben to find out what's going on. Somehow we get there first so we can watch the mist in a forest clearing dissipate to reveal a spaceship. This revelation is actually not badly done, but it's by far the best thing about the entire film and it merely involves blowing away some mist, hardly rocket science. The rocket science came a minute or two earlier when the filmmakers showed us a stock footage rocket taking off in reverse. No, I have no idea why that was there. Perhaps they thought it just looked cooler than anything they could come up with themselves. They were right.

Before the Gordons turn up, we watch a flap open at the bottom of the spaceship so a carpet monster can trudge out at very low speed. It creeps, I guess, but that's one of those words that works best in literature or old dark house movies with dim lighting and secret passages, rather than forest clearings in broad daylight. There were up to eight people inside the polyurethane contraption at any one time. One tried to stand up inside the front part with its sort of vaginal passage, while a bunch of others humped each other underneath the back end. That's what it looks like to me anyway. These unknown extras were apparently ranch hands at the Spahn Movie Ranch in California, where the Lake Tahoe scenes were shot, and one of them was the film's assistant director, Randy Starr. Five years later, the Manson family would live at this ranch while committing the Tate/LaBianca murders in Los Angeles and Starr would provide the gun.

The cheapest thing about this film is its sound, because it really doesn't have much of it, and I don't just mean the carpet monster because that does roar inappropriately every now and again. How many slugs do you know that roar? Yeah, this one. That's it. It doesn't roar too often either, only odd times like when Uncle Ben finally turns up to crawl under the ship and be eaten.

It's not clear whether the whole film was shot silently to begin with or whether the soundtrack merely disappeared along with Arthur N White, but Thourlby realised that he had a lot of silent footage with a few snippets of out of sync dialogue. He decided to do some overdubs, but possibly gave up when he saw how badly it was turning out. Whatever the reason, he mostly went with hiring Larry Burrell to narrate almost the entire story to us instead, often rambling on about nothing to ensure that we don't get bored. So we get lines like, "Shortly thereafter, Dr Bradford arrived," and "He was a much younger man than one would imagine him to be." In other words, he's driving up to the scene, we can hear the car already and he has to be good looking because he financed most of the film.

Dr Bradford is apparently the "world's leading authority on space emissions." There's a juvenile joke in there, I'm sure, especially as he's played by a Marlboro Man who didn't die of lung cancer, but I'm above that. I'll just point out that these sprawling alien carpet slug turd monsters use control panels utterly like our own with switches, dials and gauges, the works, even though they don't have eyes, arms or anything else remotely like anything we have. Perhaps I shouldn't be seeking logic in a movie this bad. "It could be one of our missiles," says the sheriff before he gets eaten. "Or one of theirs," replies Brett. That's the second good thing about this film. There aren't any more. Trust me.

31

What happens next? "A series of tragedies," says the narrator. Had the public been warned, none of these would have happened, apparently, but because the public wasn't warned they die slow horrible deaths instead.

The first death scene sets the tone for the rest. A half naked couple gets it on in the forest, oblivious to the tortured roars of the terror shambling towards them. When it can't be ignored any longer, the boy runs away and the girl is scared into climbing into the maw of the creature. This thing moves so slowly that old men with zimmer frames could outrun it. You wouldn't even have to run, just amble away at your leisure. In fact, you could moonwalk slowly backwards and laugh at the huge slug thing waving its horrendous mouth vagina at you. But no, what you'd do if you were in this movie is climb inside it to meet your gruesome death, while showing as much leg as possible on the way in.

Then it's Bobby and his fat granddad out fishing. The boy is Pierre Kopp, the son of the film's composer, so his casting was presumably part of a deal that saw him pony up that six grand towards the budget. The granddad is Jack King, who only got older and fatter but still somehow managed to end up in movies full of naked chicks, such as *Hillbilly Honeymoon*, *Sam Dobbs and the Guru Gangbang* and *One Million AC/DC*. Then it's Betty Johnson who makes something of a production number out of waving goodbye to her husband, just so she can get eaten by the carpet monster.

Eventually it's a school picnic, where most of the kids simply wait to be eaten, and a local community dancehall where one eager dancer gives up on his reluctant girlfriend to grab someone else's, proceeding to leap around rather like the average mad scientist's hunchbacked assistant. There's even a drunk staggering through scenes and stealing drinks. I couldn't help but focus on details because it takes the carpet slug so damned long to get there.

I also wondered where the hero had got to while his town was being eaten. Well, while all this mayhem is unfolding, Martin Gordon is busy necking with his wife. You see, the moral must be that if you're a young lady and you get fast and loose with the guys, you're surely going to get eaten by an alien carpet. Play your guitar in public and you're slug food. Just visit Lover's Lane and the shag monster won't merely eat you, it'll hump your car and then it'll eat you. Following the path of righteousness, however, will keep you safe. Get married, like Martin and Brett, and the nasty monster will just leave you alone. It's as if this huge slug is a metaphor for the clap or some other venereal disease that happily married couples are physically unable to contract in Production Code controlled, morally justifiable 1960s movies. You can even make out on the couch right next to Deputy Barney. I simply can't resist quoting the accompanying narration verbatim:

"Barney and Martin had been bachelor buddies for years," says the narrator. "But now that Martin was settling down to marriage, they were slowly drifting apart. Barney, naturally, was still dating all the girls in town, and he couldn't understand why Brett and Martin didn't pal around with him more than they did. He couldn't comprehend that married life brought with it not only new problems and duties, but the necessary togetherness of husband and wife as well. Despite Brett's most tactful considerations, such as inviting him over to dinner quite often, Barney was growing resentful of her, or at least she felt that he was. Since time began, this change in relationships probably happened to all buddies in similar circumstances. Life has its way of making boys grow up and, with marriage, Martin's time had come. His life was now Brett, a life that he thoroughly enjoyed."

And you thought this was a monster movie.

Then again, with a monster like this one, perhaps it's best to avoid it. There is a second monster, as the army discover when they crawl inside the ship. It looks more like a garbage heap with the sort of corrugated tubes that kiddie craft books told us to stick onto our alien monster attempts. None of what we created would have passed muster in a monster movie and, amazingly enough, neither does this one. It's there because Jon Lackey, the artist who created the carpet monster, somehow took offense when he didn't get paid so he left with his other creation, leaving the filmmakers to create a backup, which unfortunately reminds us of a humungous turd.

Of course, the point is that none of this was ever intended to be seen. Arthur N White only wanted money. He didn't expect that anything he shot would see release and he didn't care. How many other movie cons never saw the light of day merely because they didn't have a William Thourlby to finish them?

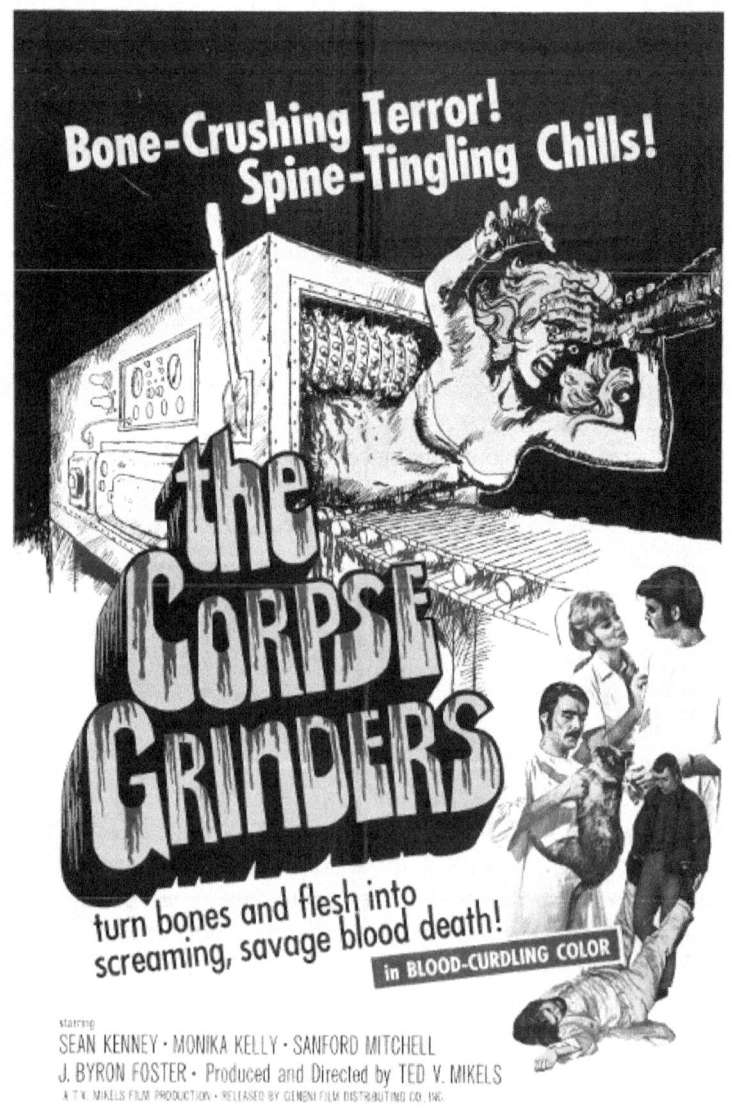

D is for Debt:
The Corpse Grinders (1971)

Director: Ted V Mikels
Writers: Arch Hall Sr and Joseph Cranston
Stars: Sean Kenney, Monika Kelly, Sanford Mitchell and J Byron
Foster

Eight years after *Blood Feast* invented the gore film, along came
The Corpse Grinders with one of the most memorable titles in all of
exploitation cinema. Then again, it was created by Ted V Mikels,
creator of titles as glorious as *Blood Orgy of the She Devils*, *The Black
Klansman* and *Girl in Gold Boots*.

Sourced from a script by Arch Hall Sr, which was clearly a lot
more imaginative than the story he wrote for *Eegah*, it was Mikels
who renamed it from *The Cat and the Cannery*. That's hardly a bad
title itself but drive-in audiences wouldn't have been familiar with
the pun's source, a 1922 play, *The Cat and the Canary*, that had been
filmed a few times but not in America since 1939. While Mikels had
directed six very different films since 1963 and always has a host of
projects on the go at any one time, he hadn't shot a feature since
The Astro-Zombies in 1968. While he had a mere $1,700 to work with
here, this became by far his biggest success.

And that was a really good thing, because he made it to clear a
debt. Always interested in new filmmaking technology, Mikels had
become one of the first independent filmmakers to dabble in
commercial home video, on reel to reel tape as the video cassette
was still being developed. He did well, but the business spun out of
control and his two partners disappeared leaving him with $475,000
in debt. Never one to give up, Mikels offered a deal to the lawyer
handling his creditors that if he'd allow him to make a movie,
which of course is what he did best, he'd pledge half of the film's
income to clear the debts.

Given that Mikels has almost unparalleled experience of almost
every aspect of the moviemaking business, this surely had to have
been a delaying tactic, as honest as his intentions may have been, as
he never saw a dime from many of his films. Yet this had an

immediate impact, outperforming multi-million dollar Hollywood pictures in the drive-ins.

The Corpse Grinders actually sets itself up pretty well. A cat violently attacks her owner as she lets it in out of the rain. At the Farewell Acres cemetery, complete with convenient fog machines, Caleb bickers with Cleo over an open grave. He's a big and burly mountain man. She's small and nuts, as evidenced by her cooing over a little doll like it's a baby while Caleb tries to concentrate on how much Landau owes him for meat. Landau is a partner in Lotus Cat Food, a company cheap enough that its business sign is a poster on the wall in the main office and its employees seem to be escapees from an insane asylum. It's not much of a stretch to put this three piece jigsaw puzzle together, with or without the help of the rather descriptive title. Yes, Caleb sells Landau corpses for him to grind up into cat food, only for the cats that eat it to turn on their owners. This isn't rocket science, but it's a ludicrous setup that is also sheer exploitation genius.

It helps that all the characters are interesting even when unsympathetic. Caleb and Cleo are a backwoods hick and a lunatic redhead. Landau is a sleazy businessman whose company sports a gloriously awful pun for a slogan: 'for cats who like people'. Maltby, his partner, trusts him so much that he splits the cash two ways on a daily basis, so we just know that he'll be taken care of soon enough. The workers at Lotus are a riot: Willie is insanely nervous and inquisitive, while Tessie has a shock of red hair but only one leg, so she hobbles around on a crutch. She's also deaf and dumb so Landau talks to her in sign language. Across town, there's also a sexy nurse and a drunken doctor. Angie Robinson feeds her Siamese a can of Lotus Cat Food, so she and Dr Howard Glass can swap tongues and commiserate over his latest failed operation, while Baby Socks attacks him without provocation. Until that point this scene was daytime soap opera territory.

I was distracted throughout by the lovely Monika Kelly, who plays Angie, as she's delightfully easy on the eye and she's a great deal more charismatic an actor than anyone else in the film. She's also something of a mystery: IMDb lists her as being born in 1921 but there's no way she's fifty in this picture. It also suggests that she was working real estate in Las Vegas in 2003, apparently as a spritely 82 year old. The film's press pack suggests that this was her fifth film but only *Love Minus One* is listed anywhere. Who is this woman? I'm sure she has stories to tell, especially as she flirts outrageously with the inebriated Dr Glass while pulling away from him physically. I get the impression that the actors really didn't like each other. As all the salaries were deferred, her career as an actress, if she even had one, can't have been lively. All the actors hired were hired for their willingness to work for potentially nothing.

That can't have made casting particularly viable, so I wonder how much of Hall's script, which he had written with Joseph Cranston, dealt with the characters, and how much Mikels tailored them to fit the actors that he ended up with. The most experienced was Vincent Barbi, an Italian prize fighter who had played Al Capone in 1955 and racked up small roles in everything from *War and Peace* to *Sweet Sweetback's Baadasssss Song*, via *The Blob* and Adam West's *Batman*. Charles 'Foxy' Fox hadn't acted since *The Undertaker and His Pals* in 1966, a picture that Mikels had re-edited from a gore movie into a comedy. I'd like to see him in more films, but I'd also like to see Drucilla Hoy and Ann Noble even more. Noble is the joyously insane Cleo, but she only made one more picture, *Sins of Rachel*, though as both writer and lead actor. Hoy, so memorable here as Tessie the deaf mute cripple, also only made one other film, 1969's *Sinner's Blood*.

As fun as they are, it isn't the characters that people remember most from *The Corpse Grinders*, it's the corpse grinding machine, which cost only $17 to build, constructed from odds and ends from a lumber yard, lawn mower parts and a ramp. Almost thirty years later, when Mikels shot a sequel, it cost him $200 for the ramp alone. This version is one of the greatest examples of PG exploitation in the history of film, as it doesn't generate the gorefest you'd might be excused to expect. When Landau and Maltby put corpses through the machine, the worst we see is Maltby lustily eyeing a corpse but our minds fill in every gap. The grain goes into the hopper, but the corpses go onto a conveyor belt to be run through the huge machine, still in their underwear. I don't know whether human bodies or their underwear would be worse for cats! The room is bathed in red and green light, and the puréed corpse is brown. It's all glorious misdirection.

In fact the entire film is glorious misdirection. The title indicates highly graphic violence and yet there's really nothing on screen that's inappropriate. Everything we see follows the same logic as this textbook scene: we see things like bodies, spinning steel and icky purée, but only our minds provide the connection between the three as none of it is actually shown. The storyline is about food for cats rather than people, but there are constant connections drawn between corpses and food to keep a cannibalistic thought in our brains. While Caleb counts the proceeds of his bodysnatching business, Cleo pours soup for her doll. While an assistant cackles insanely, a mortician explains that the money Landau pays him for corpses will send him back to school to become a chef. As the heroes figure out what's going on, they throw out man-eating tiger analogies. Yet it seems like there's more corpse grinding machine in the trailer than in the film itself.

There's no nudity, various ladies only disrobing down to their underwear. There's no swearing at all. There's not really any gore either. The worst we get is a cat autopsy, which has Dr Glass lift fake intestines off the belly of a stuffed cat to examine. There's a little blood daubed around the throat of Annie, its owner, but we don't see the creature gnawing on her jugular and we certainly don't see spouts of blood afterwards. We just see a crazy lady on a bed and a wild bearded wino rushing up the stairs to rescue her when she screams. It's hardly X rated stuff.

In fact once Annie is taken to Dr Glass and he does some lab work, thus actually setting up the rest of the story, we can get ready to pause the DVD to surreptitiously catch the most adult part of the film. To investigate Lotus Cat Food, Angie and Howard go to the Food Adulteration Agency and there on the wall is a bizarre picture, some sort of bondage fantasy that's mysteriously absent in a later shot. That's it.

It seems strange to focus on such inconsistencies when the underlying structure is so sound, every scene moving the story forward another inch, but this film is full of them. The FAA hasn't heard of Lotus Cat Food, but Angie explains that it's the most expensive on the market. Landau kills off characters who know too much, only to bury them instead of feed them into his corpse grinder. There's a scene at Lotus where dismembered bodies are scattered all over the place for effect but surely they'd grind those up too. They grind people without taking off their clothes, so why would they remove legs and arms? Best of all is when Donna, the FAA secretary, goes home. She enters her apartment through the balcony, places a can of Lotus on the kitchen counter for her Siamese to lick but forgets to open it. Yet five minutes after she strips down to her underwear to pose on the couch, I mean relax with the TV and a Budweiser, the cat attacks her anyway.

Of course I can hardly fail to mention the change in Dr Howard Glass. When we meet him, he's a surgeon who gets drunk at work because of "hazards of the trade" and whose girlfriend doesn't seem to want to touch him, but without any background change he suddenly becomes a capable scientist able to make wild but needed intuitive leaps, a full on 70s movie star prototype: strong and capable, with a knitted sweater and a moustache. He's more than happy to follow his sexy nurse around town investigating, presumably because she's so fond of her little Baby Socks that she can't accept that it doesn't like her boyfriend. She changes too, daring and determined like many Mikels leading ladies for most of the film, only to inevitably turn all screamy and girly when in actual danger. Landau is sane all the way through the picture, just a particularly ruthless businessman, but when it all falls apart he goes completely wacko. There must be something in the air.

Certainly *The Corpse Grinders* made a similar transformation itself. Next to no money was spent on the film, the actors not being the only ones working from deferred payments. Mikels managed to talk a studio owner, against his better judgement, to let him to shoot there on the same terms. On later receiving his cheque in full, that owner pointed out that it was the only time that such a scenario resulted in his getting paid. Expensive looking props like the Farewell Acres gates were just part of the Glendale castle Mikels lived in. The camerawork is traditional, because Mikels had to teach first time cameraman Bill Anneman how to operate the camera as they shot. The acting ranges from capable at very best to outrageous. Sean Kenney has moments as Dr Glass but only Monika Kelly has any charisma and she can't carry the film. The taboo element is all that keeps an edge to the piece, which otherwise could even be described as boring. Yet it grossed $190,000 in a single week in the greater Los Angeles area alone and it continues to make money today, over forty years later. Mikels shot a sequel in 2000 and he has a third in the series in the works too. That's pretty good going for a movie whose actors probably had no expectations of ever being paid.

Perhaps it succeeded because it has heart. It's a pure exploitation picture that thrives on its outrageous theme, businessmen buying corpses and killing homeless guys just to make catfood, but the way it goes about telling this story is so inherently nice. It feels less like a gore movie and more like a 1950s horror flick with a slightly evil edge.

Whatever the reason, this one worked. "The easiest thing is making the film," Mikels has often suggested. "The toughest thing is getting the money. The second toughest is getting it back." He didn't always succed in the latter, which surely highlights how important doing so here was to his abiding and fascinating career.

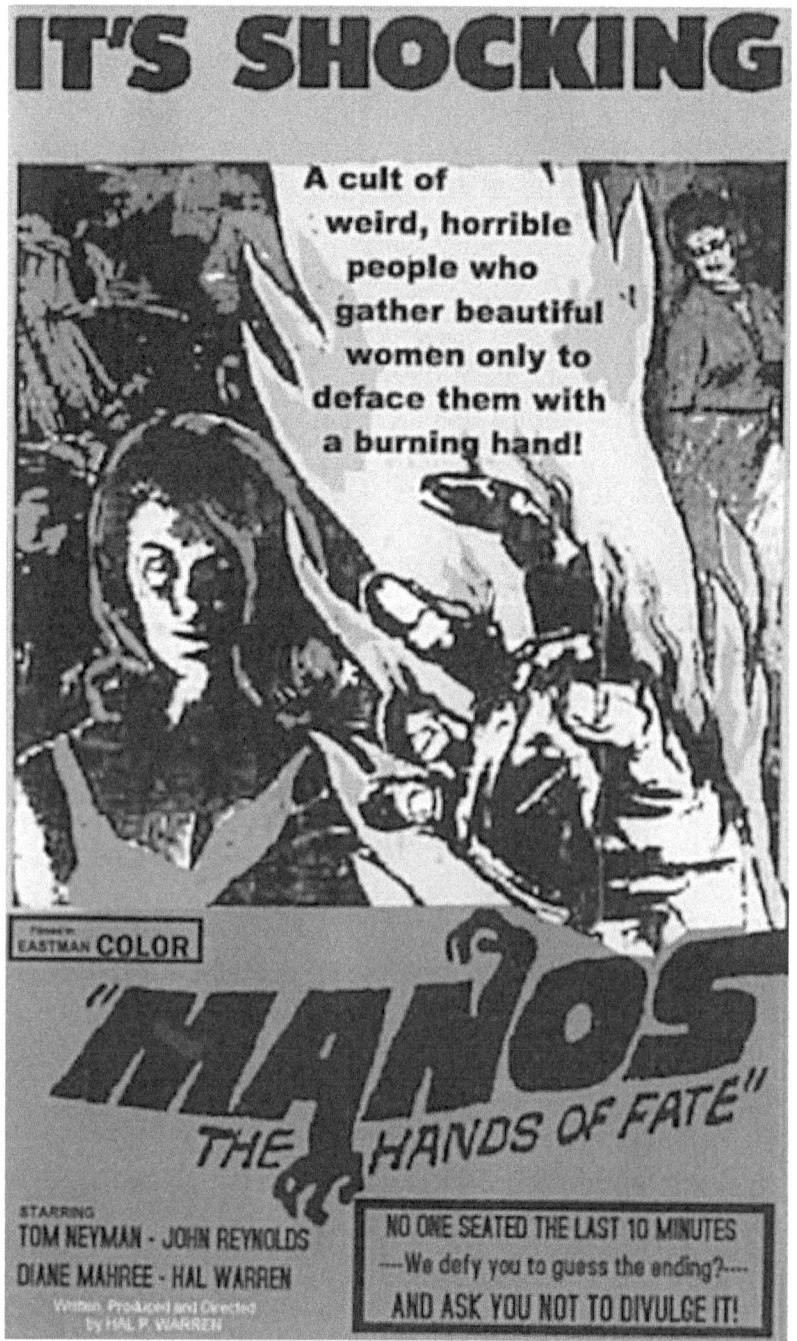

E is for Ego:
Manos: The Hands of Fate (1966)

Director: Harold P Warren
Writer: Harold P Warren
Stars: Tom Neyman, John Reynolds, Diane Mahree and Hal Warren

Ask any random moviegoer to name the worst film of all time and they'll generally say *Plan 9 from Outer Space* because they just don't know any better. It's surely the most widely seen bad movie of its era, it features more outré celebrities than any John Waters movie ever made and it got special attention in the high profile Tim Burton/Johnny Depp biopic of its director, *Ed Wood*, so it's simply the easiest choice. Of course, it had been enthroned with that precise title in the 1980 book, *The Golden Turkey Awards*, by Michael and Harry Medved.

Yet, if you ask the sort of people who actually know about really bad films, people like Elvira, Mistress of the Dark or the writers of *Mystery Science Theater 3000*, and the answer will usually be *Manos: The Hands of Fate*. It was fully intended to be a horror movie but Quentin Tarantino, who owns a 35mm print of the film, calls it his favourite comedy of all time. I can certainly understand why.

Manos: The Hands of Fate is a man's movie in every way, right down to owing its very existence to a bet, one conjured up in a Texas coffee shop between a fertiliser salesman/insurance agent, Harold P Warren, and a television screenwriter, Stirling Silliphant. They'd met before, as Warren played a bus driver in an episode of *Route 66*, which Silliphant wrote, but this time they talked about movies and what it took to make them. Warren, who was active in local theatre, believed that anyone could do it, so he bet Silliphant that even he could conceive and complete a movie, beginning right there in the coffee shop by writing out plot details on napkins. He won that bet, of course, by conceiving *The Lodge of Sins* and completing it as *Manos: The Hands of Fate*. He even premiéred it at the Capri in El Paso in 1966, which gave it a brief theatrical run, meaning that Warren got further to the big time than most would be filmmakers.

Warren raised an estimated $19,000 from friends and family. The most obvious way he had to cut costs was to become the writer, producer and director and also cast himself in the lead role of Mike. The second was to not pay anyone, promising them instead a share in the film's profits, which never materialised. To be fair, he gave seven year old actor Jackey Neyman a red bicycle and her pet doberman, Shanka, fifty pounds of dog food, but nobody saw any money. The third was to dispense with any opening credits, so we're thrown right into the action, or the lack of it. Mike is taking his family to the Valley Lodge, but he's lost and unwilling even to ask the cop who pulls him over for a broken tail light for directions. So they drive around for a while, as the non-existent credits fail to roll, passing the time by singing *Row, Row, Row Your Boat* until they find a sign for the place and drive straight into the Twilight Zone and cinematic history.

If the existence of the film isn't enough to tell us that Mike, Margaret and their little girl, Debbie, are heading for trouble, a couple of very old teenagers necking in their car underline it for us. "I wonder where they're going?" asks the girl. "Like there's nothing up that road," the boy adds.

The girl was supposed to have a more substantial role but Joyce Molleur, also uncredited for stunts, broke her leg during filming, so ended up stuck in the car. As Bernie Rosenblum, uncredited as the film's stunt coordinator, promptly got hired to smooch with her throughout, it wouldn't be tough to conjure up a conspiracy theory. As he was also the film's key grip, that could easily be combined with risqué jokes. Stranger things have happened and, well, they mostly happened on this film, as Warren's ambition wasn't matched by any moviemaking experience and the small cast and crew were sourced from a local theatre and a finishing school, so didn't have any either.

Strange things are about to happen to Mike and his family. Lost again, they turn round, only to find that the road they drove up has disappeared, to be replaced by a dead end. Turning round again, they immediately stop at the house that apparently just appeared out of the ether. Yes, you read that right and Warren surely knew how dumb it must have seemed too, as he wrote a line of dialogue to explain the gaping plot hole. "Where did this place come from?"

Mike asks. "It wasn't here a few minutes ago." His wife simply answers, "I don't care," and that's all we need to know. You can turn off your sense of logic now because it would help.

Maybe this isn't a regular holiday at all, it's really a family acid trip to the countryside, thus explaining why they arrive at the headquarters of the local polygamous demon worshipping cult instead of the Valley Lodge, to be greeted by what must be the single most amazing character in the history of bad cinema.

"I'm Torgo," says the freaky guy on the porch, "I take care of the place while the Master is away." It isn't the beard, the shredded hat or the iron staff with a hand on it. It's that we can completely believe the rumours suggesting that actor John Reynolds was strung out on LSD throughout the entire shoot. There's just no way that he wasn't tripping on something. Robert Guidry's camera lingers on him as he twitches around like he's battling the worst case of ADHD possible or using an army of fire ants to irrigate his colon. He continually repeats himself. He answers questions nobody has asked. He continually repeats himself. He can't even walk, hobbling around instead like he's auditioning for a paraplegic performance of *Riverdance*. The character of Torgo is uniquely magnetic, commanding our attention for all the wrong reasons, but it's acutely painful to watch Reynolds suffer through his performance, even before we discover the sad reasons behind it.

Reynolds was one of the actors Warren knew from the Festival Theater in El Paso, as was Tom Neyman who played the Master. Both were method actors and they approached the character of Torgo very seriously. He's supposedly a satyr, half man and half goat, so Neyman built a metal harness out of wire and foam for Reynolds to wear. Much has been written about the resulting prosthesis causing him acute pain, possibly by wearing it backwards, which led to an addiction to painkillers that lasted until his suicide six months later, a month before the premiére of his only film. Certainly that's believable, given what we see, and especially sad as the film utterly ignores that he's a satyr, suggesting that he tortured himself into agony and suicide for nothing. More recently though, people involved with the film have suggested that his addictions were recreational, perhaps sourced from his time, while the harness was safe and used properly.

Whichever is the truth, I find it difficult to understand how Warren could have failed to notice the condition that Reynolds was in, or for the sake of his project, to have cared. After all, his bet with Silliphant was to simply complete a movie. Delivering his cast and crew to the Capri by limousine for the première, at which he was made an honorary deputy of the city, suggests that he wanted something more out of his film.

To hindsight, he couldn't have done without Neyman, who didn't just provide Torgo's satyr harness but most everything else too. He created the artwork and the costumes. He provided many props up to and including the convertible that we see so much of in the early scenes. He plays one of the key characters and his daughter plays another. He even brought his dog along with him. Yet Reynolds only played Torgo, so ought to have been easy to replace, through ironically Reynolds is now the most fascinating facet of the entire film.

If anything, Warren played up Reynolds's trainwreck of a performance. He used a Bell & Howell 16mm camera, one that had to be manually wound and only allowed 32 second shots. Yet even with that inherent restriction to work under, his best editing aims to extend shots like one that sees Torgo trying to stand up, because he apparently couldn't do it within 32 seconds. Clearly reluctant to waste anything, other scenes cut back and forth to extended footage that may only contain Torgo squirming uncomfortably in the blazing sun that constitutes night in this picture or his wavering hand getting slowly closer and closer to Margaret as she stands waiting and waiting to be able to scream. There are even extended shots of a painting that serves to introduce us to the Master and his dog, painfully extended shots that aren't enhanced by repeat viewings or by shots of Mike and Margaret looking at it. "Sinister isn't descriptive enough," says Margaret.

Of course, if we don't watch the truly fascinating Torgo, who would we watch? Mike and Margaret are so annoyingly traditional that they may just be the reason why the counterculture happened. Mike is the tough all American alpha male, who can't ask directions and takes charge even when not at home. He rudely orders Torgo around and browbeats his wife. After Torgo thankfully takes him down with his staff and ties him up, he annoyingly escapes by simply standing up. Yet, when things go bad, his best suggestion is, "We'll hide in the desert. Someone will help!" Margaret only encourages him. She's a stereotypical damsel in distress, unable even to open the door as her husband comes to her rescue. She falls over every couple of yards in the desert, for she won't take off her high heels, and she quickly gives up thought of escape. "Let's go back," she whines. "They'll never think of looking for us at the house."

If Mike and Margaret are the old way, perhaps the Master and his six wives are supposed to be the new way, living together in some sort of polyamorous occult commune, so misogynistic that the women paralyse themselves when the Master goes to sleep on his stone slab and turn into decorations. Neyman, who doesn't show up for half the film and then conducts his moody rituals like a tribute to The Crazy World of Arthur Brown, is so powerful a master that he can dominate Torgo into submission just by looking at him but he's unable to deal with any his wives, let alone all of them. If they're the new way, they're surely also the failure of the counterculture to come up with meaningful change. He has no less than six wives, aspiring models plucked from a local finishing school called Mannequin Manor who wear granny panties beneath diaphonous gowns and catfight like it's performance art. Yet the Master is clearly henpecked.

Manos: The Hands of Fate, a clearly redundant title given that it translates from Spanish as *The Hands: The Hands of Fate*, is legendary for making every mistake in the book. Warren shot his night scenes at night, which meant that nobody could see anything, least of all us. One amazing scene has two cops start into the desert to investigate a shot, only to turn back after two steps because they couldn't see enough to put one foot in front of the other. Warren is obviously more a writer than a director, given the concepts he uses here that sound fine on paper but look inane on film. The Master dominating Torgo with his eyes sounds cool, but it's just two people looking at each other in a movie. We're never told who Manos is, though he's presumably a deity who requires his followers to commit every cliché in the book, from wild staring to maniacal laughter. That's before the bad acting, the continuity errors, the conveniences, you name it.

But, at the end of the day, Warren won his bet. He even rubbed Silliphant's nose in it, by having the El Paso elders attend the premiére: the mayor, the alderman and the chief of police. His film has even undergone a massive resurgence of interest after *Mystery Science Theater 3000* riffed on it in 1993, today more popular and famous than Warren ever imagined it could be, even if it's for being the worst movie of all time.

Yet, I've never seen what Silliphant thought. He may never have known that he lost. He may well not have cared, given that he went on to win an Oscar for *In the Heat of the Night*, while Warren failed to garner any interest whatsoever in the production for a second movie, *Wild Desert Bikers*, but Warren certainly did. He started with nothing and he created a complete film. I'm not sure whether to admire him for that achievement or to condemn the ego of the man that prompted this cinematic abortion to be made.

Huh? An A-Z of Why Classic American Bad Movies Were Made

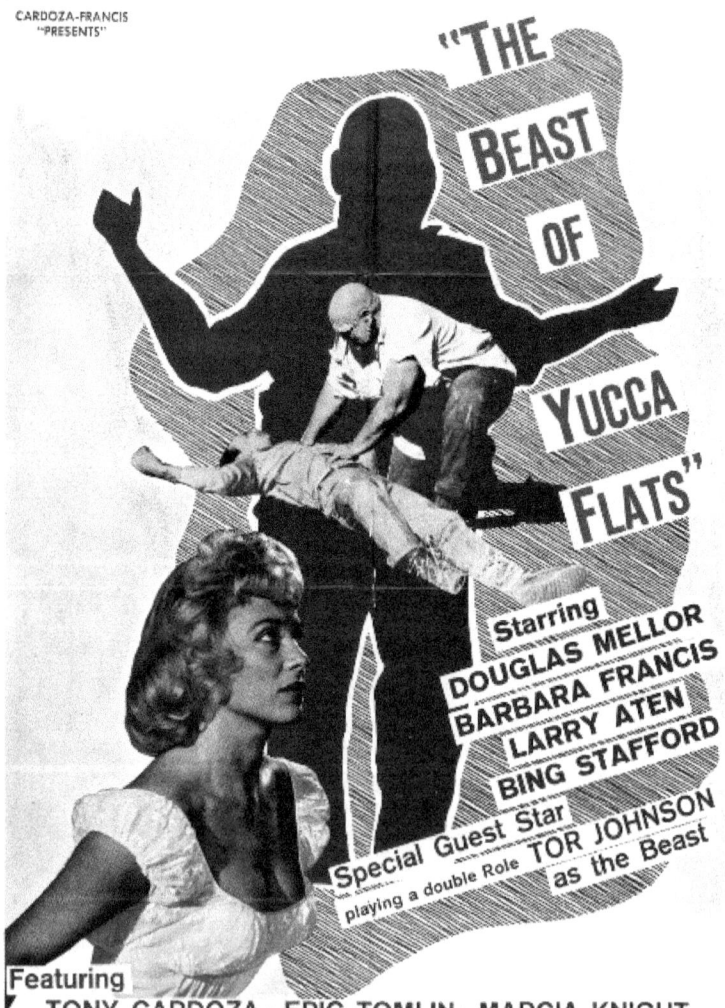

F is for Frustration:
The Beast of Yucca Flats (1961)

Director: Coleman Francis
Writer: Coleman Francis
Stars: Douglas Mellor, Barbara Francis, Bing Stafford, Larry Aten, Linda Bielema and Tor Johnson

Before I started deliberately delving into the worst movies of all time, *The Beast of Yucca Flats* was the yardstick that I judged others by. Bizarrely, as the 19th worst film of all time in the IMDb Bottom 100, at the time of writing, it's the highest rated of the three that Coleman Francis wrote and directed. These ratings suggest that he only got worse, but at least they gave him exposure and that's what he wasn't getting elsewhere.

Francis wasn't without experience, having moved to Hollywood in the forties and landing a succession of bit parts, like the deliveryman he played in *This Island Earth*. Yet it took ten years before he obtained a credit, as a detective in *Stakeout on Dope Street*, Irvin Kershner's solid directorial debut in 1958. By this time Francis had built up a reputation for liking the bottle a little too much, so, frustrated at trying to succeed as an actor in other people's movies, he started to make his own, if only to be able to call the shots himself.

It's hard to suggest that he succeeded, given the results he came up with, but he did get some impressive credits, not only for himself but for his family. On this film, he was the writer, editor, producer and director, as well as appearing in two bit parts and narrating the entire thing. He wrote and directed *The Skydivers* two years later, again playing two bit parts as well. For *Night Train to Mundo Fine* aka *Red Zone Cuba* in 1966, he wrote, produced and directed, took the lead role for himself and narrated the film. He cast his ex-wife, Barbara Francis, as the leading lady here and their children as her character's kids. All three of them returned for *The Skydivers*, but presumably wanted no more after that. They never acted again.

The rest of the cast were made up primarily of people that

Coleman knew or people that his producer knew, including the main reason that most people watch the film today, Swedish wrestler turned actor, Tor Johnson.

Johnson is one of the gems of exploitation cinema. Because of his powerful presence and size, he'd played bit parts in better films than Francis ever managed: *Road to Rio* with Bing Crosby, Bob Hope and Dorothy Lamour, *State of the Union* with Spencer Tracy and Katherine Hepburn or the Rodgers and Hammerstein musical, *Carousel*. Of course, if you're reading this, you're likely to know him better from Ed Wood movies like *Bride of the Monster, Night of the Ghouls* and *Plan 9 from Outer Space*. If he hadn't achieved screen immortality after those, he had after this.

He's Joseph Javorski, a high profile Soviet defector who flies into the atomic testing ground at Yucca Flats with secret data on a Russian moon shot stowed away in his briefcase. Francis wanted him for this film and somehow found the name and phone number of Anthony Cardoza, who had lost a lot of money investing in *Night of the Ghouls* but hadn't lost his passion for the industry.

Cardoza got Tor Johnson, of course, and found the money to pay him. At this point Johnson was 58 years old and in terrible shape, a bloated 390 pounds. Mostly supported by his son Carl, who used to fight him in the ring but was now a police chief in San Fernando, he wasn't going to say no to a paycheck but his contribution to this film is primarily iconic. He literally ambles into the desert to avoid the bullets of KGB assassins, before a nearby atomic blast wipes them out and transforms him into the beast of the title, who terrorises anyone who might drive by. He looks suitably vast, with powdered toilet paper pasted onto his face to mimic burns, but he obviously couldn't run more than a few yards at a time or stand up without the aid of a wall. Four of the crew had to literally haul him by rope up to the old mine that substituted for the beast's cave, two pulling and two pushing. It's a testament to his constitution that he lived another decade.

Of course, we're not supposed to recognise how ineffective he would have been. He's a fiend, a monster, a prehistoric beast in a nuclear age! These descriptions, like almost everything else in this film, come to us from the director's narration. Whether the Mitchell camera used couldn't record sound, whether Cardoza couldn't raise funding to buy any sound equipment or whether Francis simply thought it would be less work this way, the entire film was shot silently. Later, in post production, Francis added in a few sound effects, music and a little dialogue, having shot everything in such a way that he wouldn't have to be too careful synching it up with the action. Guns are fired, but their muzzles are always off screen. People speak, but their lips, if not their entire heads, aren't visible. At one point, one couple, Hank and Lois Radcliffe, walk back to their car to talk. They stand outside and chat while we watch their chests through the window.

Almost everything comes from the narration, because there's so little else. Francis had to fill up the vast 55 minute running time somehow, but he chose to fill it with a slow, fragmented stream of consciousness narration that makes us wonder what he was taking at the time. "Flag on the moon. How did it get there?" he asks nobody in particular. "Secret data. Pictures of the moon."

It feels like he recorded all this in one session, improvising most of it with any random words that came to mind. Maybe all these phrases could be rearranged into something that makes sense, but that would take a sadder man even than I to even attempt. Given that the narration fails to reflect the visuals on a regular basis but somehow remains our best source to keep track of the plot, what little there is of one, *The Beast of Yucca Flats* becomes a hallucinatory experience, as if we're somehow experiencing two completely different things at the same time.

If we can separate the two, we can keep a vague track of what's going on. A vacationing couple have the bad luck to break down in the middle of the desert, right in front of our atom scorched killing machine, so that's the end of them. What's most amazing here is how this four hundred pound radioactive Russian can sneak in and out of the back of the car without anyone noticing, including the young lady in the front seat. Maybe he's an atomic ninja. Then again, she failed to notice the atomic explosion five minutes earlier, so she's hardly reliable. She's killed and carried off to the beast's cave.

A couple of desert patrolmen, each independently described as "caught in the wheels of progress", roam the desert for twenty sun-filled afternoon hours, finding the girl but not the beast because he's playing peekaboo with them. Massive doses of radiation do wonders for the mind. Just ask Spider-Man. Or ask Coleman Francis. "Touch a button. Things happen," he narrates.

So, the only thing for it is to put Jim Archer's paratroop training to good use and head on up into the sky with a rifle. "Shoot first," his partner tells him, "ask questions later." Vigilante killing is a common theme in Coleman Francis movies, as are light aircraft. You'd think that with so little in his films, it would be tough to find commonality, but the little there is in one film is in the others too. Most of it ties to "man's inhumanity to man."

Fortunately for the next vacationing family to conveniently break down on the same stretch of desert highway, Jim may have been trained as a paratrooper but he's so terrible a shot that he couldn't hit something hot with a heatseeker. Even lined up for a *North by Northwest* style swoop in open desert, that film a potential inspiration given that it was released only two years earlier, he's unable to take down a man running in a straight line at a consistent speed. "A man runs." the narration tells us. "Somebody shoots at him."

Bizarrely, the acting isn't a downside. Perhaps it's because nobody really gets an opportunity to act. They just walk into frame, towards the camera or into the desert. They're rarely called on to display emotion because those scenes are mostly shot with them looking away from the camera.

Barbara Francis does get to look worried a lot, with her boys lost inside an atomic testing ground, but that can't have been much of a stretch given that she could probably see how the film was turning out and her name was prominent on it. She's billed behind only Douglas Mellor, who has all those running scenes while Jim Archer was shooting at him.

Only Tor Johnson is really asked to do anything else and his only task is to look big and menacing, which frankly he could do in his sleep. The worst thing any of these people did was choose to be in the movie to begin with, but they probably thought it was a lark. I'd have shown up for free if Coleman had asked.

There is one notable actor that I haven't mentioned yet. She's Lanell Cado, an uncredited Italian girl from New York, who's the first person we see on screen and who gets pride of place because she was willing to get naked. She climbs out of the shower, dries herself with a towel and puts on her panties. Even in the regular public domain cut, we see a nipple, a fleeting shot in the mirror but one that in a 1961 monster movie makes us rewind the DVD to make sure we saw right. In the full version, there's a further nineteen seconds, mostly of Cado's breasts.

We don't know who she is and we're never told, as she's only here to remain strangely compliant and utterly silent while being strangled to death. There's a hint at necrophilia as someone lifts her legs onto the bed, fitting for the title but misleading in every other way. If this is supposed to be Javorski, he isn't a beast until the atomic blast makes him one. If it isn't, it's never mentioned again.

Cardoza has pointed out that Francis added this scene after the picture was completed, for no better reason than he liked nudity. Apparently he didn't see a problem, because he went along with it and continued working with Francis on his other two pictures. After that, he stopped for a while because he had a wife and two kids, was working full time as a welder and realised that he was doing all the hard work on these movies, raising finances, sorting out distribution and trying to sell the pictures, while Francis just wrote and directed.

It was a great deal for Francis, who was finally getting real credits and thumbing his nose at the establishment in the process, a possible further reason for the Cado scene as the Production Code would have barred that from a studio film. However it's telling that once Cardoza's involvement was over, Francis didn't write or direct again. I wonder if these three films would exist if he'd never found Cardoza's phone number.

Francis did continue to work in pictures, but they were hardly major productions. Only *PJ* was made by a studio and he was an uncredited actor. The rest were indie films for indie directors. Three were for Ray Dennis Steckler: he narrated *The Thrill Killers*, appeared in a couple of segments in *Lemon Grove Kids Meet the Monsters* and played himself, or at least a character named for him, in *Body Fever*. Two more were vanity projects for Titus Moede, an underground maverick with ties to Steckler: *The Last American Hobo* and *The Dirtiest Game*. The others were for Russ Meyer: *Motor Psycho* and *Beyond the Valley of the Dolls*, his last role, in which he played Rotund Drunk, a fair description of what he had become. Three years later he was dead in the back of a station wagon with a plastic bag over his head, forgotten by most. Like Harold P Warren, it took *Mystery Science Theater 3000* to resurrect his name. He'd be happy it has a place in history.

Huh? An A-Z of Why Classic American Bad Movies Were Made

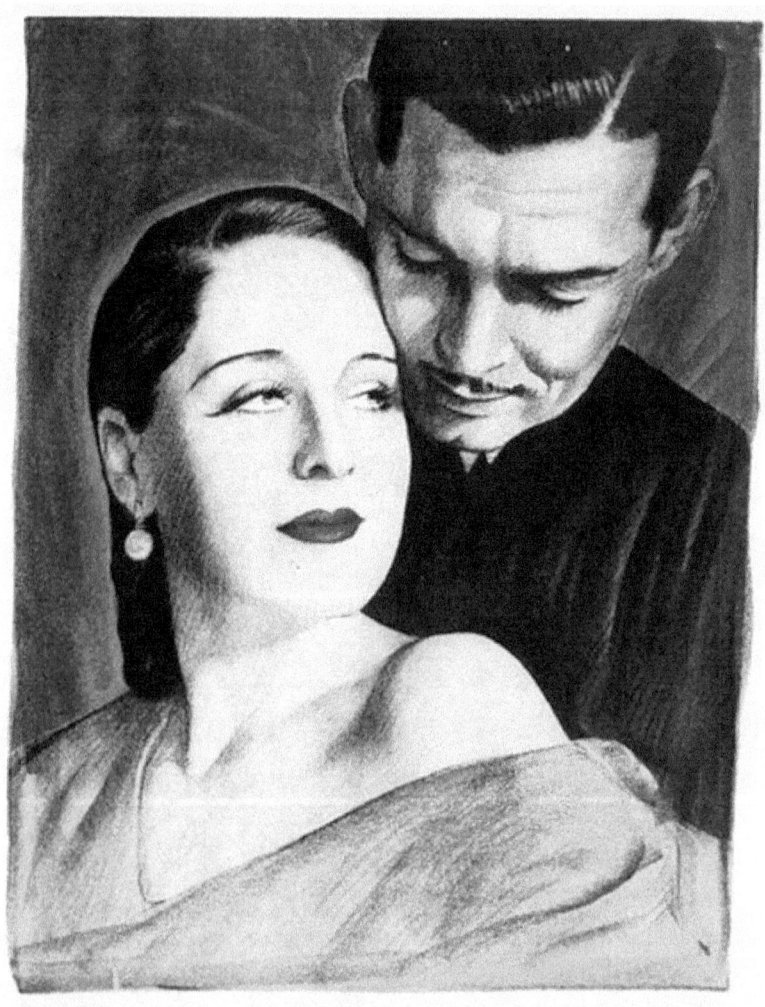

G is for Gimmickry:
Strange Interlude (1932)

Director: Robert Z Leonard
Writer: Eugene O'Neill, from his play
Stars: Norma Shearer and Clark Gable

When this project morphed from being about classic bad movies into why classic bad movies were made, *Strange Interlude* was an immediate choice.

It wouldn't have fit well otherwise with my other reviews that were mostly of genre flicks, often low budget in nature, a basic sampling of what people have traditionally called the worst movies ever made. By comparison, this was a big budget production from the biggest studio of them all that featured many major names. Yet the reason for its rather spectacular failure fits perfectly here, because it has to live or die on its gimmick, a scenario that it shares with many of those low budget genre movies. Not only does it die, it dies horribly in ways that would have swept the Razzies, had they existed in 1932. Even back then, this must have felt horrible, but the passage of eighty years has only worsened it. Now, it's frankly impossible to see this quintessentially serious picture and not laugh. Well, laugh or cry.

Like many pictures from the early thirties, when movie sound technology was still in its infancy, *Strange Interlude* was sourced from a play. It's an experimental piece from the groundbreaking American playwright Eugene O'Neill, who wrote it in 1923, with two Pulitzers already to his name for *Beyond the Horizon* and *Anna Christie*, though it wasn't staged until 1928, when it won him a third. He'd later make it four with *Long Day's Journey into Night*.

While O'Neill was established as a playwright, he wasn't yet well represented on film, perhaps because of the talky nature of his work, four of the five screen adaptations of his plays made earlier than this being of *Anna Christie*, including the famous "Garbo Talks!" picture in 1930. *Strange Interlude* played for 426 performances on Broadway, even though its nine acts meant a four hour running time that became increasingly broken up over two nights or with a break for dinner halfway through.

While the Hollywood of the thirties was drawn to popular plays like a kid to candy, you might have thought that it would have paused for thought at such a length. While epic films are nothing new, D W Griffith's *The Birth of a Nation* and *Intolerance* each running over three hours even in the mid-1910s, this isn't an epic story, it's a melodrama. MGM hacked it down to 100 minutes.

You might have thought it would have baulked at the subject matter, which had often led to the play being censored or banned outright. Even in the relatively free days of the precodes, films were allowed less than plays. This material was all cut, prompting O'Neill to call it the adaptation of his work that he liked the least and that MGM had "censored it into near-imbecility."

Most of all, you'd think that they'd have seen flags in the gimmick, which to my eyes is an idea inherently rooted in the stage and utterly unsuited to film, except in parody, as Groucho Marx ably demonstrated in 1930's *Animal Crackers*.

This gimmick is a modern adaptation of the soliloquy, a theatrical convention that allows an actor to temporarily remove himself from the body of the play and speak his thoughts aloud. It's an age old convention well used by Shakespeare, who wrote some of the most famous soliloquys, such as "To be or not to be" from *Hamlet* or "Romeo, Romeo, wherefore art thou, Romeo?" in *Romeo and Juliet*.

Usually grandiose in nature, it mostly disappeared from the stage when playwrights moved more towards realism, but O'Neill brought it back with a vengeance. Rather than give his characters a few long soliloquys, he wrote them many brief ones, more like asides not aimed at the audience, and they pepper the dialogue continually. To avoid staginess on film, they were provided here in voiceover, as the actors pause to look pensive and act out their thoughts with facial movements or body language. Unfortunately, this breaks the flow, prompts overacting and looks stupid.

Revisiting *Strange Interlude* after almost a decade, it looks even more stupid than before, because now I realise just how important these actors are. When I first saw it, I didn't have much of a clue. I had seen May Robson in *Lady for a Day* and *Bringing Up Baby* and Maureen O'Sullivan in Tarzan movies, but I only really knew Clark Gable at this point and even there I hadn't yet realised what importance his precodes had, as he singlehandedly redefined the concept of masculinity by slapping his co-star here, Norma Shearer, a year earlier in *A Free Soul*. Now, I realise that this was a major cast, not only Gable, who would literally be voted King of Hollywood in 1938, but Shearer, the epitome of the liberated woman on film and the wife of MGM's wunderkind, Irving Thalberg; Ralph Morgan, a perennial screen villain who co-founded the Screen Actors Guild and served as its first president; and Robert Young, who later found fame on TV in *Father Knows Best* and *Marcus Welby, MD*.

Unlike some critics, I don't believe the actors were miscast, even Gable clearly there to serve as the masculine ideal, as he did so often in the precodes. However they're as clearly hamstrung by the gimmick as the film is by its relentless bowdlerisation.

The story revolves around Nina Leeds, who begins as a histrionic young lady pining for Gordon Shaw, a World War I flier shot down and killed in action. In turn, a family friend, Charlie Marsden, pines for her but can't confess his love. She decides to honour Gordon's name by caring for disabled servicemen in a sanitorium, only to turn into a tramp. She marries Sam Evans, a likeable but forgettable soul, but is then warned by his mother that hereditary insanity in his family means she shouldn't have kids. So she bears the child of Dr Ned Darrell, his best friend, whose career can't afford a relationship, while pretending that it's Sam's. As you can imagine, she falls for Darrell and heartrending melodrama ensues.

I tried to imagine how this would all play out without the gimmick. Back in 1932, it would surely have been much better, audiences generally being far more accepting of melodramas. Nowadays, it would still be improved, though the result would be painful nonetheless. Perhaps going back to the original play might work, as the 253 minute television adaptation for *American Playhouse* did in 1988, but I haven't seen it or the play, so I can only assume that it all unfolds better as O'Neill wrote it rather than as Hollywood crippled it.

One major problem here is that there isn't a single character worth caring about or rooting for. O'Neill is known for his pessimistic realism, so it may be that he's as responsible for that as the Hollywood screenwriters who attempted to adapt his work. Certainly the soliloquy gimmick enhances the pessimism, almost every voiceover thought being negative, if not downright bitchy, and, yes, I'm talking about the men too.

If it would be a poor film without the gimmick, it's a truly abysmal one with it, as highlighted by the few scenes that are fast paced enough to disallow the possibility for thought.

The best scene in the film is probably the one where Nina's mother-in-law explains the insanity in the family and rushes her upstairs to look at Sam's crazy cackling aunt. Without time to think, this is traditional and capably shot, but it doesn't run long, and any dramatic tension it builds is lost with the first thought that follows.

You see, every thought means a pause, not just by the actor who's thinking but to the action unfolding or the conversation in motion. We discover in the very first scene that two characters can't think at the same time because they would interfere with each other, so the thoughts unfold in serial rather than parallel. Soon afterwards, there's a thought conversation in which Darrell and Marsden politely take turns thinking while the actors mirror it all in facial tics.

Perhaps the definitive scene of the picture has the four main characters fall into thoughtful poses in close quarters, while Nina thinks about her "three men". It's a well composed shot, beautifully put together, and Nina's thought underlines how picturesque it all is: "That makes it perfect!" she thinks. The catch is that it's not the result of happy characters thinking happy thoughts, it's the result of miserable characters thinking miserable thoughts, so it becomes a perversion of the picturesque, a parody in which three of the four characters in shot look utterly downtrodden. Only Sam, apparently immune from such misery, is happy and in being so, appears to have photobombed the scene.

The definitive scene for the gimmick is the one when Marsden becomes Sam's silent partner entirely as a dig at Darrell, after figuring out his and Nina's big secret through a surreal Mexican thought standoff. Thoughts here are musings far less often than they're weapons.

While the gimmick has aged terribly, the film has aged even worse, though not always on its own merits. While melodrama has been out of style since the 1940s, the sort of story that feels like it's being depressing for the sake of being depressing has been out of style since the 1970s, after the kitchen sink drama ran its course. Those films succeeded because of their grounding in working class struggles, eliciting at least some sympathy at the plight of others. This kitchen sink drama is from an era where the characters never need to see the kitchen, let alone the sink, and there isn't any sympathy in their misery. They dug their own holes and frankly, we don't want to see them climb out. We don't care about characters like this any more, who spend years sick because they don't want to be well, flounce around for sixty years not declaring their love or describe falling in love and getting pregnant as "that scientific afternoon," even if only half of it was planned.

Some of it is pure coincidence and utterly not the fault of the filmmakers at all, but still telling to posterity. When Robert Young tells Clark Gable that he ought to spank him, it isn't just sexually inappropriate, it's the punchline to a cinematic joke that hadn't been written yet. It's as wrong as Jackie Chan having to fight Peter Fonda. Ralph Morgan cornered the market on polite heels who were less gentlemanly than those given to George Sanders, but his endless scheming in thought makes him reminiscent of Jonathan Harris in *Lost in Space*. Suddenly Good Old Charlie becomes Sinister Dr Smith and any power in his acting is gone. Even worse, translating the play's gimmick to voiceover as actors pause for effect feels like a gift to *Mystery Science Theater 3000*. As each thought is more histrionic than the last, as well as the speech that preceded it, it's increasingly difficult to avoid hearing these thoughts as inserted comments by Joel and the bots.

Some of it is less forgiveable. Having Shearer get more and more melodramatic, even as she says, "I can't feel anything at all," sounds like deliberate irony, but it isn't. It's incompetent writing. When she falls into Charlie's lap and confesses that she's been bad and wants to be punished, that may have been free of sexual innuendo in 1932 but it certainly couldn't lead to Charlie telling her that she should marry Sam in anything but a bad script. Given that Shearer brought life to a vast array of Adrian's famous gowns in MGM movies, her truly awful dress here that serves only to highlight that she isn't wearing a bra is a major mistake.

Perhaps aging the adult characters two decades for every one young Gordon Evans grows is a deliberate commentary on how misery adds years but I doubt it. It's just overdone makeup, even if it gave Gable his first screen moustache. Above all, the gimmick isn't forgiveable at all. Even William Castle couldn't have made it work.

Huh? An A-Z of Why Classic American Bad Movies Were Made

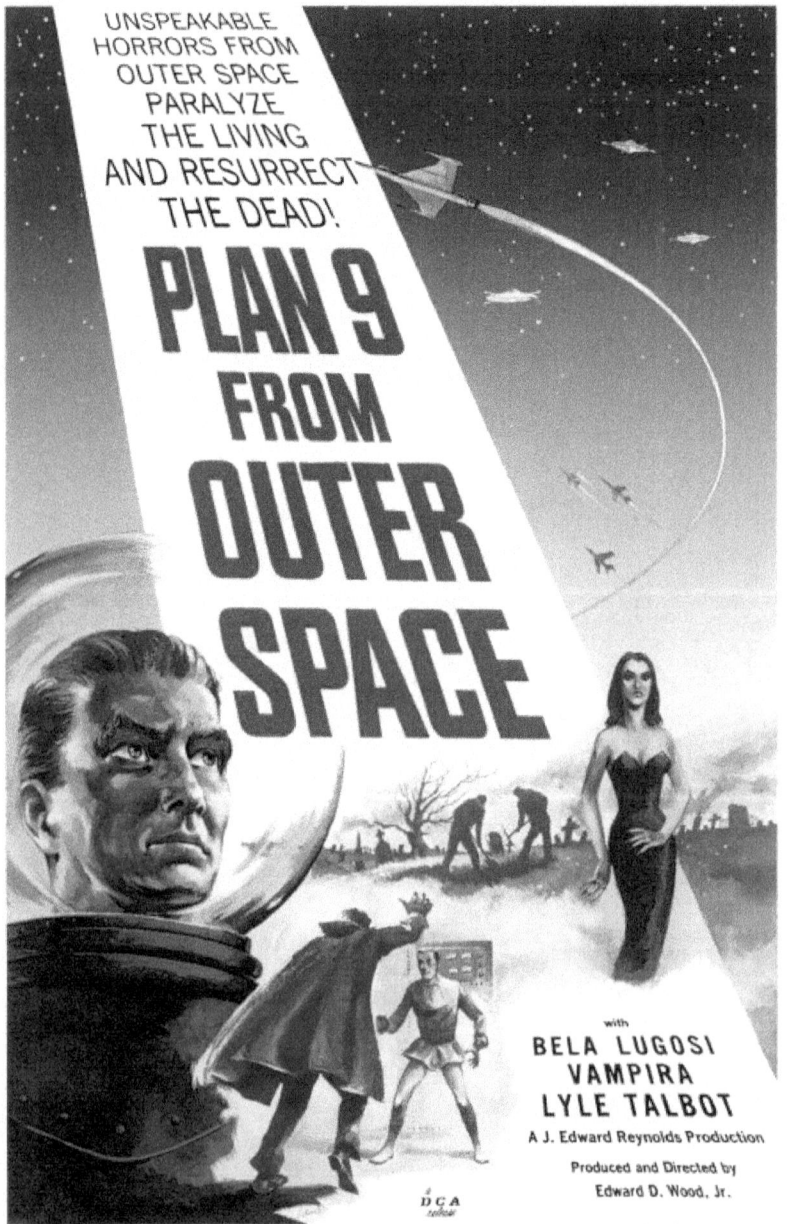

H is for Hubris:
Plan 9 from Outer Space (1959)

Director: Edward D Wood Jr
Writer: Edward D Wood Jr
Stars: Tor Johnson, Vampira, Tom Keene and Gregory Walcott

Whenever I review *Plan 9 from Outer Space*, I can't help but compare it to *Manos: The Hands of Fate.* After all, they're the two films most frequently regarded as the worst ever made, the latter slowly taking over from the former as it creeps out into the public eye. Both are as easy to pick apart as any films made, because their respective flaws leap out of the screen and slap us silly.

However, they really are works from completely different worlds and *Plan 9 from Outer Space* is superior in almost every regard, the comparison serving mostly to highlight Wood's unique position in bad movies as a professional. Put simply, he knew how to make a movie. The key to understanding him and his work is to realise that he made what he wanted to see and he focused on the things that he wanted to see most. Like Quentin Tarantino or Rob Zombie, he created patchwork quilts of everything he had seen and thought was awesomely cool. Wood merely didn't care about the stitches.

And that's where his arrogance, his hubris, comes in. His pictures contained everything he loved from other films, but he expected audiences to pay to see them. In that, he's far from alone in the movie business, but he also expected them to see them how he saw them. He cared about the stars, enough to build his own bizarre ensemble company of them to populate his movies. He cared about the ambience of B movies, the Transylvanian castles, the haunted graveyards, the laboratories of mad scientists. He cared about the monsters, the fun gimmicks, the cheesy dialogue. In short, he was a fan. What he didn't care about was how bad most of those films really were, so he ignored how bad most of his films really were when he set out to replicate it. When a tombstone gets knocked over in an Ed Wood movie, he never reshot it because to him it really wasn't important. He would have ignored it, therefore his audience would ignore it too.

With *Plan 9 from Outer Space* though, he added a whole new level of arrogance. He made it and marketed it as a Bela Lugosi picture, even though Bela Lugosi was dead before he began. That does take a special type of arrogance, even if he may also have intended it quite sincerely as a tribute to a dear friend and colleague. He did have some brief graveyard footage of Lugosi that he'd shot for another project, called *Tomb of the Vampire* or *The Ghoul Goes West*, so he found a way to splice this into graveyard scenes in this new picture, not caring that some were day and some were night, so the sun magically appears and disappears frequently as we switch between characters. Wood also had some footage of Lugosi walking down Tor Johnson's front path, so he added a voiceover that explained how tortured this old man is by the death of his dear wife and promptly has him put out of his misery by an off screen car that leaves his shadow untouched.

This is the sort of thing that's remembered by people who cite this film as the worst of all time, and frankly I'm not going to argue with them because they're right. However they tend to forget what else Wood does here.

Plan 9 from Outer Space has crisp visuals, synchronised sound and capable tracking shots. There are some decent special effects alongside the bad ones, excellent make up work and an appropriate soundtrack. It has opening credits too, cool ones with names carved into tombstones to boot. Harold P Warren couldn't even dream about any of these things. Then again, Wood had three times the budget to work with, even a decade earlier and working as cheaply as he possibly could. That's $60,000 to procure real film to shoot on, and use of real sound stages and studio lights, so that whatever happens in the film, at least we're able to see it. Cameraman Bill Thompson knew how to put them to decent effect. It even has a great poster.

Where Warren had El Paso theatre actors and aspiring models, Wood had a whole smörgåsbord of cult actors that would have made this film famous even if there were no other reason. There's Vampira, the original TV horror host with her delightful cleavage and her tiny waist. There's Tor Johnson, the bald wrestler with his thick Swedish accent, who became the Beast of Yucca Flats. There's the Amazing Criswell, a phony psychic famed for his stunningly inaccurate predictions. There's the flamboyantly gay but still rich and influential drag queen, John 'Bunny' Breckinridge. And of course there was Bela Lugosi, however much of him is really Tom Mason with a *Dracula* style cape held up to his face to hide how different he looked from the star he was substituting for. Of all things, Mason was the chiropractor of Wood's wife, hired when the filmmaker saw a similarity in his eyes that he thought he could use to good effect.

The story is laughable. There are flying saucers over Hollywood, wobbly flying saucers that the stock footage army can't shoot down. They're here because mankind has developed explosive technology far too quickly for its own good and we're apparently on the verge of destroying the universe. We know this because we watched *The Day the Earth Stood Still*, the characters in the film know it because they've secretly managed to build a language computer that can translate every language into American, except perhaps English. What's more, the aliens know it so they broadcast a plea to us in an attempt to get us to pay attention. They do speak fluent American but we're not supposed to notice that. We're not supposed to notice a lot in this film, but we are supposed to notice the plea, unlike the authorities who missed plans one to eight. So now these persevering aliens are mounting plan nine.

What's plan nine, you might ask? Bunny, as the alien leader, lets us in on their secret: "Ah, yes. Plan 9 deals with the resurrection of the dead. Long distance electrodes shot into the pineal and pituitary glands of the recently dead." In other words they want to scare us by having zombies march on the nations' capitals, in an echo of what Ozymandias would later do in *Watchmen*. And I thought *Night of the Living Dead* was really about communism! Apparently it was a wake up call from aliens to stop building bombs. How naive I was! At least I'm not naive enough to know that plan nine will succeed where the others failed, because if anything has been drummed into us by bad movies, it's that pesky aliens with electrode guns and nifty space age costumes never win out in the end over superior human intellect. For all his outsider sensibilities, Wood was all about the formulae that the movies he loved adhered to, so he adhered to them too.

Fortunately these aliens have a good whack at it first, shooting long distance electrodes into the pineal and pituitary glands of our cult cast, turning them into the coolest zombies that cinema ever saw. Vampira is an unnamed lady, fortunately buried in a glorious gown with stylish rips to expose a tantalising amount of cleavage. She's supposedly the wife whose death Bela's old man is so tortured by, Wood not explaining why they would be married, given that Vampira was 35 and Lugosi over 73. He just has aliens resurrect them both. Tor Johnson is killed and resurrected too, playing Inspector Daniel Clay with a vitality that doesn't even hint at what terrible shape he would be in for Coleman Francis's *The Beast of Yucca Flats*. That was released a mere two years after this, but the films were shot five years apart, this one filmed as *Grave Robbers from Outer Space* in 1956 and completed in 1957, but not released until 1959.

There are expected subplots that we're supposed to pay attention to. An airline pilot named Jeff Trent is hassled by a flying saucer, hanging outside his plane's window on a string. Conveniently, he also lives right next to the graveyard that it decides to park in and glow at us from. There's a general at the Pentagon, played by Lyle Talbot, who is investigating the aliens and he sends a colonel to California to investigate. There are cops galore, nearly as many as there are Baptists, who all got bit parts because they financed the movie, but none are any use whatsoever. These aren't Keystone Kops but if they'd stayed around for thirty years until Rodney King's day, given that it's precisely the same neighbourhood, he'd have kicked their asses and saved Los Angeles from "53 deaths, 2,383 injuries, more than 7,000 fires, damages to 3,100 businesses, and nearly $1 billion in financial losses." Let's hear it for idiot Hollywood cops.

I can partially watch this with the childlike innocence that Ed Wood would have wanted me too, concentrating on all the outrageous lines, monsters and old school shock moments, because to be fair they're pretty cool from that mindset. However I much prefer his previous film, *Bride of the Monster*, on that level. To my way of thinking, that's a heartfelt tribute to the horror movies of the thirties and forties which were going out of style and it works in the same way the films it references worked. This one is wilder but less controlled, so I end up watching it as a bad movie fan, enjoying my favourite zombies lurch around their cardboard graveyard while picking out all the best continuity errors that Wood would want me to ignore. The flying saucers are described as cigar shaped when they really are shaped like saucers. Soldiers leave shadows on backdrops that should be sky. Pilots fly planes without controls and with scripts on their laps.

And I do all of this with a grin on my face, because whatever else this is, it's entertaining. That's the only reason why *Plan 9 from Outer Space*, regarded since at least *The Golden Turkey Awards* in 1980 as the worst movie ever made, doesn't show up in the IMDb Bottom 100 list any longer. *Manos: The Hands of Fate* has a solid place near to the bottom. Every film Coleman Francis ever made follows close behind. Other grade Z classics reviewed in this book, like *The Beast of Yucca Flats*, *Eegah* and *The Creeping Terror* have consistent places there too, but this doesn't. It's too much fun to watch. It carries with it, albeit in an outsider way, some of the Hollywood magic that Wood was so in love with. It really was 'Made in Hollywood', magic words back in 1959 without the negative edge that they carry today. Wood was the ultimate Hollywood outsider, but he was still part of the big Hollywood story. Few indie filmmakers of the day could honestly say that.

I for one am thankful for the arrogance that called Ed Wood to make movies. He had an urge to create that has been rarely matched. In *Incredibly Strange Films*, Jim Morton wrote that, "Lesser men, if forced to make movies under the conditions Wood faced, would have thrown up their hands in defeat." Yet he completed a wild set of pictures, including *Glen or Glenda*, *Jail Bait* and *Bride of the Monster*, before descending into softcore and eventually hardcore pornography, in film and on paper, writing at least eighty sex or crime novels. His relationship with Bela Lugosi, including the sheer hubris that prompted Wood to put him into *Plan 9 from Outer Space*, ended up winning Martin Landau an Oscar for playing Lugosi in Tim Burton's *Ed Wood*. He got baptised to secure funding for this film, but ironically is now the focus of his own religion, the admittedly tongue in cheek Church of Ed Wood. Who am I to argue with the arrogance of a god?

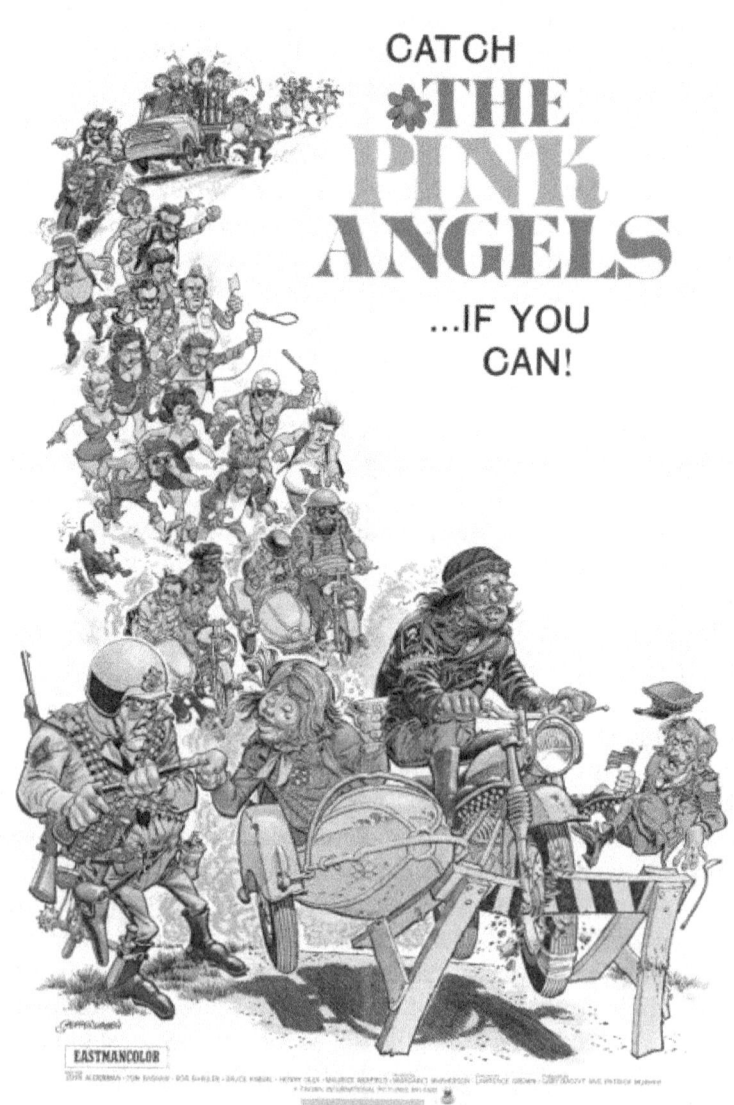

I is for Insanity:
Pink Angels (1971)

Director: Larry G Brown
Writer: Margaret McPherson
Stars: John Alderman, Tom Basham, Henry Olek, Bruce Kimball, Maurice Warfield and Robert Biheller

The most obvious reason *Pink Angels* was made was because of a bet, as with *Manos: The Hands of Fate*. Someone bet Gary Radzat that he wouldn't be able to make and obtain US distribution for a motion picture. I don't know who bet him, when the bet was made or whether he ever got his winnings, but Radzat certainly won that bet as Crown International released *Pink Angels* to five thousand theatres.

Beyond being bet winners, Harold G Warren and Gary Radzat couldn't be more different. Warren was an inept filmmaker who chose to serve as writer, producer, director and star anyway; Radzat took a saner approach and hired others to make his picture, restricting himself to the role of producer. Warren's budget was $19,000, while Radzat surely raised a lot more than that. Warren's career died as it began but he would have made films forever if only people would have let him; Radzat seems to have had no interest in making another movie.

Perhaps because of those differences, the results are light years apart. Warren made an unholy and incoherent mess, thoroughly amateur in every regard and full of every mistake in the book. I'm still not sure what Radzat made, but at least it feels professional. It's certainly watchable and yet unlike anything you're likely to have seen before. It could easily stake a claim to being ahead of its time, with its nearest comparisons coming a quarter of a century later: *The Adventures of Priscilla, Queen of the Desert* and *To Wong Foo Thanks for Everything, Julie Newmar*.

So I should explain who the Pink Angels are, given that if you google for them you're going to come up with paintball guns and Japanese rape fantasies. Initially they seem to be a random bunch of bikers, in their denim, leather and Nazi memorabilia, but we soon find that they're really drag queens, not just gay but really gay, heading down the Californian coast in disguise to a cotillion.

The scene in which we discover the charade is one of the great "Huh?" scenes of cinema. The six leads drive into an A&W, paired up in three motorcycle sidecars, and play up biker stereotypes, disrespecting their surroundings and hinting violence to the counter girl and the hitcher they'd just picked up. It's all obviously fake but their true selves become readily apparent. One gets jealous and calls his bitch, get this, a "fickle pringle," only to have his fake beard ripped off in return. "We're being watched," one points out as a crowd gathers. "Everyone is looking at us!" So they deepen their voices again and start a food fight with condiments. "Hit me hard, you fool!" one cries as the ketchup and mustard fly like they're in a Jackson Pollock action painting. No wonder the hitcher runs. However, it's apparently some sort of revelation to him that, "Jesus Christ, you're all faggots!" Did he miss the white garter the gang leader wears on his arm?

It was here that I first wondered just what the motivation for the picture was and everything that unfolded from that point on merely added to my wonder. Put simply, I could see two audiences for the movie, bikers and gay men, which were both seemingly written away from. The opening scene in terrible light is only discernible as some sort of standoff with authority at a hotel pool, though I'm not sure if it feels more like an acid trip, aided by experimental music, or a bad frat comedy of the sort that has drunken pledges dressed in drag. It's followed by a general being chauffeured to his base, where we later find him sitting in front of the stars and stripes fondling a riding crop while listening to reel to reel tapes that rail against deviants and sex criminals. The credits unfold against a gloriously cinematic backdrop looking like nothing less than a Pink Floyd album cover, a sort of graveyard for huge concrete conduit.

Obviously we're setting this up as a clash between freedom and oppression, hardly a surprising theme for a biker movie, but it's a really bizarre way to frame it. Maybe *Pink Angels* can only be understood by looking at what was happening in the wider world of the counterculture at the time. Bikers had been a dominant image since the fifties because they felt they could opt out of society and live free on the road. Was there ever a more blatant threat to society than Brando in *The Wild One?* When he's asked, "What are you rebelling against, Johnny?" he famously replies, "Whaddya got?" Biker movies were an exploitation genre of their own in the late sixties and early seventies, after the massive success of *Easy Rider.* Another key genre at the time was porno chic, as for a short few years porn was fashionable, vaguely feminist and near mainstream with *Deep Throat, The Devil in Miss Jones* and *Behind the Green Door* playing to celebrities in mainstream theaters.

It's hardly surprising that audiences were reevaluating sexuality and authority, given a backdrop of free love, Vietnam war protests and the civil rights movement. Changes in the world of cinema helped that to be reflected on screen. By the late sixties, the Production Code which had defined morality on screen since 1934 proved to be no longer enforceable, allowing filmmakers a much broader palette to work from.

Also studio bosses lost touch with the youth audience, which had drifted away to a growing world of independent exploitation cinema. They attempted to address this by hiring film school gradutes to make Hollywood movies with million dollar budgets and complete artistic freedom. The so called New Hollywood directors, such as Dennis Hopper, Peter Bogdanovich and Francis Ford Coppola frequently came from Roger Corman's companies and made movies rooted in the counterculture that changed the face of American film.

So with this background, was *Pink Angels* an argument that gay men were just as marginalised as outlaw bikers in the American society of 1971? In combining these two oppressed minorities, was it highlighting their similarities or suggesting that bikers had become more accepted than gay men, given that the latter have to disguise as the former to get by? Regular folk don't mess with bikers, bars have prostitutes all ready and waiting for them and even cops understand how to deal with them. In fact, while there's a suggestion here that homosexual and transvestite are synonyms, it's the latter that gets a particular nod in a telling scene that has our leading ladies pulled over by the cops. While they have trouble with the bikers being fairies, one of them being black, confederate flags not withstanding, and one being a Liverpudlian poet without a driving license, it's the women's clothing that really throws them and seems the biggest disconnect.

Half of me believes that *Pink Angels* is a product of its time, when it seemed natural to question things and raise issues in film, especially independent film, just as a matter of course, and it's natural to explore what those questions and issues are, especially when the story is as wild and unexpected as this. Radzat freely admits that his film was shot as cinéma vérité, a varied style that seeks truth through provocation.

Yet the other half of me seems pretty convinced that I'm just searching for meaning in a picture that doesn't have any. The filmmakers may have set up scenes to be improvised through but there may be no truth to be found. The writing credit is to Margaret McPherson, who never earned another one, suggesting that maybe she didn't actually have a lot to say. How much was she responsible for the plethora of what now seems painfully stereotypical gay behaviour and how much were the obviously improvising actors?

The latter is a good possibility, because for a movie built off a bet it has a substantial cast from which you'd recognise a few faces. Mostly it was cast from film school students at the University of Southern California, male and female, but also from independent exploitation film regulars.

Two of the six leads were prolific: John Alderman as Michael, the leader of the gang, and Bruce Kimball as Arnold, the big guy with a fake beard. With credits back to 1958, Alderman appeared in what seems like every exploitation subgenre in the book, all the way to hardcore porn in the eighties under the pseudonym of Frank Hollowell. Kimball had been working since 1966, often in biker movies like *Chrome and Hot Leather*, *Wild Wheels* and *Run, Angel, Run!*, though not always as a biker. He was also a regular in softcore hicksploitation for Bethel Buckalew and featured in other exploitation titles from *The Mighty Gorga* to *Dracula vs Frankenstein* via *Love Camp 7*.

Henry Olek, who plays Eddie, the Liverpudlian in John Lennon glasses, was just starting out but he became a regular face on American TV throughout the seventies. Ronnie, the black queen, is Maurice Warfield, who retired from the screen but returned in 2000 for a few film and TV roles. Robert Biheller plays Henry, the most flagrant sissy of the group, who looks like a moptopped Monkee. He made a few films in the sixties but this was it between 1968 and 1993. He earned a lot of TV credits though, including a long run on *Here Come the Brides*, which has nothing to do with this film, I promise.

Rounding out the Pink Angels is Tom Basham, who reminds massively of Bill Murray as denim clad David. He returned to the screen in 1975 for *The Psychopath*, which was written, produced and directed by this film's director, Larry Brown. In that he played the lead role of a children's TV show host who stalks and murders abusive parents.

Half an hour into the picture our fake biker gang meets up with a real biker gang and there are even more recognisable faces there: Michael Pataki and Grizzly Adams himself, Dan Haggerty. Pataki is their leader, channeling Jack Nicholson and building up his counterculture presence a bit from his mime role in *Easy Rider*. He was prolific in the seventies, on TV and film, but stayed active, earning his last credit in 2010, the year he died. Haggerty is in amazing shape as one of Pataki's barechested bikers. He'd been in *Easy Rider* too, though uncredited as both an actor and a motorcycle builder. Obviously part of the scene, he was also a bodybuilder, animal trainer and stuntman, but most of his parts at this point were as bikers. It isn't surprising. If he walked down the road towards you at this point, he wouldn't look like a mountain man but a biker. Amazingly neither of these two get much to do, beyond wake up in make up and with bows in their hair.

Admittedly the last third of the film involves a vague pursuit plot as the real bikers chase the fake ones to "kill those bananas" but they end up picking them up instead, as they'd switched into drag and these bikers are idiots. It's all ignorable, just as the brief scenes with the General, played by *Putney Swope*'s George Marshall, amount to nothing more than a vague excuse for the blisteringly out there ending, which apparently was shot later because, as Radzat describes him, "the director was insane" and had forgotten to film one.

To our eyes, the General is a cross between Henry Gibson's character in *The Blues Brothers* and General Jack D Ripper from *Dr Strangelove*. As he doesn't connect with the main story whatsoever until the last minute, I'm sure his few scenes were shot along with the ending. It's as outrageously hamfisted an ending as I may ever have seen and it's hard to believe that they couldn't come up with a better one.

The way in which the ending doesn't fit in the slightest highlights the suggestion that there was no script at all, merely a set of locations that the actors got to improvise in so a vague picture could be edited together after the fact. The whole film has a destination which never arrives, so perhaps the only way to end the film is a surgical strike, quick and painless, which the General does at the 80 minute mark. There was a film, now there isn't.

There's one final view that comes totally out of nowhere but it can't seriously be considered as part of the film proper. The last few minutes can be safely ignored as we go back to the most overt cinéma vérité, as the Pink Angels realise their women's clothing is lost and so have to outfit Ronnie afresh from local stores, ones apparently run by their real proprietors, given the shocked and bemused reactions captured on camera. I'm sure mine looked rather similar but for different reasons.

Ultimately, after all the questioning and analysing, I'm still not convinced this isn't just a one joke movie. If the film was constructed during the editing phase from however much footage they shot in potentially useful locations, maybe that's all it is. It's a situation comedy designed around having limp wristed caricatures pretending to be tough bikers. That's really not a funny joke to begin with and it doesn't get any better, though it might improve with a serious quantity of narcotics.

The funniest part may well be when David can't pick which bathroom to use at a gas station, but when he finally picks the gents, Henry prances out of the ladies. Maybe it's when David is dropped back with the others by a couple of girls who have apparently raped him and stolen his jeans. Surely it can't be the picnic scene, with red tablecloth and candelabras. Let me lend this to a gay friend and see if he can find anything remotely humorous. I doubt it.

In fact I should do that anyway to try to discover the audience. While this is a film built around gay characters and oppression, I have a feeling the gay audience would be offended by the use of stereotypes and inaccurate merging of subcultures. At least when our leads become ladies, they adopt drag conventions and refer to each other by persona rather than name.

Yet what would a biker audience make of it? Surely having tranvestites pretend to be bikers is about as offensive to them as having a black audience watch white men in blackface playing dice and carving up watermelon. If they can get past that, what would they think of the real bikers, who are the densest in the whole film.

Were stoned hippies going to drive ins in 1971? Maybe at the end of the day, there was no audience, there was just a bet. Whatever else this film achieved, it won Gary Radzat a bet. Yet, I can't get past his statement that "the director was insane."

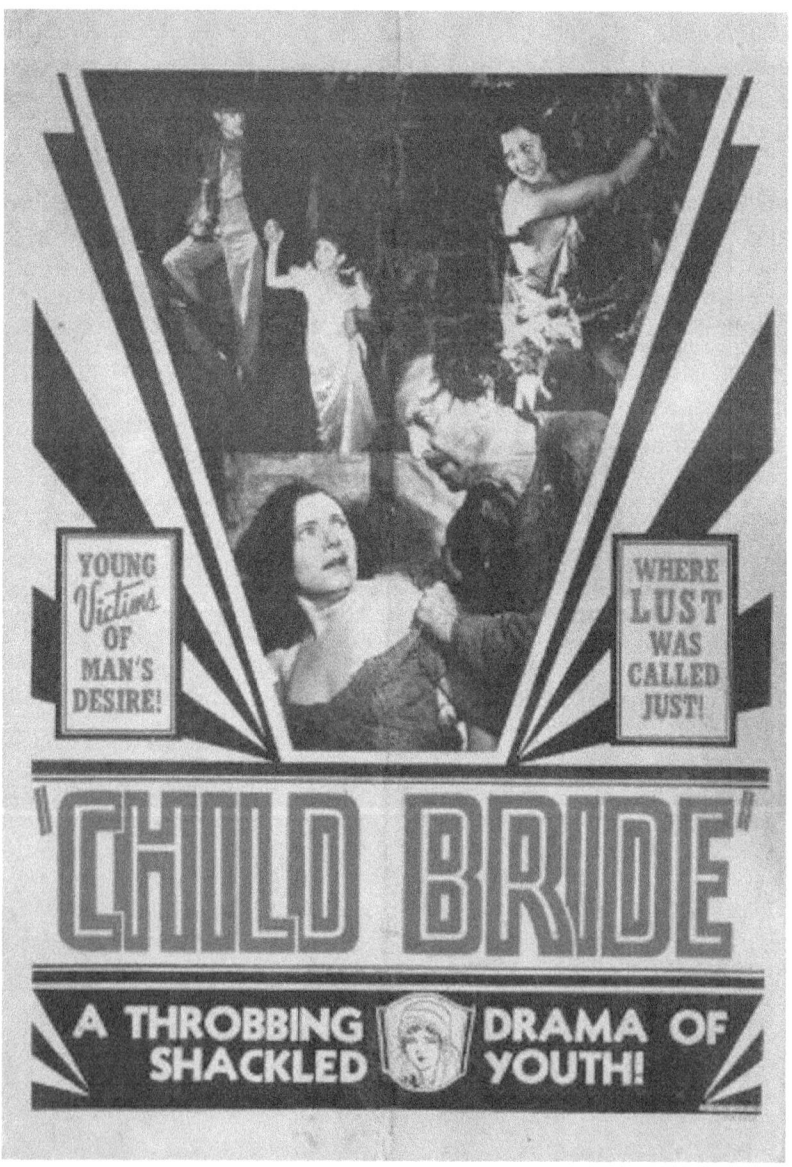

J is for Justice:
Child Bride (1938)

Director: Harry J Revier
Writer: Harry J Revier
Stars: Shirley Mills and Bob Bollinger

While many films reviewed in this book were riffed on *Mystery Science Theater 3000*, three have particular strong ties to that show. The folk who wrote it saw *Monster a-Go Go* as the worst picture ever made until they discovered *Manos: The Hands of Fate*, which promptly took over the title until the 20th anniversary celebration of the show at the 2008 San Diego Comic-Con. With almost every major contributor to the show sharing a panel, they were asked if they'd ever passed on anything even worse. Their answer was 1938's *Child Bride*, which they described as "Appalachian kiddie porn from the '30s". They chose not to screen it, even though it wouldn't have been difficult to use a cut version that doesn't include the controversial skinny dipping scene. The film is in the public domain and almost every version available omits that scene, for obvious reasons. Only Alpha Video have it available uncut and while the MST3K description is a little unfair, it's definitely a disturbing film.

It's also a rather unique one in many ways because it doesn't fit well with the only obvious category of films that springs to mind. Back in the thirties, the studio system had control of both production and distribution and, as of 1934, their films were subject to the Production Code, which substantially restricted the content of the pictures they made. To include salacious subject matter in your movie, you had to make it independently and book it into theatres not owned by the studios. Many people enjoyed this creative freedom and made outrageous pictures, often drumming up custom as if they were carnival barkers and then skipping town after the show.

While these folk weren't subject to the restrictions of the Production Code, they still had to stay on the right side of local censorship laws, which varied from town to town, so they tended to phrase their stories in educational terms, often with a speaker warning about the dangers of the topic at hand and selling pamphlets decrying it.

And so there were indie pictures about every social ill known to 1930s America: drug use, teenage pregnancy, abortion, STDs, prostitution... you name it. In every instance, these films spun melodramatic stories around their topics, occasionally illustrated with nudity, which ended up highlighting in no uncertain terms how dangerous it was not to be an upstanding moral citizen. Thus the films got by whatever local censorship was in place and audiences saw things that they couldn't possibly see in pictures from the major Hollywood studios.

One notorious example is 1945's *Mom and Dad*, which was shot in six days for $63,000 but grossed over $80m, ranking it the third highest grossing film of the entire 1940s and still one of the most successful films ever made, based on return of investment, up there with *The Blair Witch Project* and *Paranormal Activity*. Inept in most regards, it had one magic ingredient to draw in the crowds: it included real footage of a baby being born. That's all it took.

Child Bride may appear to fit in that sort of company, especially as it was made by a fly by night producer whose cheques bounced and promises remained unfulfilled, but the more you analyse it the more it's an uneasy fit. Sure, it's a crusading picture, but its particular cause stands up today as valid, perhaps as it didn't need to rely on misinformation. Sure, it has an outrageous story, but it's a believable one for a change, because it plucked an outrageous story from the headlines and didn't need to embellish it.

Most anomalous, though, is the fact that its lead actor remained proud of the film and her part in it until the day she died. Reactions like that are so rare with this sort of film that I can't cite another instance. Real actors, not that many real actors were involved in such films, tend to look back with raised eyebrows at such low points in their careers, or just avoid looking back at all. If they had careers, they tended to predate these pictures rather than follow them.

Yet Shirley Mills, who was only twelve at the time she shot *Child Bride*, remained proud of the film and her work in it until her death in 2010. She had every opportunity to avoid remembering this, her feature film debut, but she played up to it and what she felt it had achieved. She was already established on stage, singing and dancing in vaudeville venues as 'Seattle's Shirley Temple' since she was a toddler. She also built a minor career, especially in the forties, as a supporting actress in Hollywood, including a slot as the young daughter of the Joads in John Ford's *The Grapes of Wrath*. Before she retired from the screen at 26, she had made 27 films for directors as highly regarded as Michael Curtiz, George Cukor and Alfred Hitchcock. Yet she highlighted *Child Bride*, saying that, "I was proud to appear in that film," and explaining on her website that it took a filmmaker working outside of the system to make a picture that educated the public on a very real issue.

That issue was child marriage, of course, but it hadn't sprung out of nowhere. It was inspired by a real wedding that took place on a dirt road in Hancock County, TN on 19th January, 1937 when Rev Walter Lamb, a Baptist preacher, married Charlie Johns and Eunice Winstead. They had a license, albeit one obtained through false information; Tennessee law prohibited issuing them to girls under twelve, so Johns claimed Winstead was eighteen. Nobody checked. In reality she was nine to his twenty-two.

Lamb dismissed criticism on the basis that they'd have got another preacher to marry them if he'd said no. There was no undue influence as they really wanted to wed. It was a shock to Winstead's parents but they gave their approval on the basis that they'd been married under God and they didn't want to risk hellfire for their daughter by undoing that. Winstead found the concern unfathomable. They remained married until her husband died at 82 and she gave him nine children.

But the country took notice. After word got out, the story was covered by major newspapers, such as *The New York Times*, and major magazines, such as *Life*, who visited the couple in their cabin and published photos which brought home to the American public just how young Eunice Winstead was.

Married for less than a month, they had sparked a national debate. It soon became apparent that child brides were far from uncommon, ten states allowing boys to marry at fourteen and girls at twelve, so with opposition building nationwide and states hastily updating their laws, it was all ripe for adaptation to the screen by an enterprising producer. So Frederick Falcon of Falcon Pictures rolled into rural Columbia, CA in 1938 to lease its recreation park for a year so he could shoot *Child Bride* on location with a few stars and a host of local talent and follow up with a new picture every six weeks. However, Falcon was really Raymond L Friedgen and Falcon Pictures didn't exist.

Naturally the locals, naïve to the ways of huckster filmmakers, leapt on board, extending credit all around town and eagerly helping out in any way that they could, building sets and playing extras. Of course all they got out of it was an experience, because 'Frederick Falcon' rolled on out of town again at the end of the two week shoot, never to return, and paid all his bills with rubber cheques.

It was an eye opener for Columbia, whose residents unwittingly paid in time, money and effort to be volunteers on a movie being shot in their town. Most of them probably never even saw the finished product, which gradually found its way onto the exploitation circuit under the inevitable collection of alternative titles like *Child Brides of the Ozarks* or *Dust to Dust*. At least, in this instance, the film was shot professionally enough and it did get finished. Many rural towns, especially in California, probably have similar stories to tell about films that never even got finished.

I wonder what those townsfolk who did get to see *Child Bride* thought about it, because it's a heavy handed morality tale, one that somehow stamps its approval on a range of inappropriate behaviour while consistently opposing the institution of child marriage. For instance, it's apparently fine to be an alcoholic wifebeating bootlegger or to kill someone in cold blood in front of already traumatised children, as long as you're against child marriage. Emotional blackmail is fine, thrusting cleavage is fine and giving up your kids to save your own neck is perfectly fine, just no child marriage.

This sort of thing starts at the very beginning, as the Coltons, good guys because they read *Child Marriage: A Crime*, happily dress their twelve year old in a skimpy outfit conveniently ripped up the front to highlight that she doesn't wear underwear. Within the first two minutes, young Jennie sprawls in the pigpen mud and indulges in a water fight with her friend, Freddie Nulty. No exploitation here, right?

The story is instigated by Jennie's teacher, the only one in this fictional community of Thunderhead Mountain, so her class is attended by children of all ages. Miss Carol is a local girl made good, who claims to be a mountain girl even though she wears posh frills and make up and won't leave to be with her boyfriend, the assistant DA, until she's obliterated child marriage in the area. She stirs up enough resentment in the local men for them to robe up and kidnap her by torchlight to be tarred and feathered at somewhere called Spooky Hollow, but she's rescued by Ira Colton before we can see any more of her than her naked back.

Colton is an equal opportunity bootlegger, his staff consisting of Angelo the dwarf, Happy the retard and Jake Bolby, the villain of the piece, who of course is one of the riled up torch carriers. Colton has already beaten him up for robbing Angelo, so he mounts a dastardly plan for murderous revenge that, not accidentally, ends up with him landing Jennie as a wife. He's seen her swim naked in the creek, you see, and he's completely smitten.

Now if seeing twelve year olds skinny dipping in the creek is enough to turn a hot blooded man into a murderous paedophile, then we're all in trouble because that's what we get for what feels like a two hour scene. Really it's a few minutes but they're long minutes indeed.

The reasoning for it is so that Jennie can explain to Freddie that he can't go skinny dipping with her any more because Miss Carol says it's not OK. So he's stuck on the bank, wondering why he can only kiss her when they're both fully clothed, while she swims around naked. Clearly it's really there to get child nudity past the local censors, which is possibly the most exploitative thing any exploitation filmmaker can do.

Shirley Mills, twelve at the time, really did strip down to the buff and doggy paddle around in the shallows on camera, but she couldn't swim, so the longer shots are of thirteen year old body double Bernice Stobaugh Ray, who looked different enough from Mills that her pubic hair had to be shaved for the scene.

By the time we get to the just as exploitative finalé, we're not sure who we're supposed to root for. Never mind character ambiguity, the good guys are clearly bad guys. Ira Colton, hero of the day on two separate occasions, bootlegs liquor for a living, drinks like a fish and beats his wife. Even Miss Carol, the saintly schoolma'am, conducts her crusade through emotional blackmail and gives up on it the moment she's confronted with a clear example. She wins out in the end, when her boyfriend persuades the governor to sign a law banning child marriage, but can't be bothered to save the girl from being ravaged in the matrimonial bed after being hitched under threat of blackmail. The hero who saves the day in her stead does so in a way that nobody should ever condone.

None of this is ever addressed by the plot, so unlike the rest of the dubious educational exploitation pictures of the time, I can't see how they imagined this would get past local censors. In many instances it didn't.

At heart, *Child Bride* was made for the most classic of all reasons: to make money. Friedgen was merely a crook who offset his costs by getting the town of Columbia to foot most of the bill. I have no idea if he followed that model on his further films, but it wouldn't surprise me. Director Harry Revier was at the end of his career and probably thankful for a last shot; he never directed again. They cut costs by having their respective ladies play prominent parts: Dorothy Carrol, who plays Jennie's mother, may or may not have been Revier's wife, and Diana Durrell, who plays Miss Carol, may or may not have been Friedgen's fiancée. It's within the bounds of possibility that they were merely mistresses.

Only 2'11" Angelo Rossitto is recognisable today, credited as Don Barrett but playing a character with his own name, Angelo the dwarf. His career spanned seven decades, memorable in films like *Freaks* and *Mad Max: Beyond Thunderdome* and TV shows like *HR Pufnstuf* and *Baretta*.

What makes *Child Bride* unique amongst its peers is that, to hindsight, it seems to have achieved something. It didn't directly, as by the time it was ready for release in late 1938, the problem had already been taken care of, at least to the satisfaction of the offended public. States had brought in new laws to enforce minimum ages for marriage. While young girls continued to be married, as in some states wives didn't have to go to school, none would be quite so young as Winstead was and occasionally their husbands would be whisked off to jail.

Yet the film, unlike every single one of its peers, finds itself to hindsight firmly on the side of justice. Until her death Shirley Mills continued to proclaim how proud she was to be part of a film that helped change the social fabric of her country, thus elevating it in the eyes of posterity. Really it was made for money, a con on a lesser level than *The Creeping Terror*. Over time it somehow morphed into what it pretended to be, a crusader for justice.

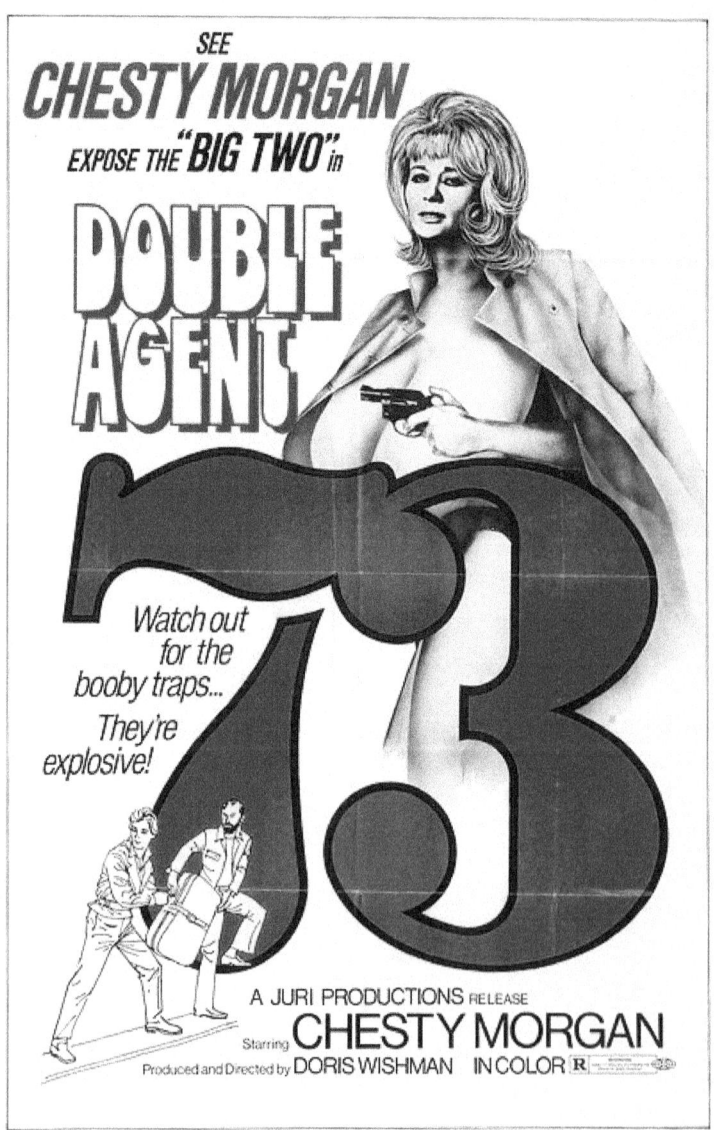

K is for Knockers:
Double Agent 73 (1974)

Director: Doris Wishman
Writer: Doris Wishman
Star: Chesty Morgan

Exploitation films are so named because their filmmakers exploited something to bring in their intended audience. That something could have been anything, like a trend, a name or an event, anything to persuade people into spending their money on watching this particular picture over anything else. Doris Wishman, knew that she was onto a winner when she found Chesty Morgan and I dearly wish I could discover how that happened.

Morgan was a freak of nature, a popular one who made a lot of money out of a particular physical quirk that Mother Nature chose to gift her with: a 73FF bust. This makes her look rather unlike anyone you've ever seen, as it isn't the result of implant surgery; porn stars with silicone balloons in their chests aren't remotely like Chesty Morgan. Constrained by an ambitious bra, her assets provide a truly daunting cleavage; when freed from captivity the laws of gravity ensure that they reach almost to her waist.

And of course they're the entire point of this movie, so we get to see a lot of them. The excuse Wishman generated to make that possible is that she's a spy with a camera implanted into her left breast so she has to get topless just to partake in the plot.

Of course, all three films that she ended up in cared only about her six foot rack. She shot this back to back with *Deadly Weapons*, in which she smothers mobsters to death with her cleavage to revenge her boyfriend's death. Wishman planned a sequel to this film but was fed up with Morgan's prima donna attitude and constant lateness, so killed her off at the outset of *The Immoral Three* in the form of another actress. Federico Fellini had Donald Sutherland chase her 'woman with big boobs' round a table in *Casanova*, but the scene was cut. Thus her cinematic legacy is limited to a Something Weird double bill and a deleted scene only viewable in an Italian documentary. So it goes.

The sad thing is that her life has been a fascinating one, even without bringing her knockers into it, one plagued by tragedy from her birth as Lillian Wajc to a well to do Jewish family in Warsaw in 1937, hardly the luckiest timing to begin a young girl's life. She escaped the ghetto to a Israeli kibbutz but neither of her parents made it out: her mother was hauled away in a boxcar and her father was shot dead during a Jewish uprising. In her twenties she married Joseph Wilczkowski, an American who co-owned a couple of Brooklyn meat markets and gave her two children. He was killed with two of his employees in an armed robbery dubbed 'the icebox murders', leaving her forced to overcome a thick accent to provide for her children. By the time her daughter and second husband, a National League baseball umpire, had died in unrelated traffic accidents, the latter sandwiched between two parked cars, she had become a legendary exotic dancer.

Why is open to question, as she's far from sexy. She was only in her late thirties in her Wishman pictures, but she's unpalatable throughout, topless or not. It's true that 1974 was clearly a nadir in the worlds of fashion and home decor. Morgan's clothes here are scary beyond imagination to anyone fortunate enough not to have lived through this era as an adult. It's hard to see anyone wearing them without wanting to take them off, though that may have been the point, given the material. She's obstructed by more frills and ruffles than can comfortably be imagined and she flounces in elephant bell bottoms, platform boots and a platinum blonde wig. Her blouses don't attempt to hug her figure, thus making her appear deformed: from behind she looks normal, but from the front or sides it looks like she has a midget stuffed up her dress. She's heavier here than in her days as a 73-32-36 stripper but she's not fat. It's the boobs and clothes that horrify.

What's more, she was old school on stage. She never appeared nude and relied as much on the tease as the strip, a scary proposition as she shows no style here, freeing those zeppelins from captivity almost frantically. She's topless throughout the opening credits, heaving her left boob to take photos of things we don't see with an implanted camera we don't know exists yet.

You won't be too surprised to hear that Wishman is often described as 'the female Ed Wood', as they shared an inability to appreciate plot consistency, but she wrote both her Chesty Morgan films with her niece, Judy Kushner, so perhaps that ran in the family. Her other trademarks, confusing for anyone without a background in her work, are soon apparent: shots of shoes, ashtrays and other inanimate objects, or pans that go nowhere or not far enough. One early shot has an actor apparently walk into the camera, crotch first, and we can't tell if it's ineptitude or a clever segue.

The story, if you can call it that, is set up quickly. Morgan plays a secret agent with a license to kill by the name of Jane Tennay, whose code name, Agent 73, matches her bust size. She's sent to assassinate the key members of some sort of gang, though with hints about drugs and hints about microfilm, we're never quite sure why. The key may be in the last words of another agent. He points to his eye and mutters, "Toplar, scar," before dying, thus telling us that Ivan Toplar can be identified by a scar on his ear. Remember plot consistency is unimportant in a Doris Wishman picture.

She's quickly able to locate an enemy agent, while hindered by a flowing hospital gown of turquoise frills, strangle her to death with a telephone cord and test her new camera implant, proving beyond doubt that "Toplar's agents are everywhere?" Get it? Topless agents are everywhere? That a pun is the greatest intellectual achievement of this film amply highlights just how awful it is.

This camera is an insanely poor exploitation gimmick, or an insanely great one, depending on your perspective. Of course, Agent 73 needs a camera, as she's tasked with photographing any important documents she can find, along with the corpses of those she kills, but I'm confused as to how this implanted camera can do the job. How many pictures can it take? How can they be retrieved? Tennay never changes the film, not that it's a viable option. How does it get past the barrier of skin? Where's the lens? If it's where the implant went in, then how does pointing at the ceiling take a picture of something in front of her? She certainly has an astounding aim, as she can't even see the camera and the photos that she takes end up with higher picture quality than this film! Of course, it seems rather obvious to mention that this gimmick only aims to showcase the twin stars of the film and bring a whole new meaning to the term 'flash photography'.

Given that, I'm still confused about the scene when Agent 73 is called in for Operation Highlight One. She's in a nudist colony, a common location for Doris Wishman pictures, but she's clothed. Let me run that by you again. The star of the film isn't naked, or even topless, in a nudist colony in a sexploitation movie that revolves around her getting her tits out.

There's even a volleyball game going on that has the players on our side of the net naked as jaybirds but those facing us wearing shorts. I do find the attempt to avoid full frontal nudity in a film about Chesty Morgan's 73" breasts frankly hilarious. It doesn't help that she looks like nothing less than a cheap whore in red shorts and platform boots, huge sunglasses and earrings, and a black bra that has no tie but hangs down somewhat akin to a hammock. Morgan's wardrobe in this film is notably scarier than the monster in any horror movie I can think of.

Maybe the star was just having a bad day. We've already discovered that the most talented crew member is the girl who dubbed all Chesty Morgan's lines as even Doris Wishman couldn't understand her thick accent. Beyond discarding her voice, the next scene suggests that Wishman would have liked to have discarded her star as well. In interviews she's claimed that Morgan was the most difficult and only unccooperative actor she ever worked with. It's painfully clear that she doesn't want to be there, for Tennay to hear her boss explain her assignment, and it's not clear whether everything we see during this scene was shot for it. Morgan appears to be drugged and is out of focus much of the time. She sighs often and smiles uncomfortably at one point. Most of her lines are delivered with her off screen. The suggestion is that Wishman would happily have sent her packing if only her boobs could have stayed behind to provide the gimmick she needed.

Bizarrely, Tennay doesn't use those gimmicks as exclusively as she did in *Deadly Weapons*. In that film, they were her only lethal technique. Here, she explodes her victims with lipstick, kills them with earrings that act as throwing stars, drowns them with ice cubes. Only one killing uses her breasts, coated with poison to be licked off by someone who doesn't recognise that the 73" monsters don't belong to his wife.

This may sound innovative but it's as numbing as the movie.

When Agent 73 turns the tables on a hitman, for instance, was I supposed to be looking at the horrendous pink chairs, the prominent bong that she uses as a weapon, the hallucinogenic pans over her breasts, her innovative choice of murder technique, the fact that she strips topless to pour a drink in her own apartment or just her perpetually pissed off expression? Never mind those mammoth mammaries, it's the technique and the 1970s style that bludgeoned me.

As Joe Bob Briggs detailed, "Doris was not a filmmaker so much as a film manufacturer." She got into the trade by accident. Her husband, Jack Abrahms, was a partner in a film exchange, but in 1958 he dropped dead of a heart attack at the age of 31. Wishman only made her first movie, 1960's *Hideout in the Sun*, so that the exchange would have something to sell. She learned her craft as she went along, by simply asking people.

That first picture was a nudist film, one of the first to ignore the usual educational excuses for the setting, because she was bright enough to see the potential for an indie distributor. Ironically, she was very modest, enough that she was embarrassed to watch her own movies. As times changed, her pictures changed with them, but her modesty never did. She shot roughies, which were much nastier than innocent nudies, and even a couple of hardcore pictures, though she left the room during the sex scenes.

Throughout her career, she was an anomaly: a modest lady making films all about sex, a non-filmmaker making films, a female filmmaker making exploitation films. It's inevitable that she brought something different to them than her competitors.

It wouldn't take much to paint her with a feminist brush, her Chesty Morgan pictures clearly showing the power of the female and the female form over that of the male. *Deadly Weapons* may be as unsubtle as feminism gets, given that it has an exotic dancer, a symbol of the exploited female, literally using her breasts, the most obvious of female attributes, as a weapon to kill men, one of whom is played by Harry Reems, who as a famous porn star is an obvious symbol of male oppression. *Double Agent 73* doesn't reach that level of blatancy but it's still about a stereotypical male fantasy proving her dominance over men by killing them, even when they're proposing marriage.

Feminist or not, both Morgan and Wishman became highly successful. Morgan is living comfortably in Florida off the proceeds of her career as a stripper, not having descended to any depth that stereotypes would suggest. Wishman also moved to Florida, after the unmitigated disaster that was *A Night to Dismember* in 1983. Though completed, it was half destroyed at a processing lab that went bankrupt; a disgruntled employee vandalised the place, making fresh completion a nightmare.

She died in 2002, amid a strong resurgence of her career, even making *Dildo Heaven* and *Each Time I Kill* in her late eighties. She certainly did it her way, even though she was offered work by her cousin, Max Rosenberg, who founded Amicus, the British studio known for its horror anthologies. When times changed, she found fresh gimmicks, from the possessed penis of *The Amazing Transplant* to real life transgender patients in *Let Me Die a Woman*.

Her biggest gimmicks though, in both size and earnings, were Chesty Morgan's knockers.

Huh? An A-Z of Why Classic American Bad Movies Were Made

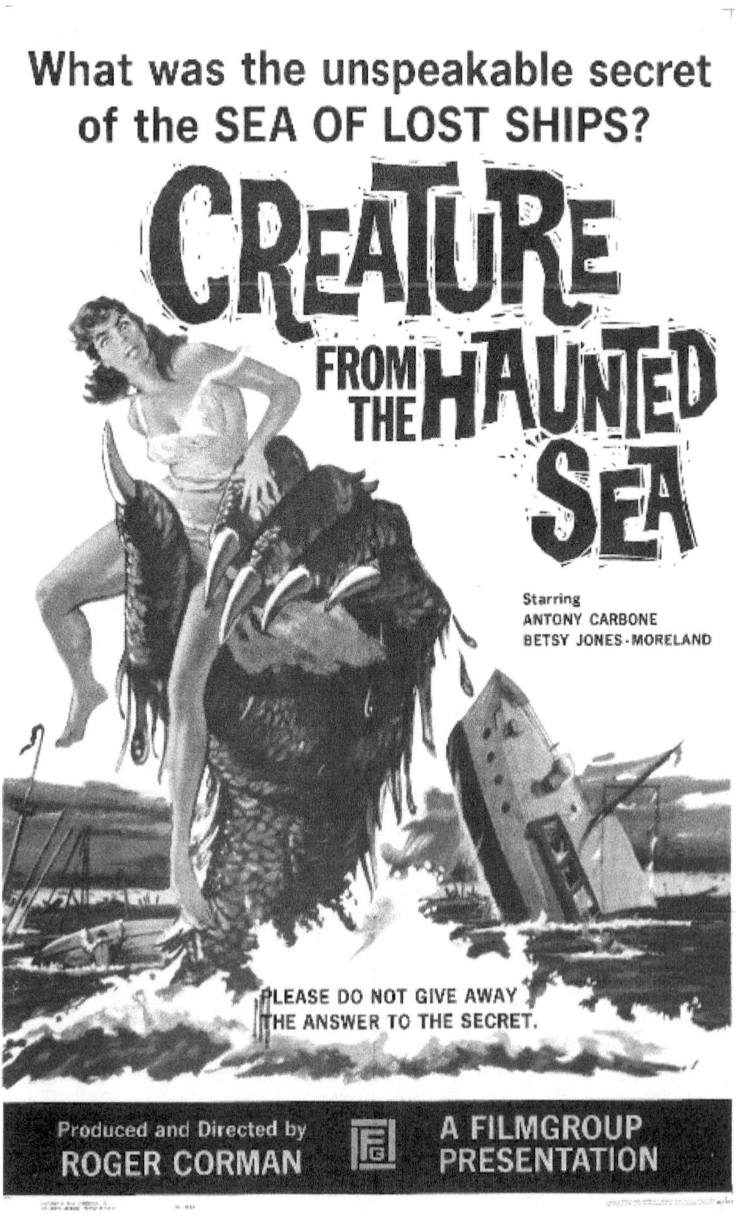

What was the unspeakable secret
of the SEA OF LOST SHIPS?

CREATURE
FROM THE HAUNTED
SEA

Starring
ANTONY CARBONE
BETSY JONES-MORELAND

PLEASE DO NOT GIVE AWAY
THE ANSWER TO THE SECRET.

Produced and Directed by
ROGER CORMAN

A FILMGROUP
PRESENTATION

L is for Location:
Creature from the Haunted Sea (1961)

Director: Roger Corman
Writer: Charles B Griffith
Stars: Antony Carbone, Betsy Jones-Moreland and Edward Wain

Sometimes it seems like legendary exploitation film director Roger Corman wrote the book on how to save money while making a film. He didn't invent every idea he used, but he put them to better use than anyone else. His autobiography is titled *How I Made a Hundred Movies in Hollywood and Never Lost a Dime* and, while that isn't strictly true, his unparalleled win/loss record is due partly to his ability to make big films with little money, meaning that he could compete with much more expensive pictures with a fraction of their overhead.

Trained as an engineer, he thought logically and occasionally went a step too far, like when he optimised lighting setups on *Oklahoma Woman* by splitting up shots based on which direction the characters were facing and shooting everything facing one way before setting up afresh and shooting everything facing the other. It made logical sense and sped up production but the actors got confused and he discarded the idea in the future.

Other ideas were as logically sound but much more successful. After Allison Hayes broke her arm while shooting *Gunslinger*, he shot close ups of her looking in every direction while waiting for the car to take her to hospital. He shot other scenes with a body double later to edit in. Even on *Five Guns West*, the first film he directed himself, he avoided costly and complex scenes in an elegant way, by having a soldier look through binoculars at a band of stock footage Indians on horseback, then explaining that, "The Indians are over here. Let's head over there." He shot *Atlas* against the plentiful Greek ruins for background colour and had a character explain that two centuries of civil war had destroyed everything. For the same film, he donated to the Greek Army Charity Fund to gain five hundred soldiers to overwhelm Thenis in panoramic style. Only fifty arrived so he filmed close ups instead and changed dialogue to reflect a small trained force defeating a large rabble.

Most successfully, he found ways to use or reuse what was already around him to do something cheaply or for free. The burning cane fields in *Thunder Over Hawaii* were a regular stalk burnoff that he scheduled around, costing him nothing. When he had to burn down the mansion in *House of Usher*, he found developers about to demolish a nearby barn and paid them fifty bucks to burn it instead while his cameras rolled. When *The Raven* wrapped a full two days ahead of schedule, he made the best use of his cast, his crew and his magnificent gothic sets that he could: he had them shoot another movie, *The Terror*. He didn't even have a complete script so he couldn't film the whole thing, but he shot what he could and had assistant directors complete it later. Perhaps his most famous film, *The Little Shop of Horrors*, was shot on a standing set that another film had left empty, in two days and one night, with three more for rehearsals.

In low budget pictures at the time, the most expensive thing around often wasn't the star or the set, it was the location. A film could elevate itself above its competition simply by sporting exotic locations, but of course it cost money to get to them. So when he was hired in 1956 to direct *She Gods of Shark Reef*, a South Pacific picture, by a lawyer who wanted to produce, it made a lot of sense for American International to hire him to direct another movie, *Thunder Over Hawaii*, back to back with it, halving many costs for both companies and gaining AIP an exotic location in the process.

Corman took that to heart. When he went to the Black Hills of South Dakota to shoot *Ski Troop Attack*, his brother Gene came along for the ride to produce *Beast from Haunted Cave* at the same time and share the costs. His most productive back to back shoot, though, was in 1959 when he travelled to Puerto Rico and shot not two but three pictures back to back.

Originally Corman was slated to produce a war picture called *Battle of Blood Island*, driven by tax incentives to 'manufacture' in Puerto Rico, but he scheduled in a second, *Last Woman on Earth*, to maximise the use of San Juan, the Caribe Hilton hotel and the beach house he'd rented. The writer on the latter was Robert Towne, just starting out in 1959 but soon to become Hollywood's most reliable script doctor and later one of its most respected writers, landing a much deserved Oscar for 1974's *Chinatown* in a very tough year. Then and now, Towne's biggest problem has always been the slow speed at which he writes, not a huge deal when you're an Oscar winner working for a major studio but a showstopper when you're working on a Corman picture. He hadn't finished before the cast and crew shipped out; Corman's solution was to bring him along too, paying his way by not only finishing the script but also playing the third character in a cast of three.

Battle of Blood Island and *Last Woman on Earth* were both two week shoots that went smoothly. In fact they went so smoothly and morale was so high that a week into the latter, Corman phoned home and asked Charles Griffith to write a third picture, a comedy horror in the vein of the pair of highly successful quickies they'd shot in 1958, *A Bucket of Blood* and *The Little Shop of Horrors*. Griffith was experienced writing for Corman and he was as fast as Towne was slow, so faced with writing an entire feature in a single week for a cast that was already on site, he recycled his script for *Thunder Over Hawaii* to become *Creature from the Haunted Sea*.

It had the same leads as *Last Woman on Earth*, Antony Carbone and Betsy Jones-Moreland, with Towne thrown in to boot. Not meeting Corman's deadline for *Last Woman on Earth* therefore got him stuck with two acting roles, both of which he completed under the pseudonym of Edward Wain.

The other reason a third picture was viable was because Corman's assistant, Kinta Zabel, flew in with money left over from another movie Corman was financing back home. *The Wild Ride* came about when Harvey Berman, who taught high school drama and ran a film class, suggested that he could shoot a juvenile delinquent film with his students for a tiny budget. Corman agreed but looked over the first day's footage and found it amateurish, so he sent his art director and a pair of his stock actors, including Jack Nicholson. He gave Zabel a $30k cheque to cover all costs and asked him to bring whatever remained to San Juan.

Enough was left for five days of production. Griffith's script arrived on the last Thursday of the *Last Woman on Earth* shoot; Corman rewrote parts of it that night. They photocopied it on the Friday and gave it to the cast, Zabel locked in locations on the Saturday, they planned shots on Sunday and began shooting on the

Monday.

What resulted was a bad movie but a fun one. It doesn't have the unlikely substance of *A Bucket of Blood* or *The Little Shop of Horrors*, but it unfolds well for the most part and doesn't get boring.

The story revolves around a strongbox full of gold stolen from the Cuban treasury as Castro took over. Surviving Batista officials spirited it away but, needing a way to get it out of Cuba, unwisely decided to trust an American gangster called Renzo Capetto. They'll give him a quarter of it and use the rest for their counter-revolution, but you won't be surprised to find that Capetto promptly conjures up a plan to keep all of it. He and his henchmen will slowly bump off the Cubans at sea, while blaming their disappearances on a sea monster. They use a plunger to leave sucker tracks and a rake to leave claw marks. The catch is that there really is a sea monster and it kills Cubans as fast as they can in exactly the same way, leading to some fun confusion.

I'm sure you can imagine the sort of sea monster built with this sort of notice. Stuck designing it was Beach Dickerson, who like everyone in Corman's company ended up doing whatever needed to be done at the time. Primarily an actor, throughout a four decade career he also produced and directed, but he'd laugh to find that IMDb lists his most famous work as 'Costume Department, *Creature from the Haunted Sea*'. There to handle sound for *Last Woman on Earth*, he handled that role for this film too, played one of Capetto's henchmen and was tasked to build the monster, even though his experience with monsters was scuttling around in a crab suit in *Attack of the Crab Monsters*. He turned five helmets from *Battle of Blood Island* into one large head with tennis balls for eyes and table tennis balls for pupils. He stuck moss and brillo pads onto a wetsuit with black oilcloth to look slimy and pipecleaners for claws. It's utterly ridiculous but in a fun way.

After all, there's no way anyone could take this movie seriously; the introductions we're given to Capetto's gang hammer that home. He's "the most trusted man ever to be deported from Sicily," whose pseudonyms range from Zeppo Staccato to Shirley L'Amour. He was "rejected by the Navy, Marines and SS." Anthony Carbone riffs on Humphrey Bogart and he's fun to watch. Betsy Jones-Moreland treats his moll, Mary-Belle Monahan, to an outrageous southern drawl. She wiped out a police chief convention at the Hollywood Bowl with a tommy gun and dealt heroin at Boys Town. Her brother, Happy Jack, developed a muscle spasm from watching too many Bogie movies. This part was written for Corman but in such a way that he couldn't play it. He cast Bobby Bean, who had been in *The Wild Ride* and flew to San Juan just in case there was something for him to do. As Pete Peterson Jr, Dickerson is like the fourth Stooge, a half retarded animal imitator.

Handling the introductions is Robert Towne, who showed in *Last Woman on Earth* that for a writer he wasn't a bad actor, but you wouldn't believe it from this evidence. He wildly overplays his role as Sparks Moran, an inept American spy known as XK150. His part was bulked up in 1963 when Corman had Monte Hellman shoot additional scenes in Santa Monica to pad the film out to a more TV friendly 74 minutes. The opening scenes with Hellman's wife as fellow spy XK120 are surreal and hilarious, even though he's reminiscent of Nicolas Cage trying to look surreptitious. He kisses her goodbye suavely then trips over the staircase; the acting is terrible but the timing is awesome and they play it all delightfully straight. Griffith's script is flawed in the extreme but it has a lot of wit. Later in the film, Moran woos Mary-Belle outrageously, with no success. Jones-Moreland has great fun rejecting both him and the Cuban general, Tostada, with delightfully snarky rejoinders.

Looking back in an interview with Tom Weaver, she suggested that the movie "started out to be a takeoff on everything Roger had ever done before. It was to be a comedy, a laugh a minute. Then all of a sudden, somewhere in the middle of it, that got lost and it got to be serious!"

The second act is certainly lacking, but the third hints at slapstick as characters fall for other characters in a daisy chain of unwanted advances. Happy Jack wants Carmelita, discovered at a sorority house; Carmelita wants Sparks; Sparks wants Mary-Belle and Mary-Belle wants and has Renzo Capetto. Of course, the monster wants everybody. The poster asks us to "not give away the answer to the secret" but it's that the monster wins, in Corman's favourite of all his endings, which he dictated over the phone to Griffith. With most of the cast dead, it survives, sitting on the strongbox at the bottom of the sea in a brief shot that has led to this film being called Corman's most personal.

In his autobiography, Corman states that "the craziness of the shoot showed in the finished film," and I'd heartily agree. The serious pulp story Griffith wrote for *Thunder Over Hawaii* and rewrote for *Beast from Haunted Cave* doesn't stand up in the slightest as a parody of those films, but the energy is palpable. The leads were making their second of two films back to back, while some of the crew were making their third in five weeks, but nobody shows signs of flagging. The movie is held together with little more than goofy energy but that's precisely what they aimed for, spicing up many shots with delicious narration and dialogue heavy ones by adding movement. One has characters throwing a coconut around a palm grove while they talk like it's an American football. Tommy Wiseau must have been paying attention, though clearly not to Corman's money saving ideas.

"Nobody was making movies like these," said Corman, but that's because only he could.

Huh? An A-Z of Why Classic American Bad Movies Were Made

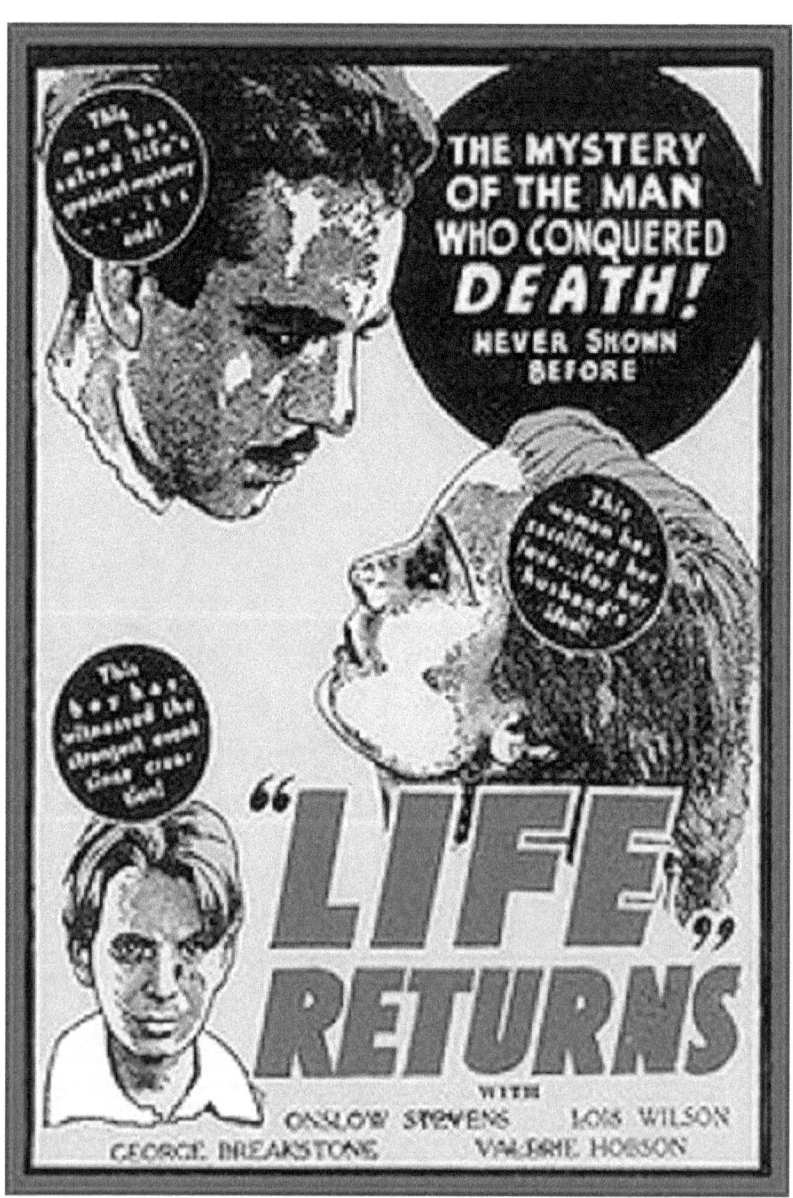

M is for Mimicry:
Life Returns (1935)

Director: Eugen Frenke
Writers: L Wolfe Gilbert, John F Goodrich, Arthur T Horman and
Mary McCarthy, from a story by Eugen Frenke and James P Hogan
Star: Dr Robert E Cornish

Horror in the early thirties belonged to Universal. Already
established in the silent era with Lon Chaney vehicles like *The
Hunchback of Notre Dame* and *The Phantom of the Opera*, they hit the
sound age running. In 1931 they released both *Dracula* and
Frankenstein, making icons out of Bela Lugosi and Boris Karloff in
the process, then followed up with *The Mummy*, *The Old Dark House*,
The Invisible Man and no end of sequels.

By 1935, they were the undisputed genre kings and to celebrate
they released what may be the best and the worst pictures in their
entire horror run, films that shared a theme and an actress but
otherwise couldn't be more different. The best was James Whale's
Bride of Frankenstein, the worst Eugen Frenke's *Life Returns*, a
partnership with the newly formed independent Scienart Pictures
to spin a hokey yarn around the true story of a real life Dr
Frankenstein, Dr Robert E Cornish, who killed dogs and brought
them back to life.

Cornish didn't live in a remote European castle with a hunchback
servant named Igor, he was an American child prodigy who earned
a degree from the University of California at eighteen and a
doctorate four years later. In 1932 he became fascinated by the
concept of restoring life to the recent dead, though I don't know if
the previous year's *Frankenstein* had anything to do with his
interest. If so, he ignored the possibility of villagers with torches
and found acclaim for a series of experiments with terriers, all
called Lazarus.

He would kill the animals by asphyxiating them, leave them dead
for short periods and then attempt to resuscitate them using a
combination of intravenous stimulation, the kiss of life and a
seesaw like device called a teeterboard to circulate the blood. *Time*

magazine reported on him often in 1934 as he found success, but unfortunately survivors were brain dead and university officials dismissed him, displeased with the attention.

If they didn't like the attention that his experiments attracted, they surely wouldn't have been appreciative of the attention this film received. Cornish only appears briefly as himself, but it's his name only above the title and the film's finalé is footage from one of his experiments, albeit spun to fit the melodrama.

Reaction was not good. It became one of only five classic horror pictures to be banned outright by the British censor, alongside the inevitable *Freaks*, Val Lewton's *Bedlam*, the 1932 version of *The Island of Dr Moreau* and a truly obscure silent and presumably lost French comedy, *Dr Zanikoff's Experiences in Grafting*. Denis Gifford, in his excellent 1973 book, *A Pictorial History of Horror Movies*, called it the most 'lost' horror film of them all: "Never seen in England, even in today's relaxed climate; never reprinted for television; unpreserved by archives, unmentioned by historians, unregistered even for copyright; yet it was the only 'documentary' horror film."

Nowadays, because Universal deliberately let it vanish into the public domain like a redheaded stepchild, it's readily available for viewing. Presumably they were aiming for a true *Frankenstein* story to accompany their fictional ones, for if reality can mimic art, then art can mimic reality or something like that. What they got was an *Our Gang* short, with every melodramatic heartstring plucked to the max, stretched to feature length and wrapped by an ego trip.

The documentary portion is transplanted from footage "originally taken to retain a permanent scientific record of our experiment" but it's badly transplanted and serves only as a dubious finalé to an unsavoury children's story. Anybody expecting a horror movie is going to be sadly disappointed with the entire thing, including the work of a number of recognisable Universal contract players who mostly seem to be confused as to why anyone would deliberately make this film and why they have to be in it.

We begin well, with three scientists talking about life being an endless playground. They're John Kendrick, Louise Stone and Robert Cornish, and they're certainly set for success: they put their studies ahead of big games and big dances, but given that they graduate alongside what looks like the entire state of California, they're surely up for some tough competition. Fortunately Kendrick sent out feelers a month before graduation and he surprises them with an invitation for the entire trio to work at Arnold Research Laboratories, which is, according to its motto, 'dedicated to the service of mankind.' Unfortunately, his colleagues aren't interested, so their goal of working together after graduation is ended. "Arnold Research is a commercial organisation," says Cornish. "They would never be in sympathy with what we want to accomplish." They'd take all the credit as well. So Kendrick goes to Arnold, while Stone and Cornish disappear from the film for a while.

That's about it for science too, partly because reality raises its ugly head and wants Kendrick to make money and partly because somehow he found time to marry a socialite and father a son. Reality kicks in when A K Arnold, the 'philanthropist' who finances the labs, decides that he can't capitalise on Kendrick's research and wants him to start working on hair restoring brushes made from pig bristles. Resurrecting the dead is the realm of graverobbers from outer space, after all, and Ed Wood was only nine years old at the time.

Kendrick is a pure scientist who simply doesn't understand what commercial gain has to do with science, so he quits and promptly goes insane, staying there for the majority of the film. His lovely wife Mary reinforces Arnold from a different angle: raising the dead may be Kendrick's great experiment but their son Danny is hers and she needs the money he makes from his two hour a day practice to keep that viable.

Onslow Stevens was riding high in 1935. He was tall and handsome and had a resonant, slightly clipped, speaking voice. After an uncredited screen debut in 1931 he quickly found regular work as a versatile leading man and this was the year that he would play Aramis alongside Paul Lukas and Moroni Olsen in RKO's big budget version of *The Three Musketeers*.

Here, however, he only has a single scene of passion after leaving Arnold, a futile effort to impress a medical board with incomplete research by comparing himself to Galileo and Madame Curie. That's it for Kendrick and Stevens couldn't find a thing to do with the part after that. He stumbles around for the rest of the film as if in a daze, somewhat like Frankenstein's Monster on sedatives. While it might be appropriate for the part, the style he adopts of effectively ignoring everyone who talks to him as if he's watching television through an invisible portal to another dimension is hardly engaging.

With Stevens an emphatic nonentity, fifteen year old George Breakston gets to carry the picture. While he was a capable actor, who played the young Pip a year earlier in *Great Expectations* and would soon become Beezy in a string of Andy Hardy films, before becoming a producer/director in the late forties, he's given the unenviable challenge of playing the the most stereotypical hard luck kid in history.

No cliché is too far for this story to grab hold of, no depth too low to sink to, no horse too dead to flog. In quick succession, Danny sells papers on the streets, mentoring a younger boy with an even more broken voice than his, returns home to find his mother dead on her birthday (and no, we don't even attempt to bring her back to life), is hauled off to court to be taken away from his lunatic father and is finally sent to juvenile hall. He escapes the courtroom to hit the high road with his little dog Scooter right behind him, hooked up to a little trailer.

It's painful to see Danny in despair, not because the six writers tried to craft a clever parallel to his father but because every shot aims to rend our heartstrings and tear us up, all for the poor little blighter with the weight of the world on his shoulders. It's embarrassing to watch his ever pleading eyes and we cringe at each inept attempt to pressgang our sympathy. "Aww gee, dad, you ain't gonna turn me down, are you?" he emotes before leaving home. "I want a father. Why, everybody's got a father. Every kid I know has got one." He ends with, "Wouldn't you sorta like to have me around?"

At least Mickey, the leader of the gang of rough and tumble kids that he falls in with, is a little more grounded, though the gang do better in their clubhouse than the public was doing at the time. He's played by Richard Quine, another child actor who graduated to the director's chair, going on to shoot *Bell Book and Candle*, *How to Murder Your Wife* and *Hotel*.

Of course, given that Dr Cornish was into resurrecting dogs from the grave, that's where we have to end up, after a succession of overdone and clumsily constructed scenes involving Scooter, the pound and the littlest boy in the gang. When the wicked dog catcher gasses poor little Scooter to death, just to make a point, it's all cunning plot development to get Kendrick back in the film, so he can let Danny down one more time as we weave our weary way to the finalé.

"Isn't Scooter as good as a guinea pig or a rabbit?" Danny pleads to his father. "I ran away from the cops so I could be with you. Well now I don't want to be with you and I'm going to the home and I'm going there for good and for keeps!" Remember, this is the best that no less than six writers could come up with. It's a blessing when these script shenanigans finally spirit us away to the stock footage of Dr Cornish's real life experiments. Trust me, that's as unlikely as it sounds.

It's difficult to imagine precisely what Universal was thinking or what audience they thought this movie would have. This would be a seriously traumatic experience for the eight year olds who might have bought into the story and a shocking disappointment to the fans of the horror films that surely inspired it. I wonder how they ever thought they could splice the various components together.

Sure, the obsessed Dr Kendrick can finally overcome his pride to perform his grand experiment, but the footage of that experiment is Cornish's and Onslow Stevens wasn't there. So Drs Kendrick and Stone provide a running commentary to explain what Dr Cornish and the team of assistants, who neither we nor Kendrick have seen before, are doing with the Lazarus suspect that happens to be a completely different breed to Scooter. Naturally, there's a happy ending, which is as disappointing and sickening a copout as you might expect.

In real life Cornish left his various terriers dead for six minutes and when that didn't work well, he lowered his expectations to two. This sort of rapid rescuscitation is routine nowadays, albeit through CPR and defibrillation rather than some magic formula, taking advantage of the timeframe where the heart has stopped but the brain hasn't died. Neither Cornish, in real life, nor Kendrick, in his futile pitch to the medical board in this story, claimed Frankenstein level achievements like being able to resurrect corpses dead long enough to be buried.

Yet that's what we see. The fake Scooter is gassed to death by the dog catcher, his corpse retrieved by Kendrick and transported to Cornish's hospital, and a team is assembled with the equipment needed (including Kendrick's mysterious formula) to confirm death and get to work on the experiment. Even ignoring the time needed to persuade the hospital management, it must be nearer to six hours than six minutes.

Most of those involved with *Life Returns* happily saw it fade into quick obscurity, mostly because the studio refused to release it. Carl Laemmle Jr, in charge of production, saw it as "not suitable for the regular Universal program." Frenke did get a release in 1938, when Universal sold the film to Grand National Pictures, but the actors, like Valerie Hobson, the wife of the mad scientist in Universal's best and worst films of the year, pretended that it never happened and moved on.

Cornish couldn't ignore it though, and it serves today as little more than a bizarre relic of a brief cause célèbre. When the University of California stopped his work in its tracks, he petitioned state governors in vain to allow him to experiment on death row convicts. That would have made for a better picture and, ironically enough, it did. In Warner Brothers' 1936 horror movie, *The Walking Dead*, Boris Karloff is executed in the electric chair but raised back to life by a scientist in a laboratory that was based on Cornish's.

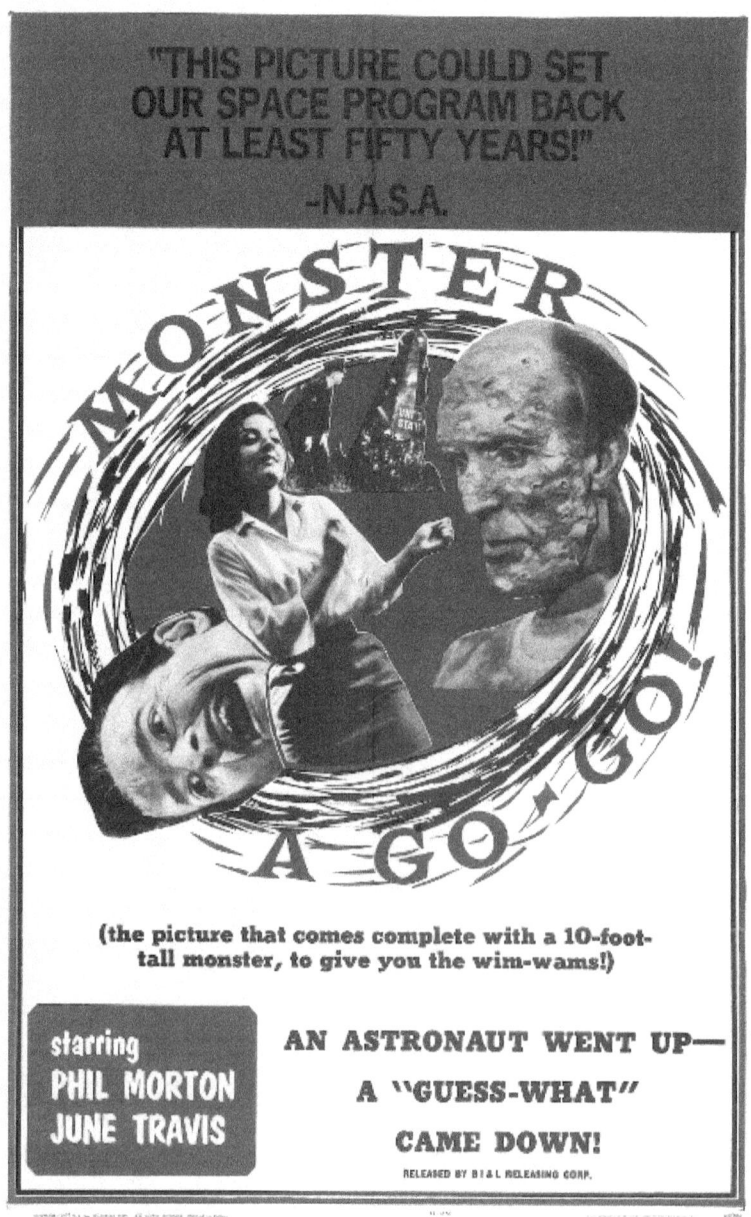

N is for Necessity:
Monster a-Go Go

Director: Bill Rebane
Writers: Jeff Smith, Dok Stanford and Bill Rebane, with additional dialogue by Sheldon Seymour
Stars: Phil Morton, June Travis and George Perry

Until they discovered *Manos: The Hands of Fate*, the *Mystery Science Theater 3000* folk regarded *Monster a-Go Go* as the worst movie that they had ever riffed. It's certainly a bad film, with bad acting, bad dialogue and bad music, along with bad sound and bad lighting that makes it tough to keep up with what's actually going on, even with a clear narration laid over the top. What makes it so notably bad is that it's also boring, which is the death knell to a picture like this. While 'bad' can be forgiven or even enjoyed, 'boring' is a much harder obstacle to overcome.

The only interesting thing about it is its history, because the man responsible for releasing it, Herschell Gordon Lewis, didn't care about it in the slightest. He merely needed a movie, any movie, to back one of his own at drive in theatres, because theatre owners couldn't withhold payment on the grounds that it was the other picture that made money when you owned both halves of the double bill.

The film he had was 1964's *Moonshine Mountain*, which cemented Lewis's growing stature as a pioneer of the hicksploitation genre by following on the heels of *Two Thousand Maniacs!* but with a focus on country music and comedy rather than gore. What he found to back it up was *Terror at Half Day*, a science fiction thriller in the Roger Corman vein, which had been in production between 1961 and 1963 but which was left languishing on the shelf of a film processing lab because the budget had evaporated.

Lewis knew about *Terror at Half Day* as he'd been brought in as a cinematographer late on; maybe Bill Rebane, who was directing his first feature, hired him for his experience, the fact that he was cheap and because he'd worked for Lewis in 1959, doing part time sales in his commercial studio. When the lab told Lewis that the footage was available, he knew precisely what he could do with it, so he bought it, reedited it completely, added a narration and gave it a new title, *Monster a-Go Go*.

He was so proud of the results that he didn't even put his name on them. He's uncredited both as a director and the film's narrator, not to mention for the cinematography that he did even before he bought the footage. For everything else he did, he did it under pseudonyms: for his dialogue he's Sheldon Seymour, as a producer he added an S as a middle initial and for production design he's Seymour Sheldon.

If the awful new title wasn't enough, his disdain for *Terror at Half Day* is made clear by the fact that he turned the serious, if probably still inept, thriller into a parody of itself, with what may well be the worst ending ever committed to celluloid, only *Chained for Life* even coming close on that front. Surprisingly, he also ditched a large amount of footage, thus minimising the presence of Henry Hite, the imposing 7'6" vaudevillian who portrays the titular monster. I can understand much of what Lewis did and why, but I can't understand why he'd throw away what are probably the best bits.

While necessity drove Lewis's purchase of the *Terror at Half Day* footage, to a lesser degree it also drove the making of the original picture. Rebane had done very well for himself as a young man but had fallen on hard times and aimed this feature film to restore some of his success.

He'd arrived in the US from Germany in 1952 as Ito von Rebane, a 14 year old Latvian kid fluent in four languages but not English; he learned by watching four movies a day for six months. After working his way up the ranks at WGN-TV in Chicago, he went back to Germany, where he did the same thing at Baltes Film, eventually directing shorts and presumably impressing Adalbert Baltes in the process. Baltes wasn't just a documentarian, producer and founder of the company, he had also designed a 360° projection system called Cinetarium that screened movies in a similar way to a planetarium. With exclusive US distribution rights to this system in his pocket, Rebane was a millionaire at 22.

Unfortunately, it didn't last. The companies he'd formed couldn't handle the strain of patent disputes, legal fees and ongoing development, leaving him close to broke. Picking himself up by his bootstraps, he returned to making films, starting out with a couple of successful AIP distributed musical shorts, *Twist Craze* and *Dance Craze*, hardly what you might expect given the sci-fi/horror films that he would become known for, but understandable when you realise that his idol was Donald O'Connor and his English immersion was through classic musicals and westerns.

The connections he'd built during his Cinetarium days, the success of his shorts and a clear confidence in his own abilities led him to shoot *Terror at Half Day*, named for a small Illinois town north of Chicago. He failed as, in his words, "going union killed the movie," but in hindsight, it was also a first step towards building a legitimate film industry in the midwest, something he's pushed consistently and successfully ever since. That's his real legacy.

What going union meant to this film was that the entire budget, all $50,000 of it, was used up by the end of the first week and by that point Rebane hadn't even shot a single scene with Henry Hite, the terror in *Terror at Half Day*. Interviews highlight that the union crew was very professional, and certainly the best footage is from that week's shoot, but also that they had no problem spending all the money without any concern as to whether the movie would get finished. Rebane's inexperience meant that he was out of budget and in a major hole with perhaps a quarter of the film shot.

When he raised a little more financing, he'd learned his lesson so hired Lewis to finish the picture without a union bleeding him dry. These scenes are all notably inferior, especially with regards to lighting, but eventually the money ran out for good, leaving the movie unfinished until Lewis bought the footage and reworked it into his own picture for his own purposes.

What we see today in *Monster a-Go Go* is almostly entirely footage from *Terror at Half Day* but it's clearly not the same picture in any other way. The commonality ties to the core idea of an astronaut being launched into space but coming back fundamentally altered.

Rebane's version is serious, the physical and mental change in astronaut Frank Douglas caused by radioactivity outside the Earth's atmosphere, meaning that the six foot tall man who went up returned as a ten foot tall radioactive monster, killing those he meets through proximity alone.

The timing was absolutely right. Rebane sought funding in 1960 and began production in the winter of 1961; in between those dates, Yuri Gagarin became the first man to reach orbit in April 1961, with Alan Shepard coming close a month later and John Glenn orbiting the Earth three times in February 1962. Studios naturally saw great subject matter, with films like 1959's *First Man into Space* even beating reality to the punch.

Rebane also had connections within Chicago, including Mayor Daley, who was interested in seeing film production return to the city for the first time since Essenay shot Chaplin one reelers there in 1915. Edison's strongarm tactics in enforcing his patents had pushed the various studios as far west as they could go, Hollywood emerging as somewhere they could make a stand and literally throw Edison's thugs out on their ear.

We're used to seeing Chicago on film today, many of its landmarks obvious in movies like *The Blues Brothers*, *Risky Business* or *The Untouchables*, but it wasn't until 1959 and another Herschell Gordon Lewis movie, *The Prime Time*, that anyone returned to shoot there. That's why Daley and the City of Chicago happily closed down the busy intersection of Michigan Ave and Oak St for two hours around rush hour for a tense scene right under Wacker Dr that has the military catch the monster. This is groundbreaking stuff, but very little of it made it into *Monster a-Go Go*.

Nothing that Rebane aimed to follow that scene made it into the released version either. He wanted a different sort of ending to the usual. After the monster is caught, he wouldn't be destroyed in the way we've come to expect. Instead, he's taken alive and eventually cured through injections of an antidote serum. "I wanted a happy ending," said Rebane. "I'm a happy ending guy." Needless to say, that's not what he got.

It's not known why Lewis changed everything in the way he did, but perhaps he saw the existing footage as a joke. There are certainly obvious flaws that put it on shaky ground immediately. Douglas's seven foot capsule quite obviously couldn't contain a ten foot monster. We're used to seeing such capsules land in the ocean to minimise impact but this one apparently touches down gently in an Illinois field without even generating a crater. Having the monster walk away from this crash is a precursor to the beginning of *Crank: High Voltage* and it's just as outrageous here.

Whatever the reasons Lewis had for changing the tone of the picture, he did it with a vengeance and he shattered any continuity the original film had in the process. He didn't actually add much new footage, just a few linking shots to support the rewritten story and an attack scene with the monster, as Henry Hite was still available. Continuity ought to have been easy to preserve, as he worked with the original cameraman, Bill Johnson, too but it apparently wasn't deemed important, as Lewis's new ending underlines.

I should emphasise that not everything that Lewis did was detrimental. Most viewers remember the shot of the spaceman striding across the cosmos over the opening credits, and that was a Lewis contribution. The catchy theme tune by The Other Three that accompanies it was his too. Mostly though, he mangled, and most of his mangling turned out to be by ditching existing footage rather than adding anything new, although his new attack scene is rather bizarrely incompetent.

To be fair, I should also add that the bad continuity began in *Terror at Half Day*. Rebane only had his lead actor, Peter Thompson, for that first week that ate up his budget. So, once he raised more money, he simply replaced Thompson's character, Dr Manning, with Dr Brent, with no explanation beyond a line of dialogue to suggest he handed over the reins. Presumably this is also why George Perry's character, Dr Logan, is killed off early in the film, but the actor promptly returns to play his brother. Perry was a beautician who dearly wanted to be an actor; he ponied up financing in return for a major part and ended up with two. At least shooting sequentially, something else that Rebane did through inexperience, helped these transitions.

That may be inept storytelling but it doesn't break the story. Lewis's most unforgivable contribution to the film does, in such a blatant and unapologetic way that it perhaps singlehandedly caused the elevation of the picture to cult status.

After the Wacker Dr scene, the biggest looking scene in the picture which Lewis cut significantly, the authorities chase the monster into the sewers. We're shown Henry Hite walking underground and, in a more traditional ending to the one Rebane wanted, Lewis planned to have him encased in concrete by pouring it into the tunnels from above. What he actually did beggars belief and I should quote verbatim: "As if a switch had been turned, as if an eye had been blinked, as if some phantom force in the universe had made a move eons beyond our comprehension, suddenly, there was no trail! There was no giant, no monster, no thing called Douglas to be followed. There was nothing in the tunnel but the puzzled men of courage, who suddenly found themselves alone with shadows and darkness!"

Yeah, the ending is that the monster never existed. Everything thus far has revolved around a non-existent monster that held the entire city of Chicago in a panic for absolutely no reason. But wait, there's more, as they say.

Dr Logan passes Col Steve Connors a telegram and Lewis dives even further into the abyss of idiocy. "With the telegram, one cloud lifts, and another descends," he tells us. "Astronaut Frank Douglas, rescued, alive, well and of normal size, some eight thousand miles away in a lifeboat, with no memory of where he has been, or how he was separated from his capsule! Then who, or what, has landed here? Is it here yet? Or has the cosmic switch been pulled? Case in point: the line between science fiction and science fact is microscopically thin! You have witnessed the line being shaved even thinner! But is the menace with us? Or is the monster gone?"

It's hard to imagine a more incoherent or belittling end. At least *Robot Monster* was honest! This is just Lewis raising his middle finger to drive in audiences, highlighting that he has their money and there's nothing they can do about it. It gave him his double bill and his percentage and as far as he was concerned, that was all that mattered.

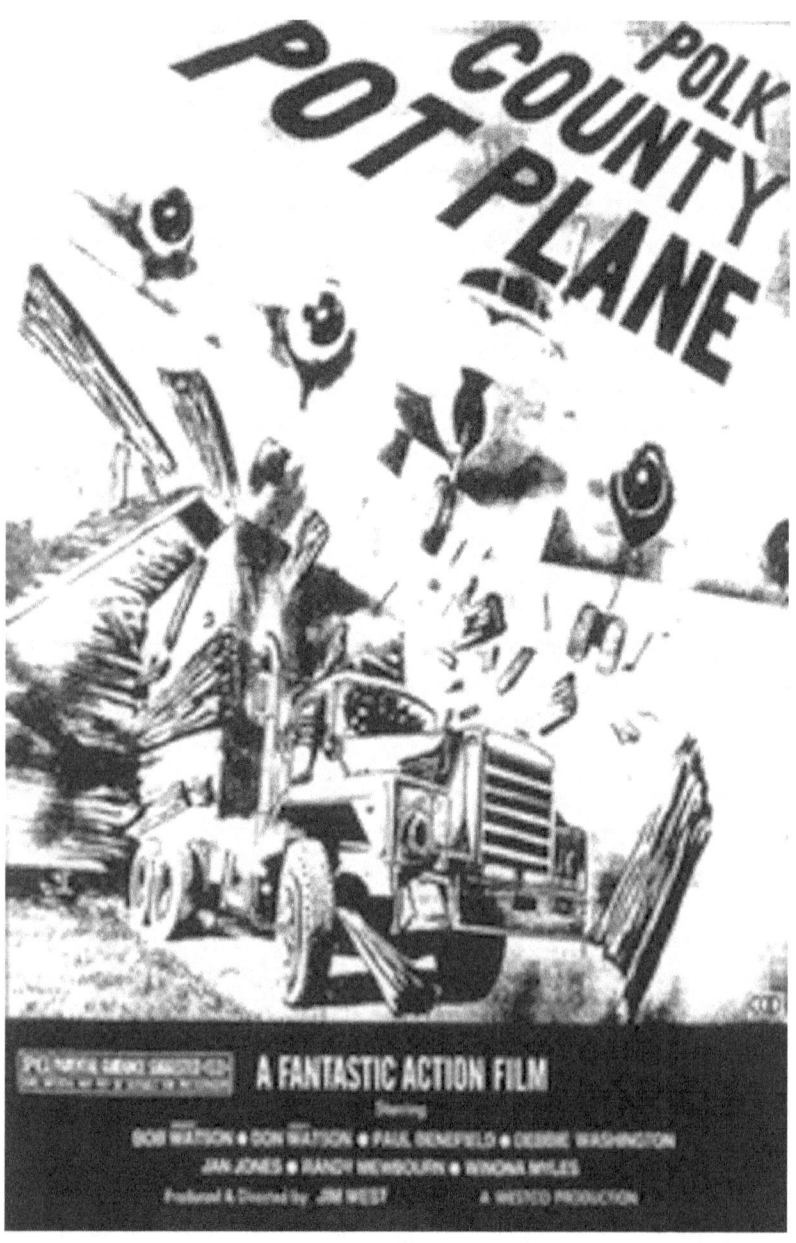

O is for Opportunity:
Polk County Pot Plane (1977)

Director: Jim West
Writer: Jim Clarke
Stars: Don Watson, Bobby Watson, Big Jim, Paul Weiner, 'Sandy' St Armour, Edward Smith, Bob Deyton, Debbi Washington and N67038 (DC-4)

We've all had good ideas for movies, just like we've all had good ideas for band names, but most of us have never shot a movie or formed a band. Georgia State Representative James I West is the exception, because a good idea for a movie literally landed in his metaphorical back yard and he made it happen.

In August 1975, someone flew a Douglas DC-4 into Polk County under cover of night and landed on the top of Treat Mountain. Designed for runways over 3,000 feet, it stopped in only 500 on a landing strip cleared by bulldozers mere hours before and lit up by strips of 100 watt light bulbs powered with a portable generator. It had clipped pine trees on the way in and needles were still stuck in the prop. It was carrying 3,260 pounds of marijuana and 75 pounds of hashish, which were mostly recovered by authorities from a rental truck a few miles away. Many were arrested but most were released, including the plane's owner, Robert Eby, as nobody could prove he was flying it at the time.

While it was a talking point all over Georgia, Jim West saw a good idea for a movie. Fortunately for us, he did everything right in turning it from the former into the latter. The federal authorities had seized the plane as evidence but couldn't figure out what to do with it, as it clearly couldn't just fly out again. Eventually they auctioned it off to the highest bidder on the courthouse steps. Ahead of the auction, West bought the 300 acres surrounding the plane, fenced it off and set armed guards to stop potential buyers from inspecting it. Once he won the plane, he hired a crew to expand the runway to 3,500 feet and flew it out himself using JATO bottles for added lift. With the set and the biggest prop in hand, he formed a film production company, Westco Productions, wrote a screenplay and set to persuading everyone he knew to take part, as cast, crew or both. Previous experience was not required and clearly didn't exist for the most part.

What's most amazing to me, beyond the background to this story itself, is how far West managed to get. His dedication must have been absolute and his word trusted implicitly. His neighbour was a house mover, so he promptly hired him to play a house mover who sets up one of the biggest stunts in the film. Howard Smith and Bob Deyton play the Clayton County police chief and sheriff purely because that's what they were. When Oosh and Doosh, the lead characters, are lifted off the roof of the Clayton County Jail by helicopter, they really are lifted off the roof of the Clayton County Jail by helicopter.

What's more, like everyone else in the film, they perform their own stunts, as presumably West just didn't know any stuntmen. These are not minor stunts and we can't forget that these folk aren't even actors, let alone stuntmen. For the more dangerous stunts, they were liquored up with 'liquid courage' first. As far as I know, nobody was hurt.

Of course, West himself was as experienced as a filmmaker as anyone else involved, which is to say not at all. This was the only film he made and it shows. While he's only credited as producer and director, it has been said that anywhere there's a Jim or a James in the credits it's really him, from Jim Clarke the writer to Jim Young the camera operator. I don't know if that's really true or not, but it's certain at least that he's Jim Whozitt as Big Jim Elliott, the pilot who flies in the DC-4 for its initial landing at the beginning of the film.

He does a capable job, very naturalistic as you might expect, but believable, and it sets the pace for the acting throughout, which is similarly shorn of any real acting in favour of authentic southern accents and conversational tone. This is actually much appreciated, one of the charms of the film, along with the relentless stuntwork and chase scenes. The film's biggest success is that nothing in it pretends to be anything it isn't.

If it wasn't clear beforehand, it becomes absolutely clear during the first chase scene that there's no effects work going on here at all, not just no CGI but no effects at all. When we see Oosh and

Doosh driving their camper van full of pot at high speed, they're doing just that. When we watch them nudging cop cars off the road, that's what they're doing. When their camper van nicks the blade of a bulldozer on the back of a truck going the other way and half the top gets ripped off, that's precisely what happened.

It feels rather surreal that we're watching a fictional story that's leading up to a reenactment of a true event, but in doing so we're watching something very real indeed. The only reasons this doesn't play out like an episode of *America's Funniest Home Videos* are that they kept getting away with these stunts and because editor Angelo Ross was one of the few professionals on the crew. His other editing job in 1977 was *Smokey and the Bandit*.

There is a plot unfolding, but that's one of the weaker parts of the affair. Oosh and Doosh work for Joe King and they're good boys the boss doesn't want to lose. They're dumb enough to get all four of their crew caught and locked up in the Clayton County Jail, but they're bright enough to talk the sheriff into allowing them all to work on the roof the very next morning with their regular clothes underneath their jail outfits. They promptly escape by helicopter, with Oosh and Doosh hanging onto the landing skids for the duration of the ride, presumably without harnesses or safety nets or anything except that 'liquid courage'. They get back to King's place to find that he's been deposed offscreen by Sandy, who shoots the helicopter pilot and puts Oosh and Doosh right back to work, this time picking up a new load from the DC-4 in an eighteen wheeler, which is promptly chased by state troopers. These cops are apparently really quick, both to find crooks and to let them go.

What follows contains a little bit of story, a little bit of humour and a little bit of violence. There's no acting talent or character building to speak of. Mostly it contains a lot of vehicles. It's a ninety minute feature but a full third of that is taken up with car chases and associated stuntwork. This would be reasonably impressive in any film, both in quantity and quality, but it's eye opening in this film because of the lack of stuntmen. Remember, if we see it, they did it for real. When a cop car crushes itself under the back of the truck, that's what it did. When another drives right under the truck and loses its top, that's what happened. And when the eighteen wheeler speeds right through a prefab house parked in the middle of the road, that's absolutely what happened. How much of the budget went on 'liquid courage' I have no idea, but most of it was surely spent on vehicles. Every time I watch I forget to count how many get trashed, but it's a lot.

This is exciting but then these are the exciting scenes. The catch is that surrounding them are other scenes of vehicles that aren't exciting in the slightest. While a third of the film is taken up with chase scenes and stunts, another third of it, if not more, is taken up by vehicles not being chased and nothing else happening that requires 'liquid courage'. We see cars driving down the road, trucks driving down the road, armoured vehicles driving down the road. We watch loading and unloading, we even watch parked vehicles waiting for someone to show up. We see cop cars waiting for something to happen. We see bulldozers at work. We watch vehicles following other vehicles, pushing other vehicles, nudging them in new directions. We're shown shots from the helicopter and the DC-4 and aerial shots of the helicopter and the DC-4. Sometimes it feels like the action was choreographed by a six year old boy playing with his hot wheels.

In some ways it's refreshing that this isn't just another seventies action flick, even just another seventies hicksploitation flick. Because nobody knew what they were doing, the film doesn't feel like anything else and that's always a good thing, even if the end result is fundamentally flawed. The building blocks may be clearly phrased like the memories of films or TV shows, but generally they're put together in whole new designs that apparently just seemed like they made sense at the time. Whole swathes of this film are completely dialogue free, occasionally accompanied by old timey music that helps set the scene as silent slapstick comedy. It's a heist movie when Oosh and Doosh rob an armoured car to pay back Sandy for the losses and damages they've incurred. It's a chase movie in its heart and in truth it's a snapshot of the seventies south, Georgia accents all the way, jeans so tight you can see the testicles and hairstyles right out of Lynyrd Skynyrd.

Eventually all this preliminary padding gets us to the point of the film, dramatised of course. Big Jim wants to bring in the biggest shipment ever seen and, despite their track record, wants Oosh and Doosh to be his ground crew. He's going to fly in ten million dollars worth of pot and cocaine from Colombia and he'll give them a quarter of a million each to make it work. He needs a 2,500 foot runway carved off the top of Treat Mountain in Polk County and five two ton trucks to carry away the drugs. And he needs it in three days.

Nobody does their job right, the ground crew not clearing as much as they should and even Big Jim arriving a couple of hours ahead of schedule, but that just means that we watch the plane fly in, clipping trees as it did in reality, wondering how Jim West managed to get away with everything he put in this film without a single stuntman on the payroll. The picture's motto is clearly, 'Just do it!' and that's what they did.

Presumably the aerial shots we see during the finalé were the first filmed, of the real plane in the real location before Jim West bought the land. They could even be news footage taken after the event, just as the radio announcements by real Atlanta DJ Van Q Temple may well be recordings from the time. Yet, as tends to be the case with this unique film, reality morphs into fiction that is in its own way, new reality.

When Jerry Burnam and his bulldozer crew clear land for Big Jim to fly onto Treat Mountain in the story, it's really Jerry Burnam and his bulldozer crew clearing land for Jim West to fly off the mountain with his new purchase and so make the rest of the film possible. When he flies back in, he's reenacting the real event in the real plane in the real location. We're impressed with his skill as a pilot, assuming he's actually flying the plane, but we're even more impressed with the unknown pilot who did it first, at night and with much less runway.

The more I see *Polk County Pot Plane*, later reissued as *In Hot Pursuit*, the more I love it. While it's not a good movie, clearly an amateur affair through and through, Jim West was bright enough to know every one of his limitations before he even began and he worked around them throughout. He knew he was working with amateur actors because they were friends, family and presumably whoever said, "Sure, I'll be in your movie, Jim," so he wrote scenes that didn't require acting. He knew he didn't have stuntmen so he persuaded his cast with a politician's silver tongue to go for it and do amazing things. The result is so intrinsically honest that it's surreal. We're conditioned to know that films are fake, but this one isn't. It's as honest as they come, not because West necessarily wanted it that way but because he didn't know how to do it differently. He saw an opportunity, grabbed it and didn't let go until he had what he wanted. Maybe that 'liquid courage' was really for him.

Huh? An A-Z of Why Classic American Bad Movies Were Made

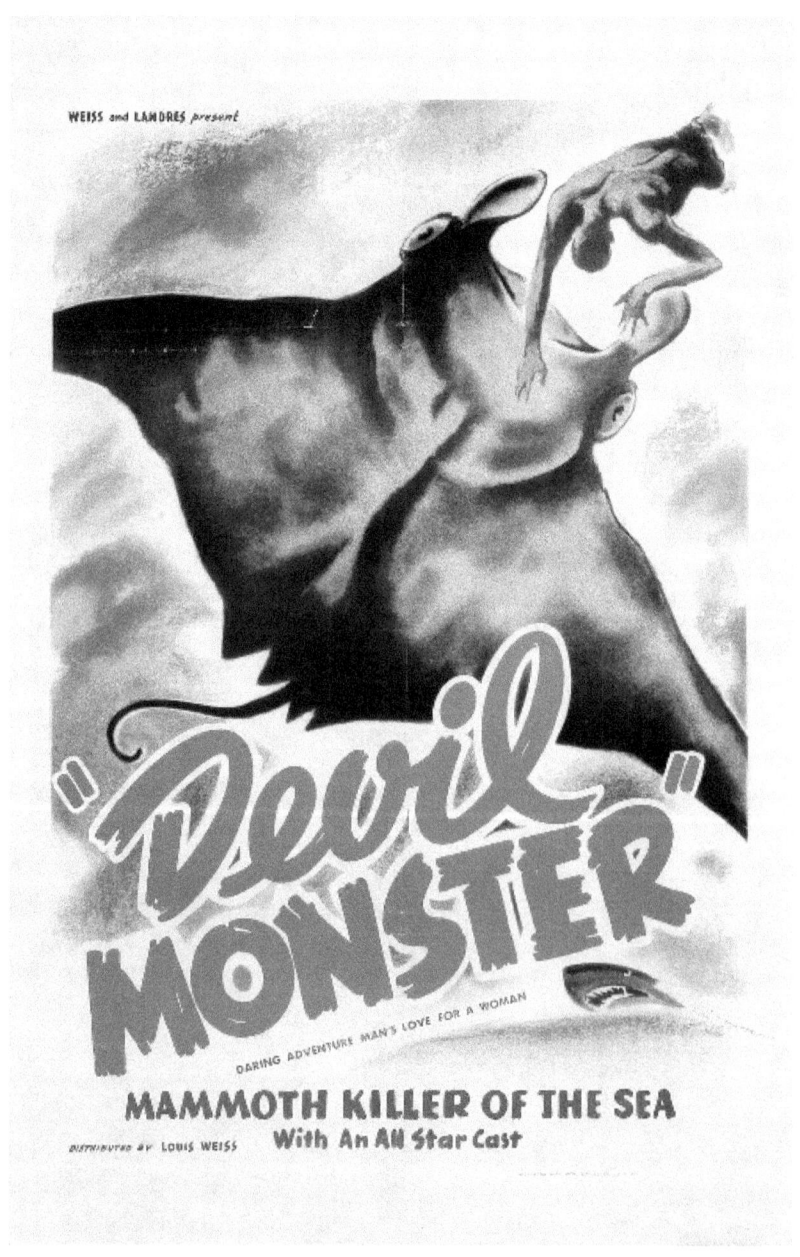

P is for Patchwork:
Devil Monster (1946)

Director: S Edwin Graham
Writers: Juan Duval and S Edwin Graham, from a story by Thelma
Brooks and Terry Grey, with narration by Tom Hubbard
Stars: Barry Norton and Blanche Mehaffy

Nowadays we have it lucky: there are so many avenues we can
follow to see classic movies that we're spoiled for choice. Back in
1946, most people only had the option of going to their local
theatre to see whatever happened to be showing and the only
choice they had was between the different movie houses in their
town.

Many would have seen *Devil Monster*, often on a double bill with
The White Gorilla, and wondered why it seemed familiar, only to
shrug it off. After all, every popular success launched a hundred
cheap imitators and many classic era films were remakes to begin
with, even famous ones like *The Maltese Falcon*. Those who paid
attention, though, may have realised that *Devil Monster* didn't just
seem familiar, it was really something they had seen before.

You see, not one single moment within this entire film is original.
Everything was patched together from stock footage and older
movies that the 'filmmakers' had bought the rights to. The details
are so convoluted that nobody seems able to confirm exactly which
piece fits where, but the source movies expose a host of business
practices commonplace in the classic era that may seem bizarre
today.

In sound's early days, pictures were often shot simultaneously in
more than one language, usually with different cast and crew. The
1931 *Dracula* was really two films, for example: Tod Browning's
iconic Bela Lugosi film and George Melford's Spanish version with
Carlos Villarías as the Count. The latter was shot at night with the
same costumes on the same sets, but it runs 29 minutes longer and
benefits from the crew watching and learning from the Browning
dailies. Alfredo Carlos Birabén, the bilingual Argentinian actor
better known as Barry Norton, who played Juan Harker in Melford's

Drácula, is the star here, his footage taken from *The Sea Fiend* and *El diablo del Mar*, the English and Spanish versions of the same film. The third associated source film is *The Great Manta*, but it's not clear precisely what this was. It starred "Barry Norton and a Big Native Cast" and was advertised as early as June 1935, so it may be another film shot alongside *El diablo del Mar*, which saw its Mexican release in December of that year. Maybe *The Sea Fiend*, a closer translation of the Spanish title, was merely the name given to the film for a British release in 1938. It was routine for B movies to be released under different titles in other countries or even other states, and the retitled films often had different running times too in order to cater to the varied rules of local censor boards.

Another suggestion is that Russ Vincent and George Moscow bought the rights to *The Sea Fiend* and renamed it *The Great Manta*, though the years don't quite add up. However closely or not they're related, the rights to all three titles apparently ended up with E M Landres and Louis Weiss in 1945 for $500.

Devil Monster is the result, a patchwork quilt composed of scenes from all three versions of the source story, along with a slew of stock footage from nature documentaries and perhaps even a few scenes from other pictures too, like 1930's *Hell Harbor*. Without seeing the source material to make a comparison, it's hard to tell, but it would hardly seem unlikely.

There are no less than five credited writers, only one of whom was new to this release. He's Tom Hubbard and he wrote the narration that overlays the stock footage, in a vague attempt to maintain consistency across entirely unrelated material. The original director, S Edwin Graham, retained his credit, but it's followed by another that reads, "Supervised by Adrian Weiss." Adrian was the son of Louis Weiss, so he had presumably been tasked with turning the footage his father had co-purchased into some sort of financial return.

It's a seafaring story, even though Robert Jackson, our narrator and hero, has never been to sea. He's a captain's son who has spent his entire life in the fishing village of San Pietro and he hangs around the docks in a sailor's cap talking about tuna runs, but he's busy getting cockblocked by Louise, which annoys him, especially while she's eating bananas. Louise is in love with a man who's missing, presumed dead: Jose Francisco, first mate of the *Miami*, lost six years earlier. To Jackson, he's "a lifelong friend of the family," but when Louise's mother shows him a newspaper clipping about a pair of bodies discovered on a beach in the Galapagos Islands, he sneaks onto his dad's boat and persuades him to search the South Seas for Jose's body, so he can finally get laid. What grizzled sea captain could resist such eloquence as, "You've got to help me! C'mon dad, don't be a grouch!" One that died four years before the film's release, of course.

And off we go into the strange land of stock footage. It really is strange as Adrian Weiss trawled many documentaries to collate his footage but found little to make consistent. There's three and a half minutes of sealions and elephant seals, which may not seem much but that's a third of the film thus far. "I hung on the rail for what seemed like hours," says Jackson and we know what he means.

At least the next section, featuring the supposed natives of a friendly island, is mostly made up of topless women, surely explaining why this film gained even the slightest success. It's a wildly multicultural island, comprised not only of the expected Hawaiians but white women and even Australian aborigines. The common factor is that they're all topless, even when one joins a native boy to put on an underwater floor show in shark infested water. Naturally the shark never shares the screen with the natives he threatens, because it's from different footage.

Some of the footage is mildly interesting, like natives running up palm trees as if gravity can be ignored, but none of it has anything to do with the story, and we were hardly given much of that to begin with. When Capt Jackson and Tiny the cook show back up to spy the wreck of the *Miami* through their telescope, it's the first time we've seen a single member of the cast for 13 minutes and 48 seconds and we're only 21 minutes into the film, a full third of its running time. The time spent with cast on the screen thus far only just edges out the time we've spent watching a battle between an octopus and a moray eel in a fish tank. It's supposed to be a lagoon but the octopus spends most of its time attached to the glass so we don't buy it for a moment. When a school of fish show up so Jackson can suggest they deliberately overcome the octopus by sheer numbers just to rescue their buddy, the moray, we wonder if we've found ourselves in a Disney movie.

You might think it a relief when Jackson announces, "Continuing the search for Jose..." but it isn't, for we're about to meet actor Bill Lemuels. It isn't just that a South Sea Island chief is played by a native of Norfolk, Virginia, who probably left it only to seek fame in Hollywood, it's that Lemuels somehow felt that he should put on a bad Bela Lugosi accent, only to prove so bad at it that he comes across more like Mal Arnold trying to channel Bela Lugosi in *Blood Feast*, merely wearing curlers and a Hawaiian skirt.

Given that Barry Norton plays Jackson roughly like William Haines would have played Marlon Brando and Jack Barty is so wooden that a native might well have climbed him in search of coconuts, he is at least a distraction. That leaves Terry Grey, an actor and writer who failed to explain why he plays a character named Tiny, obviously neither a literal nor ironic nickname. Maybe it's a self deferential reference to the size of his penis.

There is one word here that's sheer genius, though hardly in the way the writers intended. When the Jacksons ask about the manta ray that's painted onto the wall of the chief's hut, he explains that it's one of a pair of deadly killers that have plagued the island for centuries, the only objects of fear the natives have, but it was caught by the sole survivor of the wreck on the beach. "Is it him?" Capt Jackson asks his son in a huddle, after he looks out the window at this magnificent fisherman. For the duration of one word, Norton provides a masterclass performance. "Yeah," he replies with so much resignation that we can fully believe that in that single moment he's just had his world turned upside down, lost all chance of getting anything from his girlfriend, who of course won't be his girlfriend for much longer, and been rooked between the eyes with guilt for failing to look for his friend before now. It's a marvellous moment. That's all, folks.

Now Jose is having a ball on the island. He's the master fisherman of all time, spending his days making wild passionate love to Maya, the chief's daughter. "I'm one of them now," he explains to Jackson and you can't blame him. There's an easy win/win here, but Jackson aims for a lose/lose by getting the island drunk and kidnapping him. Amazingly, Jose is thankful, getting upset only when Tiny lets slip about Jackson and Louise, setting the stage for a third act in the waters of the devil monster.

Jack Del Rio, who plays Jose, is at least a better actor than those he's acting with, especially Lemuels, who gets still more ridiculous when drunk, deciding that Transylvanian South Sea Islanders need pork pie hats. Del Rio is no great star, going insane in the silent style for a couple of scenes, but his shows a dynamic edge during the finalé. Best known for being Peggy Lee's fourth husband in the sixties, he had credits in only four of seventeen films.

I should point out that the title of the film is appropriate but unfortunate, given that manta rays are about as ineffectual as any villain Nature has given to the world of film. They may be huge creatures, reaching up to 25 feet across, but unlike their stingray cousins, they're dangerous only to plankton. Presumably the hacks who wrote seafaring horror stories in the thirties didn't realise that evolution had stripped them of teeth and stingers as they became filter feeders, so conjured up outlandish plots from their size and nickname alone. Thus we howl in laughter as this gentle vegetarian of the deep is painted as a centuries old sea monster capable of ripping off human arms at the slightest provocation. *The Sea Bat*, a 1930 film with Charles Bickford and Boris Karloff, had the same problem, but at least offered something to posterity other than a textbook example of how not to construct a new film out of old material.

It's hard to imagine how Adrian Weiss could have done a worse job. Obviously he was limited by the production quality of his source material and he was unable to sync wildly disparate shots together, like the too distant with the too close, but he had total control over what material to pick and choose and how to patch it all together into something new. Diverting us from five minutes of melodrama into fifteen minutes of sealions, naked breasts and octopus war is indefensible.

In fact, it's hard to see how the source films could have made any sense even before the splicing. Jackson constantly talks as if he's an experienced fisherman but this is his first time afloat. The crew only appear on the way home, as if they've been in cryogenic storage until Jose was found. They're happy swanning around the South Seas looking for someone they've forgotten about but once he takes the helm to steer them to tuna it takes a mere hour for mutiny to be raised.

Hardest to defend is the fact that this appears to be a horror movie. It's called *Devil Monster*, for pity's sakes. The poster depicts a vast manta ray about to devour an unwary sailor, above words that read, "mammoth killer of the sea'. What would you expect going in? There's nothing there to suggest that this is really just a melodrama about a man who searches for the corpse of a family friend just so he can get laid. False advertising just doesn't come close.

It even claims "an all-star cast," though only one member of that cast could remotely lay claim to ever having been a star and then only in foreign language versions of Hollywood films. The leading lady had retired no less than eight years before this portmanteau picture was released. The leading man hadn't just fallen to the level of being uncredited in films like *Casablanca*, he'd fallen to the level of being uncredited in films as bad as *Zombies on Broadway*. By those guidelines, I'm a superstar.

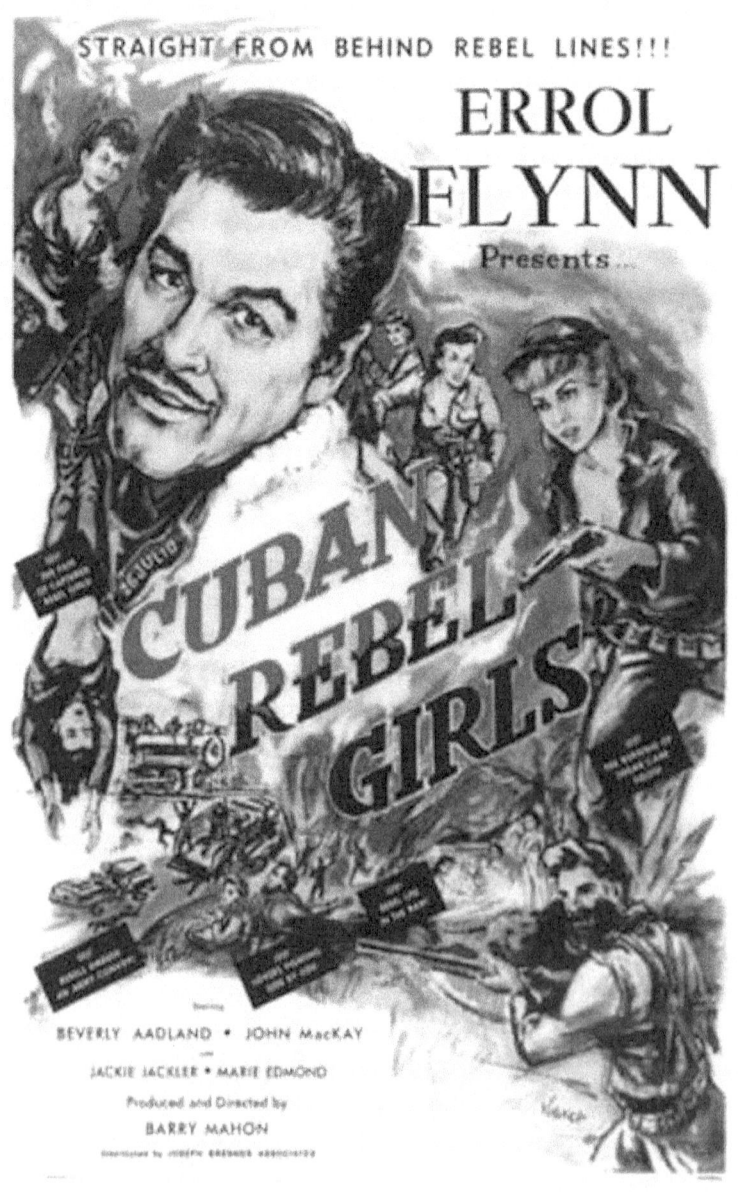

Q is for Quickie:
Cuban Rebel Girls (1959)

Director: Barry Mahon
Writer: Errol Flynn
Stars: Beverly Aadland, John MacKay, Jackie Jackler and Marie
Edmund

The last line of Errol Flynn's infamous memoirs, *My Wicked, Wicked Ways*, reads, "The second half-century looms up, but I don't feel the night coming on."

He dictated that in late 1958, at the age of 49, while living in Jamaica with his girlfriend, Beverly Aadland, as she turned sixteen, but the night came on quicker than he thought, as he died of a heart attack in Vancouver only a year later. It's unlikely that it was a surprise to anyone else, as a lifetime of hard living and harder drinking had turned him from the swashbuckling icon of *Captain Blood*, *The Adventures of Robin Hood* and *The Sea Hawk* into a bloated parody. He hadn't been healthy for years, rejected for service in 1942 as 4-F for an enlarged heart, chronic back pain, malaria, tuberculosis and a set of venereal diseases. His liver began to fail in 1952, as he contracted hepatitis. Heavy smoking had caused Buerger's disease, thrombosis of veins and arteries. His second half-century lasted less than four months.

It's not unusual for Hollywood stars to deteriorate, slowly or quickly, and die before their time, but usually they fade away. In Flynn's case, what makes it unusual is he did the opposite. 1959 might even count as his most fascinating year, even had he not died towards the end of it. He survived a bout of food poisoning earlier in the year, after eating a mixture of uncooked hamburger meat and raw egg yolks. He was plagued by the IRS, who eroded his finances so far that he was heading for bankruptcy, though his lifestyle continued as if he was still one of Hollywood's highest paid actors. His third wife, Pat Wymore, was finally divorcing him, which made his teenage girlfriend happy, as she was eager to become his fourth. Even his career was notable again, his three 1957 and 1958 films, *The Sun Also Rises*, *Too Much, Too Soon* and *The Roots of Heaven*, praised for some of the best acting in his career. Yet his final two, shot in 1959, were perhaps his worst.

Conversely, they're also two of his most interesting, as he found himself in the right place at the right time to meet a variety of personal needs. The place was Cuba, which he knew well, having long enjoyed the hedonistic lifestyle made possible by Fulgencia Batista's openness for wealthy tourists. The time was just before Batista, Cuba's president and dictator, was overthrown by the guerrilla revolution led by Fidel Castro and his 26th of July Movement.

Revolutions had long been a magnet to the idealistic Flynn, who once wrote, "Ever since boyhood I have been drawn, perhaps romantically, to the ideas of causes, crusades." He joined the Abraham Lincoln Brigade during the Spanish Civil War and condemned Gen Franco in Madrid, as he aimed "to follow in Hemingway's footsteps" as a wartime correspondent. With a new Cuban cause, he took to the hills to report it for the *New York Journal-American*, a Hearst publication. He wrote at least two features.

Clearly just as important to Flynn as this serious reportage was the need to repair his finances, so he took the opportunity not only to write about the revolution but to film it too, making two rather different pictures that went on to have rather different histories.

The one that nobody knew about for the longest time was *Cuban Story* or *The Truth About Fidel Castro Revolution*, as it saw a world premiére in Moscow before disappearing for four decades, finally being rediscovered and screened in New York in 2001. A supposed documentary, it's closer to propaganda, clearly taking the side of the rebels, with whom Flynn and film producer Victor Pahlen felt kinship. Pahlen, a Russian born American, met and befriended Flynn in Havana in 1956. They both knew and loved Cuba under its dictator, but were well aware of problems that Castro claimed he would solve, after seizing power, like restoring elections and press freedom.

As propaganda, *Cuban Story* is a mess, a paean to an ideology that didn't exist, awkwardly pro-Castro but not pro-Communist. The rebels fighting Batista were comprised of different factions with different agendas, including anti-communists; even after taking control, Castro came to the States to deny he was communist. In 1965 he became First Secretary of the Communist Party of Cuba, but Flynn saw that writing on the wall in 1959. "It is one thing to start a revolution, another to win it and still another to make it stick," he said, "and as far as this writer is concerned it ain't sticking," adding that "the police state in Cuba is not very different from that of its predecessors."

What *Cuban Story* really has is amazing footage, chronicling the changes in Cuba from the very beginnings of the revolution to after its success. When it finally resurfaced, even the head of the Cuban National Archive told Pahlen's daughter that he had never seen it before. As it wasn't all shot in 1959, clearly Pahlen was responsible for the footage, or at least most of it, with Flynn peripheral in the grand scheme of things. Maybe he helped get Pahlen and his camera into some of these places, but he doesn't appear on screen much at all.

He's there at the outset, apparently ad libbing an introduction whilst under the influence, locating Cuba on a globe that he literally tosses throws away to bounce audibly off screen. He's there early on playing cards with Aadland at the Casino de Capri in Havana, partly owned by George Raft. For a shot of Flynn with Castro though, we have to settle for a photograph. While Flynn clearly gives the introduction, it just as clearly isn't him providing the narration, though the film claims that it's "reported by Errol Flynn" and it's told in the first person as if it was. It has been suggested that it's Pahlen himself, who has the writing credit, though the accent is British with a Scots tinge, rather than Russian.

The footage in *Cuban Story* is valuable to historians of Cuba: Batista in his palace, rebels dead in the streets after the failed attack on the Moncada Barracks, Castro preparing for exile in Mexico, demonstrations, rebels hiding in the hills, Che Guevara liberating Santa Clara, former president Carlos Prío, Castro's first speech in Havana with a dove alighting on his shoulder, destruction of Batista landmarks, trials of officials, even a firing squad.

The other film Flynn shot at this point is also Cuban but valuable far more to historians of Errol Flynn himself. It's *Cuban Rebel Girls*, which purports to be a dramatised documentary of rebel life with his girlfriend, Beverly Aadland, as the star. She was a budding actress and underage showgirl in Las Vegas when he met and seduced her on the set of the Gene Kelly movie, *Marjorie Morningstar*, in 1958. She was fifteen at the time, though she looked much older. He may or may not have believed she was eighteen.

Why Flynn made *Cuban Rebel Girls* is open to debate, possibly because it was for many different reasons all at once. He knew and loved Cuba and was caught up in the revolution unfolding there. He wanted to meet and report on those behind it, perhaps seeing Castro as a hero of the people. Being out of the country also meant that he was out of reach of the IRS, at least temporarily. He'd already spent the advance for his autobiography, which he hadn't delivered yet, as well as much of what he'd borrowed from backers for a film he planned to make but perhaps didn't even exist outside his sales pitches. As some of these backers may well have been 'less than reputable', it's hardly a stretch to see him connect the dots and decide that shooting a cheap quickie in Cuba would be the best thing all around. It would deliver the film he'd promised, serving as a tax write-off in the process, unfold in exciting fashion amidst a real revolution and make his girlfriend a star.

While that sounds like a winner on paper, *Cuban Rebel Girls* is a loser on almost every front. How much money he had left to finance it is open to question, but it obviously wasn't a lot, given who he put to work on it. The only major name was his own and he didn't have to pay himself, so he's prominent, writing the script and providing narration, for real this time. He's obvious early on as 'The American Correspondent', flying into Havana where he's shuffled from contact to contact to get him closer to the rebels, then vanishing from sight for long periods at a time, resurfacing in the hills where he visibly struggles in the terrain.

To direct, he hired Barry Mahon, a fighter pilot and POW camp escapee whose experience in movies was restricted to co-producing a couple of Flynn's indie pictures in the early fifties. More importantly, he had been Flynn's personal pilot for years and had more recently become his manager. Success was clearly in his interest too.

And of course there's Beverly Aadland. Her mother Florence was a dancer who had lost her leg in a car accident, so lived vicariously through her daughter. Beverly was posing for adverts at six months, eventually becoming the Ivory Soap baby. Dance classes followed as soon as she could walk and she was doing bit parts in movies at three. Some reports suggest she was doing a good sight more than just acting, as she'd bloomed quickly to a 34-18-34 figure at the age of twelve and was allegedly willing to use it for a hundred bucks. Flynn's exploits with the ladies were not far removed from those of the characters he played, leading to the phrase, 'in like Flynn'. He also clearly liked the young stuff, though when he was brought to trial in 1943 by two underage girls for statutory rape, he was cleared of all charges. However, reading what she's written between the lines, it may well have been Aadland who seduced him rather than the other way around.

The catch is that however much experience Aadland had on stage and film, this one makes it very obvious that she wasn't a good actress. Amidst all the true and supposedly true material conjured up for Flynn's script, there's a hokey fictional subplot to provide her with a part and the film with a dynamic title.

She's Beverly Woods, an American girl whose boyfriend is Cuban and fighting in the hills with Castro. Her friend is Jacqueline Dominguez, Cuban herself, and about to mount an arms run to the rebels, so she goes along for the ride. Flynn immediately plays them up. "Some people can put idealism ahead of their own personal losses," he tells us, as they fly to Miami with $50k in their handbags, drive to Key West and hire shifty looking Capt Alvarez to sail them to Cuba. Some of this is interesting. Boxes are gradually sneaked into the hold and regular fishing trips disguise the odd run across the Straits of Florida under the eyes of the coastguard. Mostly it's ham fisted.

The action is poorly staged and poorly written: one bunch of inept rebels literally walk outside to be arrested when the polizia arrive, except for Maria who climbs out of the window and escapes slowly over the rooftops. The direction is what you'd expect from a man new to the director's seat and whose career would lead him to the heights of *International Smorgas-Broad*, *Fanny Hill Meets the Red Baron* and *Prostitutes Protective Society*.

Worst of all, the acting is poor to begin with and gets worse, especially from Aadland, who doesn't seem to realise what tone is appropriate in a rebel camp. Life is jolly, it seems: natives sing songs, the girls take baths in inlets and they all talk about military equipment. "Sounds like fun," says Beverly. "Maybe I'll get to shoot somebody." She pouts a lot, she blinks a lot and she always sticks her breasts out to pose while she talks. Most of her dialogue is about getting to see her Johnny. She clearly doesn't care about the revolution.

Her performance makes the poor drama even more tortuous. There are slight hints at suspense, strategy and action, but mostly there's only Beverly and Johnny mooning over each other. "Now I'm a rebel girl, I think I'll think about war too," she proclaims. She's like a transplant from a teen drama to a war movie, like *The Steel Helmet* with Hannah Montana. Of course, the only common ground between *The Steel Helmet* and *Cuban Rebel Girls* is that they both have three word titles and they both contain shooting.

The continuity is terrible, making it easy to lose track of who and what and why. Everyone's a terrible shot as well, making these Cubans seem rather like Imperial stormtroopers battling Imperial stormtroopers except that occasionally people die. Flynn reappears on occasion to say something chipper while looking like Walt Disney. Beverly gets radio duty on a radio that never talks back to her; she talks, frogs croak and birds tweet and it's otherwise silent and surreal.

One scene literally stops so Beverly can sew up a hole in Flynn's trousers because he scraped his knee on the way up to the camp. Bizarrely, it's the most believable scene in the film, the truest to reality in this supposed dramatisation of real revolution life. With Flynn in bad shape, he needed a lot of care and Aadland tirelessly gave him that, nursing him through recurring bouts of malaria. It was Aadland who found him unconscious in Vancouver, attempted mouth to mouth rescuscitation and called for medical assistance.

Flynn had suggested to Stanley Kubrick, casting for *Lolita*, that he and Aadland play the roles on film that they were living at the time as a surprising but devoted couple. That didn't happen. Neither did her inheritance, as the will which Flynn wrote before going to meet Castro that left her a third of his estate in Jamaica was declared invalid. In the end, what she got was the leading role in her lover's last film. It was a quickie in every way.

Huh? An A-Z of Why Classic American Bad Movies Were Made

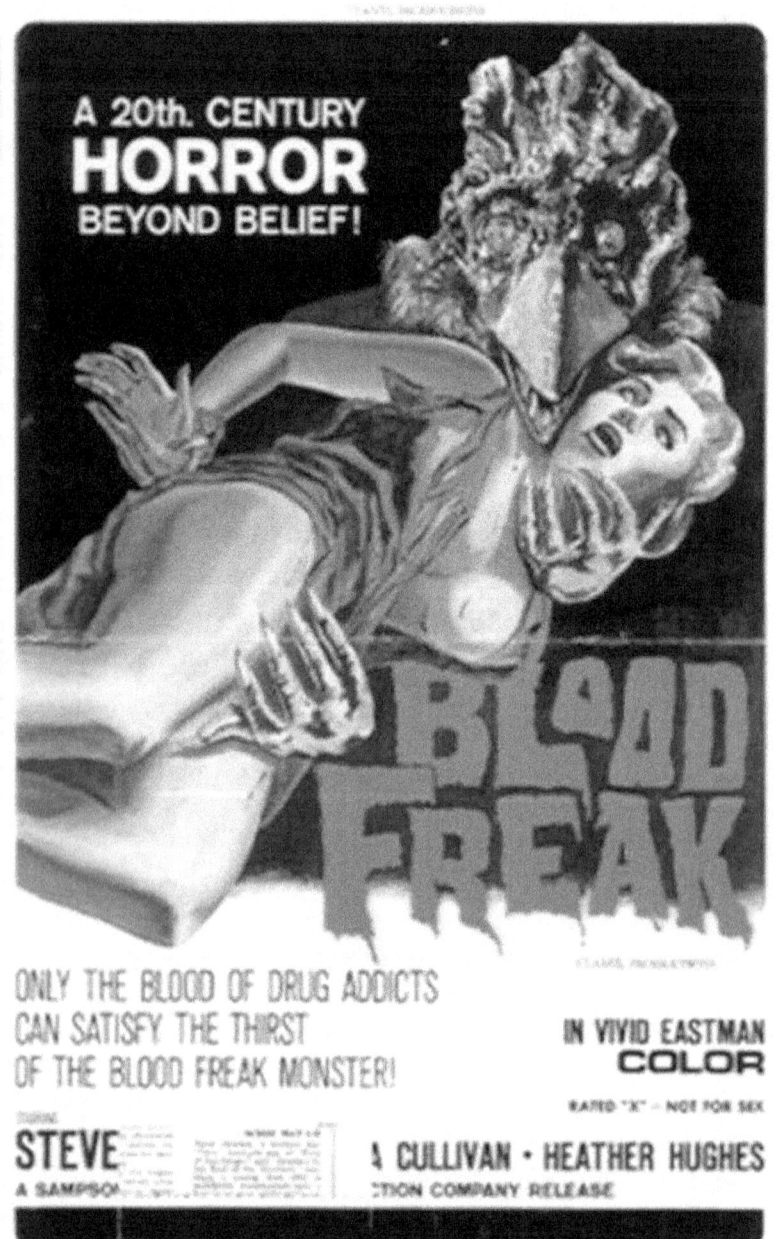

R is for Religion:
Blood Freak (1972)

Directors: Steve Hawkes and Brad Grinter
Writers: Steve Hawkes and Brad Grinter
Star: Steve Hawkes

It's hard to imagine a film like *Blood Freak* existing and it's even harder to imagine what possible motivations the filmmakers had to make such a thing. It's not just that it's so far out there that it becomes truly surreal, which it is; it's that it seems to be an anomaly in the careers of everyone involved.

I can only assume that it carried the message that its financiers wanted to be carried, but once their money supply had run out and they abandoned the film, it fell to Brad Grinter and Steve Hawkes to finish it on their own. How much they obscured that original message I have no idea, whether deliberately or accidentally, but it's certainly an unholy mishmash of a number of genres, tones and styles and apparently Hawkes, when asked about the film later in life, called it "a sad chapter in my life."

So what is it? Well, it's a pro-Christian, anti-pot, biker movie about a man who turns into a bloodthirsty freak with the head of a turkey. You know, the usual.

Grinter seems to be the focal point. He wrote, produced and directed the film, all in collaboration with Hawkes. Most of the cast are students from his film class who had never acted in anything professional before and would never do so again. His son, Randy Grinter, took a part and took charge of the sound department.

This may suggest that Grinter is precisely the sort of authority figure to make a Christian propaganda movie, a vaguely updated version of *Reefer Madness*, made thirty years on, but that doesn't seem to be the case. His main focus in life was naturism, to which cause most of his films are dedicated. He appeared in William Kerwin's *Sweet Bird of Aquarius*, in the all together; directed *Never the Twain*, which merges possession by Mark Twain with the Miss Nude World Pageant; and produced, directed and starred in *Barely Proper*, a film about a pretty schoolteacher brought up on charges of immorality for being a nudist.

While naturism was the driving force in his life, he did make other movies, appearing in Barry Mahon films as varied as *Musical Mutiny*, which revolved around the rock band Iron Butterfly, and *The Love Pirate*, a sexploitation flick in which he appeared as Capt Fu. It's as a director that he's most remembered though, chiefly for *Blood Freak* and *Flesh Feast*, a movie shot in 1967 but not released until 1970 that marks Veronica Lake's final appearance on film. Grinter turned the star of *Sullivan's Travels, I Married a Witch* and *The Blue Dahlia* into a deranged doctor trying to restore youth using flesh eating maggots.

He didn't have a long career, almost entirely centred around the year of 1970, but it's a bizarre one. If it's even possible, his collaborator on this film had even more of a bizarre career. That's Steve Hawkes, who wrote, produced and directed with Grinter, and also starred in the lead role of Herschell. He's still in the news today.

Usually known as Steve Sipek, Hawkes is best known for playing the lead in a couple of Spanish language Tarzan movies in the early seventies, even though he's Croatian. Playing Tarzan was a dream come true for Hawkes, who had survived a tough childhood through an identification with Johnny Weissmuller, but on the second Tarzan picture a set fire left him with burns that covered 90% of his body. He spent six months recuperating in hospital while the production moved to Colombia.

He was rescued from the fire by a lion called Samson, who he promptly adopted and, while he did make a few further films, including this one, he devoted the rest of his life to caring for great cats in his wildlife sanctuary home in Florida. He's spent the last forty years living peacefully with lions, tigers and panthers, making headlines only once in 2004 when his tiger Bobo escaped into the neighbourhood. I like the sign on his electronic gate that reads, "Trespassers will be eaten."

So these are the folks who made *Blood Freak* and if you can fathom how those two backgrounds generated this picture then you're a better man than I am.

We begin with Grinter himself, in one of a number of scenes that presumably exist to pad out the running time to eighty minutes once the money supply had dried up. Periodically he appears on screen to chain smoke and read to us from notes on his desk. His utter lack of charisma may help him to fade into the background at naturist colonies but as an on screen narrator he's terrible. Every time he appeared I wished for him to turn into the Amazing Criswell but he steadfastly refused to do so.

To begin with he just talks about catalysts, which is what Angel is about to become to Herschell. Angel breaks down on the Florida turnpike and Herschell is a Vietnam veteran and biker who helps her get moving again. In thanks, she takes him back to her place, but she isn't the sort of character you think.

While she initially appears to be the standard catalyst to begin a porn movie, Angel is a devout Christian who is tolerant beyond anyone I've ever met. She offers Herschell hospitality out of the goodness of her heart, but she's also offered the same to her sister Ann, who is heavily into the drug scene, along with a whole collection of her swinger buddies who sit around doing drugs all day and trying to pick up on anyone who walks into the house. "You know your body is a temple for the Holy Spirit," she tells your sister. "You shouldn't defile it."

Herschell appears to fit well with Angel. It literally takes ninety seconds for one of the girls to pick up on him and his muscles, but he lectures her on her lack of morality. "I just don't go for a girl that acts like a tramp," he tells her, "even if she's very beautiful." The responses are predictable. Angel's a drag and Herschell's a dumb bastard, but they're our heroes anyway in what appears to be a Christian home video.

They're a fascinating pair of leads. Steve Hawkes, who is so massively important to this film that he apparently needs "Starring Steve Hawkes" credits both before and after the film's title, looks like a cross between Hugh Jackman and Alvin Stardust, complete with jacket and large Elvis quiff, but he sounds more like Tommy Wiseau. He doesn't hide his burns, which are visible the moment he sheds his jacket, and he's acutely polite. He's exactly who you'd want to take home to grandma. Heather Hughes is far more attractive as Angel, not only because of her perpetually bare legs, than Dana Cullivan is as her sleazy sister Ann, but after her initial warning to Herschell about her sister, every word she says is tied to the Bible. Whether it's odd lines like, "I believe therefore I speak" and "Praise the Lord!" or whole discussions centered around the commandments, she just doesn't quit. No wonder she's driving Ann crazy, not that she wasn't halfway there already.

And so our plot unfolds, or at least the plot we think we're about to watch unfolds. The strange joy of this film is that every time we think we know what we're watching, it promptly transforms into something completely different. Thus far, it's been a positive story all about Herschell. He does a good deed for a damsel in distress and gets somewhere to stay in return. He joins her at an impromptu bible session and that lands him a job at the Midway Turkey Farm and Hatchery.

Yet just as he finds his life on the right track, he promptly derails it just because Ann calls him a coward. Sure, she throws every temptation his way but he refuses all of them because he's a character with plenty of inner strength. He's also obviously immune to the clouds of drugs that must surely float around the place but one dare later and this good guy instantly morphs into a drug addict boffing his host's sister. Talk about gratitude!

Ah, a morality play, you might think, three acts of Herschell's rise, fall and rise. Nah, we're about to turn into a mad scientist story. One solid day of throwing turkeys around and he starts his real job as a guinea pig in food experiments. The health and safety folks require proof of the quality of the meat before it can be distributed, but for some reason that eludes me they'll be satisfied by having the drug addicted new guy eat it and just tell them there are no ill effects.

Either that or Herschell is a moron, which is very possible. He has plenty of ill effects too but how many are due to the turkey and how many to the drugs that Ann has got him hooked on is entirely open to question. The only differences between his seizures before and after eating a turkey come down to the way in which he shakes. Before, he just shimmies subtly like he wants to be a motion blur but after, he contorts like an epileptic Elvis. This scene is ripe for a YouTube mashup.

Now, you might wonder why this film is called *Blood Freak* and I'm still trying to figure that out myself. Most obviously it's because when Herschell goes home to Ann, we see that he's become a monster with the head of a turkey that lusts after human blood, and not just any blood either. It has to be drug infused blood, so he's soon out searching the town for druggies, hanging them upside down, slitting their throats and drinking down their narcotic contamination.

What's most amazing here is that Ann doesn't seem to mind. There's a truly surreal scene where she tries to come to terms with his new appearance. Sure, she faints when she sees him, but it takes a whole thirty seconds to progress to the point where she calmly wonders aloud about what kind of life they'll lead when they get married and what their future children would look like. This is one of those magic moments of 1970s cinema that make you wonder what drugs your parents were on.

A more subtle reason for the title surely has to tie to Angel and her strong beliefs in Jesus. When she left the film after a mere fifteen minutes, everything was looking good for Herschell, but a full half hour has gone by without her, even though much of that was spent in her own house. Everything has gone to Hell in a handbasket without her, suggesting pretty strongly that she's the way, the truth and the light, but what sort of good Samaritan would invite a stranger into her house, then leave him alone with a bunch of hippies and drug dealers while she swans off to do her own thing somewhere else? The only time the word 'freak' is used in the script is amazingly not to describe the man who's morphed into a murderous half-man, half-turkey monster but to describe the adherence that Angel has to the scriptures. Is the title really suggesting that she's the blood freak, because her devotion to the Holy Blood was the catalyst for events to follow?

Who knows? There are some major twists to come, although you won't believe those either. It's hard to fathom anything in this picture that anyone could believe, but these twists get seriously harder to buy into as the movie progresses, so for me it inexorably comes back to that original question: what is this film trying to tell us?

Is it really a Christian fable that explains that if you don't keep the Bible thumper in your life close, you're going to quickly lapse into depression, panic, addiction, hallucination and strange mutation into a weird turkey headed monster? Did the filmmakers (or the financiers) seriously believe that any filmgoer who turned out to see a movie called *Blood Freak* with a lead character deliberately named for the Godfather of Gore, Herschell Gordon Lewis, would watch this and be persuaded to let Jesus Christ into their lives? It's hardly the most subtle attempt in the book, gore entirely aside.

Perhaps it's a straight anti-drug film, suggesting that you can not only get hooked on your first experience with even the most minor drugs but also cured by your first bad trip? The revelations at the end of the film render that approach completely meaningless but then continuity is not a strong factor in this story. Such a message would also be rendered utterly unbelievable by the sight of Grinter throwing all this moral high ground at us while literally choking on cigarettes. We never see him without one, at any point in the film, and his last monologue is ended, possibly prematurely, by a coughing fit, through which he continues to smoke with dedication. I doubt this is deliberate irony on behalf of a filmmaker bitter at the financiers leaving his film high and dry. If these scenes were padding, as is likely, they were probably shot on odd ends of film and couldn't be redone, just as the conveniences that litter the plot couldn't be ironed out.

It could all even be a vague attempt at social commentary on the American presence in Vietnam, given some of what we're made privy to at the end. If so, it's so weak that it can't even approach half baked. I've watched this film a few times and while I'm still fascinated by what drove such an incredibly strange picture to be made, I honestly doubt I'll ever get a believable explanation.

Grinter died in 1993, his last picture almost two decades behind him, with the sole exception of the unit coordination he did on *Masterblaster*, a 1987 film written, produced and partly directed by his son, Randy. Hawkes retired from the industry in 1975, happy to take care of his big cats in Florida. If any of the cast had future ambitions on the screen, they either didn't work out or were jettisoned after their experiences on this production. *Blood Freak* is likely to simply abide, a left handed treasure for film fans who are willing to be utterly amazed.

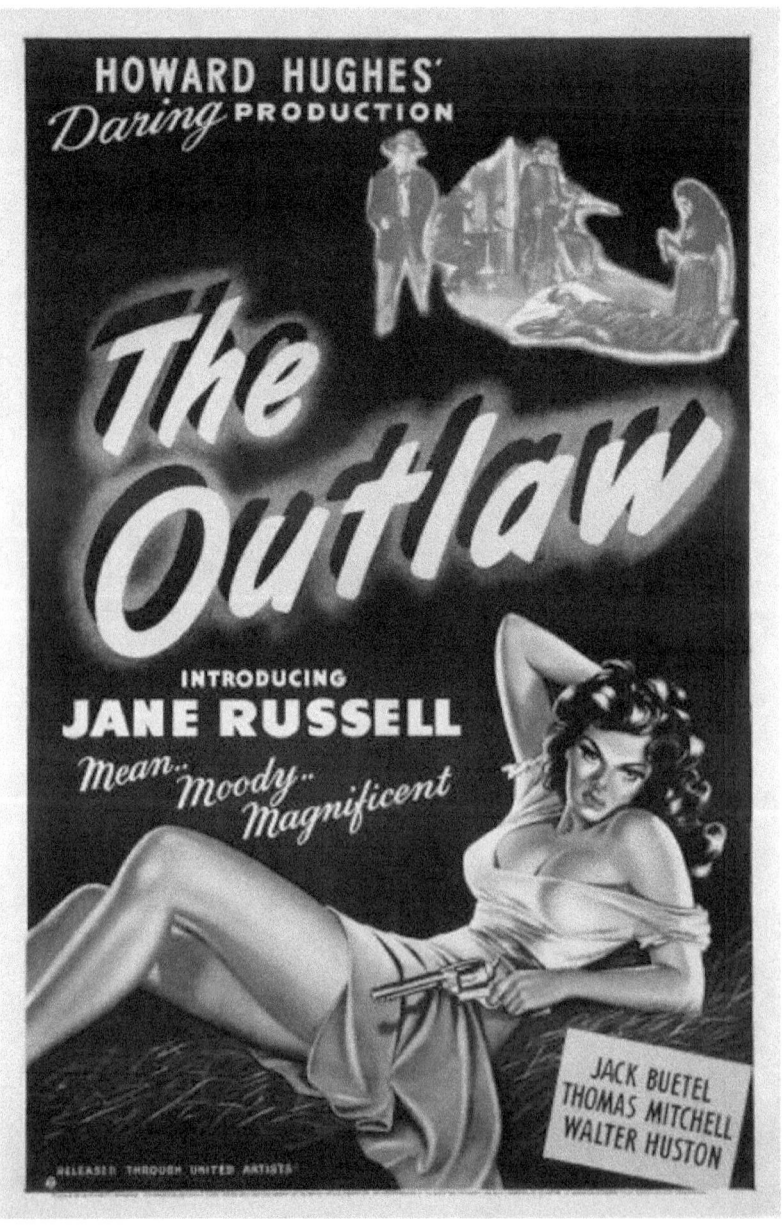

S is for Sex:
The Outlaw (1943)

Director: Howard Hughes
Writer: Jules Furthman
Stars: Jack Beutel, Thomas Mitchell, Jane Russell and Walter Huston

Bad movies aren't always made by people without enough money to make good movies. They can also be made by people with more money than they know what to do with, like Howard Hughes.

In 1941, Hughes was well established in the movie industry, having inherited the family fortune at 18 and taken his millions to Hollywood a year later to produce films. He found quick success, with his second picture, *Two Arabian Knights*, a hit with the public and the critics, winning Lewis Milestone the Oscar for Best Director (Comedy) of 1927-8. An experienced flier who would set a number of world speed records later in the thirties, Hughes spent almost four million dollars on his 1930 aviation epic, *Hell's Angels*, on which he earned his first credit as director, although he had uncredited assistance from Edmund Goulding and a debuting James Whale. His second would be *The Outlaw*, thirteen years later, which would prove just as controversial, if for different reasons.

With *Hell's Angels*, the controversies were many. For a start, there was Jean Harlow, eighteen year old platinum blonde bombshell. She'd been working solidly in uncredited roles since 1928, but this launched her to stardom, after the advent of sound overtook the film's long production and Greta Nissen, the Norwegian leading lady, was no longer viable when her role became a speaking one. Production delays also prompted a law suit, as Hughes feared that Darryl F Zanuck's *The Dawn Patrol* would steal his film's thunder before he could finish it and sued to stop its release. On a darker note, Hughes crashed a plane while shooting a scene his stunt coordinator refused to allow his men, World War I pilots all, to do. He got away with facial surgery, but four other members of the crew, three pilots and one mechanic, lost their lives during production accidents. With *The Outlaw*, there was only one controversy, spun deliberately for publicity: Jane Russell's bust.

And that's really what *The Outlaw* is about. Ignore all the many suggestions to the contrary, this entire film exists so that Howard Hughes could show as much of Jane Russell's bust as possible.

Sure, the screenplay was written by massively experienced writer Jules Furthman, who had been Oscar nominated for his screenplay for the 1935 version of *Mutiny on the Bounty*. Sure, there were also uncredited contributions by versatile producer/director Howard Hawks and his long term writing collaborator, Ben Hecht, who had met while working on 1932's *Scarface* for Hughes and ended up working together on nine films, including *Twentieth Century*, *His Girl Friday* and *The Thing from Another World*. Jean-Luc Godard called Hawks "the greatest American artist"; Richard Corliss called Hecht "the Hollywood screenwriter." Hecht won the first Oscar for best original screenplay and ended up with two from six nominations. These aren't minor names.

Neither are those they wrote about, the story revolving around wild west legends Pat Garrett, Billy the Kid and Doc Holliday, perennial Hollywood subjects in the forties, after odd earlier portrayals: Edith Storey played the title role in *Billy the Kid* in 1911, with Garrett and Holliday both originated on screen in 1937, Robert Homans playing the former in *Jim Hanvey, Detective* and Harvey Clark the latter in *Law for Tombstone*. Billy the Kid was especially popular, Bob Steele playing him six times in 1940 and 1941 and Buster Crabbe thirteen between 1941 and 1943.

The actors giving them life here are even more prestigious. Garrett is played by Thomas Mitchell, whose Oscar was for 1939's *Stagecoach*, but could equally have been for any of four other classics he made that year. Holliday is Walter Huston, who didn't win until *The Treasure of the Sierre Madre* in 1949 but had already landed three nominations. Only Jack Buetel was new to the screen as Billy the Kid.

Well, Buetel and Jane Russell, both of whom became stuck under Hughes's thumb for seven years. *The Outlaw* was originally shot in 1941, but spent two years in limbo because of how prominent Russell's breasts were in the film. While Hughes initially bowed to the requirements of those who administered the Production Code and cut half a minute of footage, his distributor, 20th Century Fox, cancelled their agreement. In response, Hughes orchestrated a counterintuitive campaign to build public outrage about his unreleased film, fuelling the fires beneath a controversy about his "lewd picture" until the demands for it to be banned generated enough publicity to reach screens in 1943. However it only lasted a week before its violations of the Production Code prompted its removal. When it finally saw wide release in 1946, Buetel and Russell had been stuck promoting for six years, locked into contracts for Hughes that disallowed them from making other movies.

Looking back from today, it's almost unfathomable how this happened. Russell doesn't get naked in the film; she doesn't even get topless. This was Production Code era Hollywood and that simply wasn't allowed, whatever imaginative publicity Hughes might have generated. She merely shows a decent amount of cleavage, but that was shocking enough. A great review at IMDb talks about how a fourteen or fifteen year old youth sneaked in to see it on original release. His friends were eager to know how fast Billy the Kid was, who shot who and how. "All I wanted to do was describe Jane Russell," he said. It's a telling anecdote, but it's not merely a reflection on Russell's charms, which gave their names to pairs of mountains across the globe and prompted Bob Hope to joke that "culture is the ability to describe Jane Russell without moving your hands." It's also a nod to how there's nothing else here to see. The time honoured stories are told at their most ridiculous.

For a while, you might think that the story is all about Doc Holliday's strawberry roan, which has been stolen. He's "about thirteen hands high and cute as a bug's ear," as he describes him and he catches up with him in Lincoln, NM, where it arrived in the hands of Billy the Kid, who swears he bought him fair and square.

Given that Doc's old friend, Pat Garrett, is working as the sheriff of Lincoln County, we get to meet all three of them quickly in perhaps the best scene of the movie. They're shot well, hardly surprising as the cinematography is by Gregg Toland, at the peak of his career after *Wuthering Heights*, *The Long Voyage Home* and *Citizen Kane*.

Unfortunately, he's the only one impressing. Huston isn't bad in his awful chequered trousers but he gets progressively worse as the film runs on. This is already the worst I've ever seen Mitchell, usually such a reliable actor, and he gets worse too. Buetel never gets the chance to impress, but this is his best scene.

Worst of all is the script. Already it's clumsy and occasionally cringeworthy, but it gets far worse than any of the actors. From this pivotal scene, it plays out like a love triangle, but one between three men. Garrett describes Holliday as his best friend and he reacts to the growing friendship between Doc and the Kid with what can only be regarded as jealousy. Each scene heightens the homoerotic undercurrents until they reach ludicrous level and then continue on regardless. The schemes and counterschemes to win the strawberry roan feel like a metaphor for their friendships.

Just in case we might take any of this seriously, the score underlines that this is all a cartoon, complete with wah wah wah noises for every disappointment. Bizarrely the music is by Victor Young, a composer who was also at the top of his game. He never won an Oscar in his life, but landed 22 nominations, sometimes four of them in the same year, like 1940 and 1941.

In another film, Doc's strawberry roan would be the MacGuffin of the piece. Certainly owning Red the roan is the primary motivation throughout for both Doc and the Kid, which means that it becomes one important factor for Pat Garrett too, yet we don't care about him in the slightest. What makes the film so surreal is that all this continues unabated even when Rio McDonald shows up no less than eighteen minutes in.

Yet this is a rather unique film because it seems to have a pair of MacGuffins, one for the characters and one for the audience. Even as these legends tussle over the strawberry roan, the viewers are wondering when Jane Russell is going to show up. After all, it's her on the posters, her on the publicity stills and her that Howard Hughes had been pushing at the public for years, in a shirt which looks like it's held up only by the power of art but would fall off if she only breathed. Hughes had even designed a legendary brass bra for her, to push up those breasts and highlight that cleavage. Yet the characters don't care about either Jane Russell, or it would seem, Rio McDonald.

We don't see her until the eighteen minute mark and then not enough to know she's female, let alone Jane Russell. She's just someone trying to kill Billy the Kid one night in a dark barn. Two minutes later they tussle in the hay, but even when she's revealed, she's fully clothed, shirt right up to her neck. After she tries and fails to kill the Kid for the last time, in revenge for the death of her brother a town or two back, it's hinted that he rapes her there in the hay. "Hold still, lady," he tells her, "or you won't have much dress left."

That's it for Rio McDonald though for quite a while. We have more homoerotic love triangle stuff to struggle through, Doc taking the Kid's side when Garrett tries to stop him leaving the scene of a deadly shootout. That spurs a sequel, Doc taking down Pat's gun and Billy two of his deputies. With a through and through to the side though, he's in bad shape and Doc takes him straight to Rio's house. Rio, it seems, is his girl.

Now, we have to pause for reevaluation here, because this is the point the script finally gives up the ghost. Rio attempted to revenge her brother by killing Billy the Kid on her own, even though she's sleeping with one of the most legendary gunslingers in the west. She didn't ask Doc to take care of it for her, she tried it herself, failed and got raped in the process, but Billy's unconscious body in her bed is all she needs to realise that she's in love with him. She does wield a knife in a threatening manner, but decides to just use it to cut his clothes off, so she can nurse him back to health, even climbing into bed with him to keep him warm. Doc's gone for a month, but when he returns, he discovers that his new friend has taken his girl as well as his horse. The Kid graciously offers him one of the two, while Rio stands there dumbstruck, and he has the bad taste to argue with him when he picks the horse. He doesn't even kiss her goodbye.

It's a strange thing when every bit of publicity material revolves around Jane Russell's twin assets but the story itself really doesn't concern itself with them at all. They're the only reason she's in the film, as her acting talent is hardly notable here and her perpetual sneer is often painful to see. Maybe it's a pout, but it's hardly sexy, even if it smoulders. I wondered if the wind had changed on her. It turns out to be her Blue Steel: disdain, defiance, disappointment, every emotion from D to D. So she's here to show off as much cleavage as the Production Code would allow. For a while, her dresses get more and more revealing until a full 45 minutes in, she leans over the Kid's body and both he and we get a great view. From then on, the 1946 audiences dreamt of a fast forward button to see how much more she'd show and how soon. Her best scene has her tied up outside with leather straps soaked so they'll shrink. The world lusted. Doc and the Kid didn't notice.

The Outlaw is a stunning failure in almost every regard. The performances are embarrassments to the talents of the actors. The story is such a stinker that Hawks and Hecht must have been truly thankful to have remained uncredited to posterity. The music is the most inappropriate score I've ever heard in a Hollywood picture. Only Gregg Toland's cinematography emerges unscathed, and even there it suffers from some awful rear projection shots. Russell didn't even wear the cantilevered bra that Hughes had carefully engineered with structural steel; instead she secretly modified her own a little and pretended.

The film would have been a great candidate for the Razzies, had they existed at the time. Yet *The Outlaw* was also a box office hit that launched Russell's career as a global sex symbol and built her 38D-24-36 figure into the latest sensation. The publicity worked in ways the film itself couldn't dream of. Sometimes all you need is sex, and sometimes it doesn't even have to be in the film.

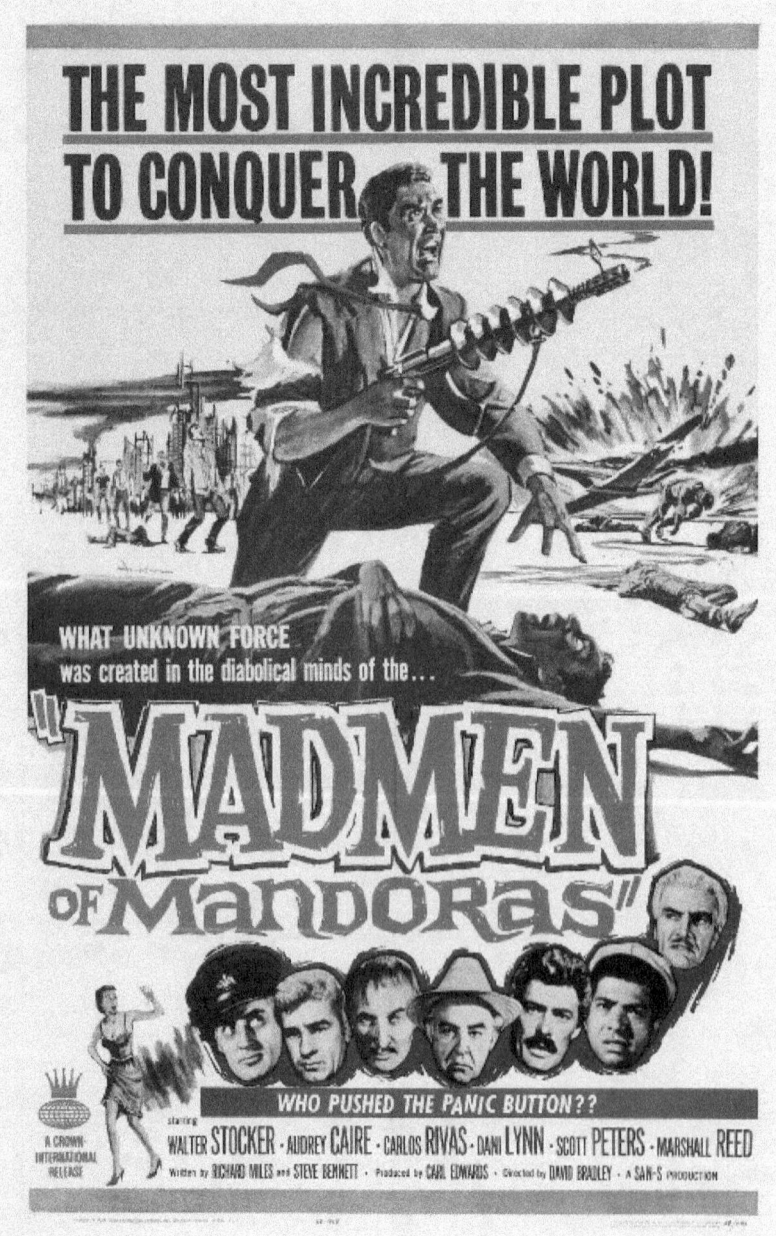

T is for Timeslot:
They Saved Hitler's Brain (1976)

Director: David Bradley
Writers: Steve Bennett and Peter Miles
Stars: Audrey Caire, Walter Stocker and Carlos Rivas

They Saved Hitler's Brain is unarguably one of the greatest movie titles in existence, one that simply exudes badness in the most awesome way. I'd wanted to see it for years, since the very moment I heard its name, not initially believing it was even real and never realising that it would highlight to me a whole new subset of bad movies that I hadn't realised existed.

You see, it's the precise opposite of something that plagued me in England growing up, when it was a rare movie I saw that wasn't on television. My first wake up call was *Star Trek IV: The Voyage Home*, of all things. I'd become a fan of exploitation movies, hooked on late night Hammer horrors, and I soon became aware that some films shown on TV were cut for content, hardly surprising given that the BBFC often required cuts for the big screen too. I knew that there was nothing potentially offensive in *Star Trek IV* because I'd seen it in the cinema, but when I watched again on TV there were scenes missing.

Eventually, I realised that it had been edited down to fit into the programming schedule. It ran a minute shy of two hours, making it a tight fit even for the BBC, which didn't run commercials, and very awkward indeed for ITV, which did. Sometimes channels used tricks to avoid editing, such as removing the credits, or when that was ruled illegal in the US, speeding them up instead, but while all this manipulation is annoying, it is at least understandable.

What I never dreamed of was that the opposite might exist as well, that films might be padded out to fill a broadcast slot that was too long. Here's where *They Saved Hitler's Brain* became a whole new wake up call for me. The regular timeslot for movies on seventies American television ran two hours, of which a quarter was devoted to commercial breaks. This was perfectly fine for regular ninety minute movies, but many distributors had shorter product on their books, often drive-in material from a decade or two earlier, that they wanted to license to TV.

One great example is a 1963 film called *The Madmen of Mandoras*, owned by a distributor called Crown International. With no viable theatrical options left and home video still mostly in the realm of science fiction, television licensing was the only viable market and they wanted in on it. The catch was that *The Madmen of Mandoras* ran a slight 64 minutes, not even close to TV length, so Crown hired Donald Hulette, a composer and director at Paragon Films, to shoot additional footage to splice in.

The film was already over a decade old, so reusing the original actors wasn't viable, even if they were still alive or working; instead he wrote new subplots, shot them with actors from UCLA whose names are mostly lost to posterity and edited them into a new, longer picture that Crown called *They Saved Hitler's Brain*, a bastard child that popped out around 1976. Hulette did this for (or to) many movies around this time and he got rather ingenious about how he did it.

However, as I'm sure you can imagine, this had a tendency to just make bad material worse. Bad movies breed drinking games and this one works on the introduction of new characters, because they never quit coming and it's tough to figure out who we should be watching.

Initially we focus on Dr Barnard, a chemist who is to bring the formula to the only known antidote to G Gas to Russ Van Pelt at CID headquarters. But, villainous Van Pelt merely aims to destroy the formula, so has his henchmen, who closely resemble the Blues Brothers, plant a bomb in Barnard's car and that's the end of him. Van Pelt explains to Vic Gilbert how his *CSI: Miami* techs proved that the formula was with Barnard when he died and that he hadn't made another copy, but Gilbert knows for sure that he copied it from the work of John Coleman, so off he goes with a chunky young investigator called Toni Gordon on some wild goose chase or other while we get some explanations.

What is G Gas, you ask? Well, it's to humans what DDT is to flies, as we see in stock footage of an elephant lying down. Many nations have the gas, but only the Americans have the antidote, and Coleman plans to present it at the International Chemical Warfare

Conference in Washington, DC. Van Pelt must eliminate him first, so he calls him over to his daughter's apartment so he and the Blues Brothers can kidnap him. Now, Gordon is mysteriously right there, and she follows them to their lair, crouches outside their window and hears them spill about a secret Nazi plot in a South American country called Mandoras. They hear her though, chase her down and shoot her dead in a phone box. With Barnard dead, Gordon dead and Coleman kidnapped, our hero surely must be Vic Gilbert, right? Gordon rings him before she dies and gives him the address to the villain's lair but he shows up, discovers the truth and is promptly shot dead too.

But, no! He's rescued by Toni Gordon, mysteriously resurrected long enough to save his life, kill Van Pelt and order Gilbert out of the house, even though she sent him there, before finally dying. What a girl! So off goes Gilbert, with the Blues Brothers hot on his tail, only to fall asleep at the wheel during a car chase, run off the road and roll into an electrical substation in stock footage from *Thunder Road*. That's it for him and we wonder who we're supposed to have been watching because everyone's dead.

Well, all we've seen is that extra footage shot by Donald Hulette and it has nothing to do with the story. It's all distraction that we could have safely ignored. Coleman is the only major character from *The Madmen of Mandoras* thus far, with a few others briefly visible in the background. His assistant is Frank Dvorak, his daughter is Suzanne and her artist fiancé is David Garrick. Also appearing here and there to look suspicious is a nervous guy called Teo Padua.

So which one do you think the hero might be? I'll bet you get it wrong. Try me. OK, he's Phil Day. Yep, Phil Day. We haven't met him yet. He's Coleman's son-in-law, having married Suzanne's elder sister Kathy, who goes by KC even though those aren't her initials any more. We haven't met her yet either. You see why this film is confusing now?

Once they do finally show up, they're thrown right into the intrigue by being kidnapped by Padua, who's promptly shot dead before he explains much of anything by the Blues Brothers at the next stop sign. Somehow the Days don't hear the shot, even though it was from a foot away from the only other vehicle on the road, so they leave the corpse in a phone booth and fly to Mandoras. Oh yes, there are leaps here. The chief of police is there to welcome them to Mandoras too, which surprises them. At this confusing point, it might be wise to back carefully away from *They Saved Hitler's Brain* and go back to the original film.

The Madmen of Mandoras begins with Prof Coleman's presentation, the one with the elephant. It's a good place to start and without all the extra material it even makes sense. The plot is relatively straightforward from there. G Gas is stupendously dangerous and the antidote that Coleman has developed is the only one, thus making him a man much in demand from all sides. The bad guys kidnap him and his daughter Suzanne, then whisk them away to Mandoras, where the rest of the action unfolds. Teo Padua is a good guy from Mandoras whose suspicious acts were merely failed attempts to reach him before this happens. So, after the fact, he enlists the help of KC, his other daughter, and her husband, CID agent Phil Day. When he's killed before telling them much, they fly to Mandoras to investigate. It almost seems like a real film. There are still problems, of course. It's just that, unlike *They Saved Hitler's Brain*, continuity isn't one of them.

There are wild and overblown claims, Coleman saying that "the loss or destruction of the formula for this antidote would mean complete annihilation of the world." There are goofs, like Coleman's antidote, which is "more powerful, with almost positive results." The dialogue is predictable but capable, as is the camerawork, courtesy of Stanley Cortez whose career veered between quality pictures such as *The Magnificent Ambersons* and *The Night of the Hunter* to outrageous material like *Dinosaurus!* and *The Navy vs The Night Monsters*. There's bad acting, certainly, but I've seen a lot worse; the actors are hindered by few characters fitting between heroic all American on one side and sinister and villainous Nazi on the other. Perhaps there's only Police Chief Alaniz, whose vague allegiances remind of a Sidney Greenstreet character, thus promoting Teo Padua's to the Peter Lorre equivalent. Nestor Paiva isn't up to Greenstreet's standards, of course.

Alaniz also meets the Days at the airport to take them to the Hotel Mandoras, which is like having a Hotel United States or a Hotel England. Maybe the nation is so small that it's the only hotel they have. Maybe that's why I've never heard of it. He's one of the secondary characters we meet in Mandoras and they're a mixed bunch.

Suzanne Coleman is an acutely embarrassing hepcat who dances the night away in a bar, almost as if she's in a different movie. I wish that she had been. Keith Dahle is almost as embarrassing as the stereotypical Texas mining executive who was the only other passenger on the plane in. He ends up pouting about not getting his own way, though why he thought he'd be able to when he's working for Adolf Hitler I have no idea. Only Carlos Rivas is really any good in a double role as Teo Padua and his brother Camino, the twin sons of Juan, the president of Mandoras, though his sincerity does get grating.

It's Camino who provides the real background to our story, which begins with the announcement of Hitler's death in 1945. Admiral Dönitz takes over, but was Hitler really dead? Teo knew, as he was a lab tech in Hitler's bunker, which the Führer rarely left, perhaps because his schnozz is so large that I expected Mel Brooks to voice him as a stereotypical Jew. All those other Hitlers with charisma enough to sway a nation at grandiose events were just bad doubles. Now Mr H (Camino is apparently on great terms) isn't dead, though not really alive either. The filmmakers do try to build suspense as to the how of that but they were more successful when the film wasn't titled *They Saved Hitler's Brain*. Yes, his entire head is kept in a glass jar, just like the *Futurama* Nixon, which is hooked up to some sort of machine. Matt Groening and Rob Zombie both obviously paid attention. Maybe their names should carry umlauts. What do they have in their basements?

While the vision of the disembodied head of Adolf Hitler kept alive in a jar is exploitation genius, having it carried around in the back of a car without a seatbelt, let alone life support equipment, really highlights the lack of budget. You might expect these Nazis to keep their Führer in a vast hall or grand Aryan shrine, but no. He's kept on a plinth in the junction of two corridors with an attempt at a swastika above his head. Not only that, it looks like the exact same junction of two corridors that was used in the flashbacks to Hitler's bunker in Berlin.

These are hardly ambitious sets, even when the lighting is good, but they're more understandable than the plot consistency problems that creep in. Palace escapees stand around outside talking while sirens wail for their arrest. Magic grenades explode in front of things, while follow up shots show utter devastation. The slow motion precursor to Major Toht's face melt in *Raiders of the Lost Ark* is a gem though.

All in all, *The Madmen of Mandoras* isn't a good film, but it's not a particularly bad one either. On its own merits, it's a cheap but cheerful sci-fi action ride, hardly essential but with some influence. Director David Bradley became best known as a professor of film and this was his last picture, but his earlier career looks fascinating, including titles like *12 to the Moon*, with its multinational pre-*Star Trek* lunar expedition, a biker movie with Fay Wray called *Dragstrip Riot* and, above all, his imaginative 1941 feature length take on Henrik Ibsen's play, *Peer Gynt*, which he wrote, shot, produced and directed as a twenty year old student of the Art Institute of Chicago. I've only seen the seven minute *Pagan Dances* section, which shows a surprising Carl Theodor Dreyer influence. Even more surprising is seventeen year old Charlton Heston, debuting on screen in the lead rôle, though he wouldn't return to film until Bradley cast him again in 1950 in *Julius Caesar*.

If *The Madmen of Mandoras* isn't good, *They Saved Hitler's Brain* is horribly worse, only worthy of memory for its salacious title and the method of its mangling. While I can certainly admire David Hulette's ingenuity in meeting the terms of his contract, his work submerges even the good parts of the original into an abyss of confusion. He shot in black and white but his style doesn't gel with the older footage and finding a black Lincoln continental to use can't bridge the gap.

Perhaps his work was doomed to failure: the new footage has to appear at the beginning as it can't interact with the meat of the story, so for half the running time we're stuck trying to figure out who we're supposed to be watching. For a while it feels like a twelve part serial where nobody can progress to the next episode, all compressed to feature length. Splicing in new footage can make sense, as even *Godzilla, King of the Monsters* shows, but it's obviously a tough and thankless task.

Huh? An A-Z of Why Classic American Bad Movies Were Made

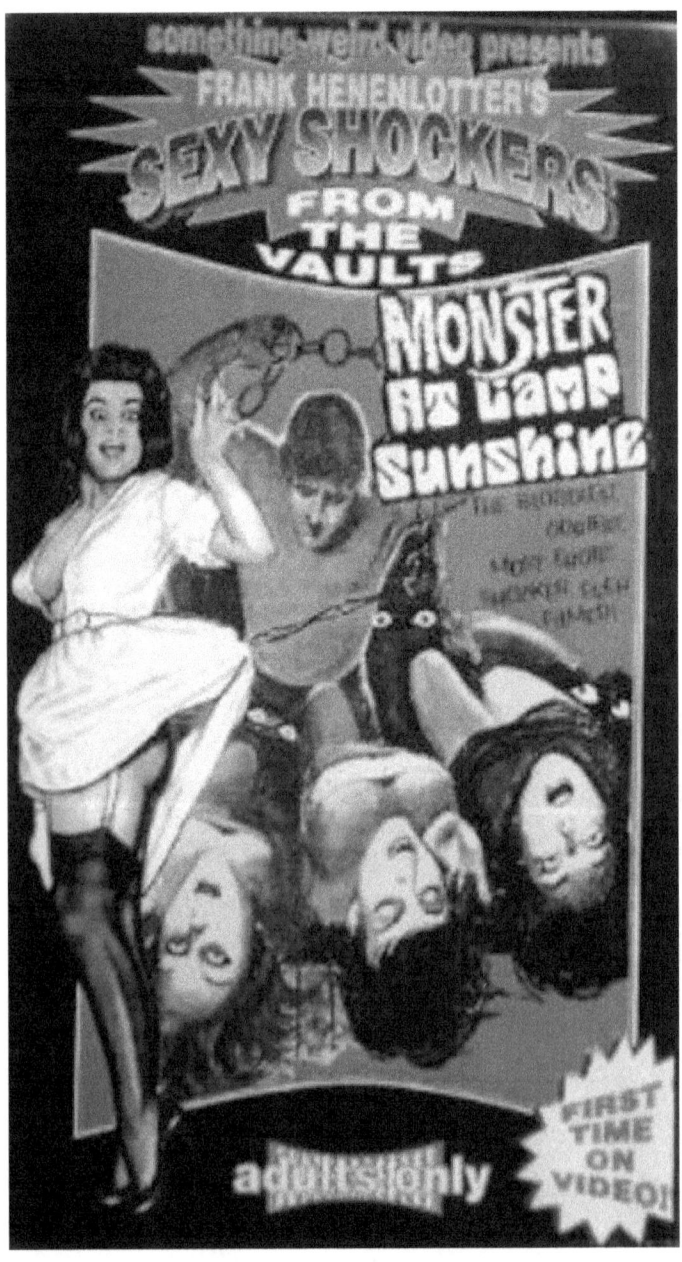

U is for Unknown:
The Monster of Camp Sunshine (1964)

Director: Ferenc Leroget
Writer: Ferenc Leroget
Stars: Harrison Pebbles, Deborah Spray and Sally Parfait

I have no idea why *The Monster of Camp Sunshine* was made and neither, it seems, does anyone else, but is there a better location in which to set a monster movie than a naturist colony? A Nazi death camp would provide opportunity for fetishistic sleaze in black leather, but a nudist camp preserves all the innocence of the old school monsters while gifting us with copious quantities of naked female flesh.

The Monster of Camp Sunshine is a terrible, but surreal, bizarre and unique picture, apparently sincere in its message about naturism but with its tongue firmly in its cheek when it comes to its outrageous monster. It also goes full out batshit insane when it feels like it, not least during the last fifteen minutes of sheer outsider genius. It takes something truly special nowadays to me to exclaim, "What just happened?" So far I can only believe it's something made by a set of highly talented people, merely ones whose talents aren't in moviemaking.

Nothing is easily explained and everything generates questions. It has a foot clearly planted in the past, as half the film is set up as a silent movie, down to the histrionic intertitles, but it's inherently forward looking, with its social commentary about animal rights, environmental horror and the freeing power of naturism. It's cultured, with topical fashions, playful wit and a feminist angle, with its two liberated female leads working in the big city and sharing a flat after having being matched up by IBM cards, but it doesn't delve too far into any of these and descends into inanity by the finalé. It even has a sense of humour, with an introductory text that might have been written by the ghost of Oscar Wilde. "The motion picture that follows is a fable," it says. "In it there are many nudists but only one monster. In life, it is generally the other way around." Yet almost the entire first hour of the film is notably boring.

Before we're ever shown Camp Sunshine or its monster, we're introduced to the leading ladies, who are so addicted to nicotine that they have an ashtray hanging from the ceiling to raise up and down between their bunk beds.

Marta doesn't like ghastly horror movies like *Monster from the Hairy Planet* and *Dracula Meets the Beatles*, yet she works at a lab full of "half crazy animals with sharp little teeth." It's a freaky place, that "upsets the delicate balance of nature," but it's still a paycheck, it seems.

Claire is a progressive model, based at a studio high up in one of New York's skyscrapers, albeit a tiny room with just enough space to strip off and wander out onto the patio. Ken photographs her in the latest risqué fashions, like a topless bathing suit, against the iconic New York skyline, as we wonder how strange it is to miss the World Trade Center before it was even built.

Claire also provides the narration when the intertitles don't do better. She gives us a hint early on when Marta drops a mirror, prompting "an adventure that came as close to costing us our lives as a hound dog comes to a treed coon," but it takes a while for her to warn us that, "Marta is about to go through the worst experience of her life."

This is as she puts a cage of white mice on a desk, while accidentally switching on an overhead toxic water cooler. An intertitle seriously reads, "Their killer instincts are unleashed." This is insane scene number one, as this thoroughly liberated woman is afraid of white mice, and I mean deathly afraid, though to be fair someone off screen does actively throw the things at her, thus clambers screaming out of the window to hang from the ledge by her fingernails, many storeys above ground. I understand that some women really are afraid of white mice, however stereotypical that may seem, but how many of them really choose to work in animal experimentation labs?

Of course, Claire and Marta are nudists, who spend their naked time at Camp Sunshine, which is run by a friend called Susannah York. No, not that one. We're even given a flashback, in a nudie cutie monster movie, to find how Claire stumbled onto Marta's stash of *Urban Nudist* mags and became initiated into the scene.

Mostly it's just an excuse to finally show us naked bodies, given that we'd spent twenty minutes without a hint of a naked girl or a monster. There's no full frontal nudity, as this is a 1964 movie, but Camp Sunshine has a clothing optional environment, as York struts around in a pair of jeans and her halfwit half brother fortunately stays clothed throughout.

He's Hugo, a rather large and sweaty gentleman who does the gardening. "There was something about his looks that gave me a chill," ponders Claire, though she's told that there isn't a mean streak in him. Apparently nobody notices how threateningly he waves his secateurs at people.

It's plot convenience time and do we have a doozy for you. Dr Harrison, who talks far more like a pulp villain than a doctor, rants on to Marta about "a million to one shot," "some combination of vicious substances" and how he thanks "the great surgeon in the sky that it happened to rats and didn't happen to human beings." He even emphasises how thankful he is that there are scientific techniques to get rid of such "vile, vicious substances." You know, like running over the road to hurl the vial into the Hudson river, that sort of scientific technique. It's promptly fished back out by some yokel with a straw hat and a pipe who likes catching hot water bottles and bicycle tyres and vials of foul smelling liquid. This moron puts it in a bucket on the tailgate of his truck so he can drive a couple of hours to his next stop and knock it into the stream, conveniently right next door to Camp Sunshine, for Hugo to drink. Guess who the monster of Camp Sunshine will be?

The Monster of Camp Sunshine came along just as the nudie cutie was becoming extinct, which may be one key reason for its disappearance. Something Weird Video found the 35mm negative on the top shelf of an old film vault, where it may have sat since it was made, never having seen the light of day. The ensuing gap of 29 years between production and release means that it's nigh on impossible to discover anything about the film and the people who made it. Most, if not all, are credited under pseudonyms. Harrison Pebbles? Sally Parfait? How about Ron Cheney Jr? Most vanished completely, only producer Gene Kearney earning another credit, though he died in 1979.

There's such a solid wall of silence surrounding this film that it's easy to be suspicious. Harold P Warren wore his *Manos* cape every Halloween. Don Barton attends screenings of *Zaat*. Shirley Mills talked about the positive change that *Child Bride* had brought. Here? Nothing.

While nobody involved has apparently ever exhibited curiosity about this bizarre chapter of their past, there is a topical connection that makes me wonder all the more. The topless bathing suit was invented by Rudy Gernreich, an avowed nudist, the summer this film was made. His muse was a model named Peggy Moffitt, who looks like Claire, down to the dangerous nipples in the famous photograph of Gernreich's monokini. Moffitt was married to William Claxton, who looks a little like Ken and who liked to photograph his wife or other subjects, like actress Natalie Wood, on rooftops against New York's skyline. Claxton was also noted for his work with jazz musicians, who provide most of this film's score. I spent some time comparing photos of these people with stills from the film and while I don't believe that Deborah Spray and Ron Cheney Jr are Moffitt and Claxton, I have no doubt that they play characters based on them.

The credited writer and director is Ferenc Leroget, maybe a real name given that it doesn't seem to translate to anything but maybe not given that he seems to be the only Leroget in existence. Perhaps it's an anagram of 'got leer'? If Ray Dennis Steckler hadn't been so honest about all his pseudonyms I'd wonder if he was Leroget, as the timing is right and this feels much like his sort of inconsistency. It's technically vastly inconsistent, half a silent movie with intertitles and half a regular sound film with badly lipsynched dialogue, and it has a flavour of the DIY filmmaking of today, with its opportunistic use of amateur actors, stock footage and whatever sets or locations were available. Also, I can't help but believe that, like so many of Steckler's scripts, this one had a wild evolution over the duration of the shoot, possibly because it was shot mostly in order. And so to the ending, which is truly something out of Ed Wood's wet dreams.

We end up back at Camp Sunshine, of course, where halfwit Hugo is now chained up in a chalet. Claire and Marta wander around, strip naked and wonder where everyone else is, while the score turns into a *Foghorn Leghorn* soundtrack of southern classics. They party with Ken and Laurie, his girlfriend, who they brought along with them because it might do her good. She's also the secretary at Claire's studio, who couldn't dream of taking her clothes off in front of anyone. She stays shy while the rest of them find ever more inventive ways to hide their genitals from 1964 morality: forget the straw hat, use an autoharp! Eventually she wanders off down to the river to strip naked in solitude and get herself stalked by the monster. Yes, Hugo has escaped, and only the broken sound could explain why Laurie doesn't hear this 300 pound zombie chimp monster clad in loose chains stomping around behind her with an axe.

Eventually Susannah turns up to explain that "mah brahther's a mahnster" and prompt all hell to break loose, not much of an understatement. The monster arrives as they're celebrating Claire's birthday, naked with sparklers, and the girls break bottles over his head. Ken turns into Rambo, complete with machine gun, sticks of dynamite and a large pair of underpants. Dr Harrison drops in by parachute, landing on a van like Captain Chaos. They call the authorities, which means one guy in fatigues and a nametag reading Bat Guano, along with what must be every branch of the armed forces the filmmakers could find in stock footage. "A monster?" cries Guano. "In a nudist camp?" In rush the cavalry, literally, men on horses with sabres, though it's hardly the place for horses given that this is now a true warzone, complete with barbed wire, anti aircraft guns, amphibious vehicles, cannon, air raid sirens, the works. Blink and you'll miss a war.

It becomes something akin to *Saving Private Ryan* with bouncing breasts, which is not exactly a bad thing, but it comes out of nowhere and refuses to quit. A nudie cutie monster movie morphs into the mother of all war movie mashups because, well, because it could. Day becomes night, night becomes day, nobody really knows what's going on but they all take their opportunity to flounce around topless in front of the camera as the military folks strut their stock footage stuff. "And that's all that's left of the monster of Camp Sunshine," Harrison somehow manages to say entirely deadpan, as the armed forces vanish into the mist and he locates the monster's brain, the only piece remaining to kick dirt over.

Anyone watching this will want to leave their seat for the first boring hour, but if they make it to the end, they'll be stuck there for ten minutes after the film finishes, still seated in sheer shock. I say again, "What just happened?"

For all that *The Monster of Camp Sunshine* is a terrible movie, and that cannot be disputed, it occupies its own space as an artistic statement. It's certainly fascinating in ways that most bad movies aren't.

It may have been a very late nudie cutie, born during the rise of the roughie, the sort of violent and frequently explicit sexploitation film that set the stage for the unique excesses of the seventies, but it was groundbreaking in other regards. As a monster movie set in a nudist colony, it anticipates the slasher craze, as well as other future sexploitation genres, standing alongside a select few titles like *House on Bare Mountain, Kiss Me Quick!* and *The Beast That Killed Women*. It opens with Terry Gilliam-esque animated title credits, five years before *Monty Python's Flying Circus* came along to shake up everything.

All I can believe is that if it hadn't disappeared into thin air for 29 years, we'd know a lot more about it and the people who made it today.

Huh? An A-Z of Why Classic American Bad Movies Were Made

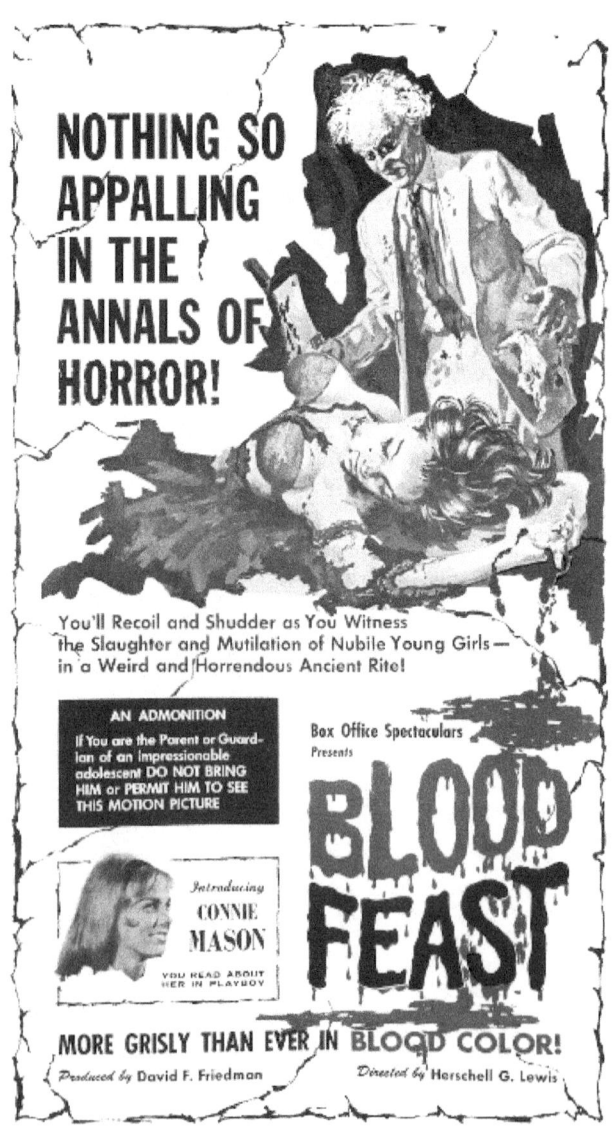

V is for Violence:
Blood Feast (1963)

Director: Herschell Gordon Lewis
Writer: A Louise Downe
Stars: Thomas Wood, Mal Arnold and Connie Mason

The tagline on the *Blood Feast* poster cries, "Nothing so appalling in the annals of horror!" Today it may seem like it might refer to the quality of this 1963 shocker rather than its contents, but then we're jaded.

To describe it, the film's director, exploitation maestro Herschell Gordon Lewis, likened it to a Walt Whitman poem: "It's no good," he said, "but it's the first," and he's right. While Japanese films like 1960's *Jigoku* technically predate it and earlier exploitation gems like Dwain Esper's *Maniac* were black and white precursors, this is the original American gore movie, arguably the most influential horror film since the days of the Universal monster movies.

Details vary depending on the reports but it was shot in around a week on a budget of less than $25,000 and became a huge instant hit at drive-ins, grossing over $4m for Lewis and his business partner, exploitation producer David Friedman. It succeeded by delivering exactly what it promised, unlike anything that went before it.

In fact that's why *Blood Feast* came about. In the early sixties, Lewis and Friedman partnered on a string of nudie cuties, films like *The Adventures of Lucky Pierre* and *Nature's Playmates* that were mere excuses to see naked women in naturist camps with a modicum of plot and a dash of humour. It was a winning combination, but also an inevitably short lived one as the market soon saturated. Even as they shot *Bell, Bare and Beautiful* in Miami early in 1963, they realised that they needed new subject matter.

Both men were canny promoters, Lewis retiring to make millions as a direct marketer, so they compiled lists of what the major studios either couldn't or wouldn't do, so as to ensure a niche audience. After Lewis saw a movie with each of many instances of violence ending in peaceful death, all tiny bullet holes and closed eyes, he returned to their HQ in Florida, the Suez Hotel, came face to face with a statue of the Sphinx and *Blood Feast* was born.

The story is a simple one, as befits something made from a fifteen page script, because this was never about the story. It was about the gore, oodles of it, that began at the very beginning of the film and continued through to the very end, literally shocking the audience into reaction. While it may be hard to imagine today, in a world where the major studios churn out endless sequels to torture porn films like *Saw* and *Hostel*, in 1963 nobody had seen this sort of blood and gore on a movie screen.

It debuted on a Friday night at a drive-in theatre in Peoria, IL, and both Lewis and Friedman kept away, not having a clue if they'd be successful or not. They drove to the theatre on the Saturday night, unable to resist the temptation any longer, and found themselves stuck in a ten mile traffic jam all the way to the screen. *Blood Feast* made half its budget back in one week at one drive-in theatre and there were 5,000 drive-in theatres in America in those days.

Today, we have to have that background to understand why this film was so successful, because it literally has nothing going for it but the sheer guts of two men to do something that had never been done before. Even during its theatrical run it started to be banned, though that was partly publicity, Friedman even getting an injunction against his own film in Sarasota to generate yet more interest in it. Generally, local authorities had to be creative as the film simply didn't break any rules: it wasn't obscene, according to the definitions then laid down, it had no foul language and the bad guy gets his comeuppance. The rules said it was fine but by the time *Two Thousand Maniacs!*, the thematic follow up, was released, some towns had enacted new laws that actually applied. By *Color Me Blood Red* in 1965, it was harder to find places to show the film, so Lewis and Friedman parted company and moved on to new genres, at least for a while.

The story follows Fuad Ramses, an Egyptian who runs an exotic catering business out of what looks like a regular grocery store. We know he's the villain because the first scene shows him killing Pat Tracey in her bathtub even before we know who he is. She looks like a Hitchcockian heroine, fitting for a bathroom murder, though the slowly beating drum that accompanies her strip isn't anything like Bernard Herrmann's shrieking strings. She conveniently switches on the radio so we can hear about another murder in the park and for the police to ask women to stay home. Pat cosies up in her bubbles with a copy of *Ancient Weird Religious Rites*, required bathtime reading for all lovely young ladies in 1963. It looks like a bible with a fake cover and given that the film was shot mostly in the Suez Hotel, this suggests that the Gideons inadvertently provided a pivotal horror movie prop. Next thing, Fuad Ramses is outdoing *Psycho* with gleeful abandon.

There's a reason Lewis is known as 'the Godfather of Gore' and this is it. One stab and Pat Tracey is missing an eye, gloriously red Eastmancolor blood pooling on her face and bloody body parts skewered on her killer's knife like a kebab. Some hacking and slashing later and her severed leg goes slowly into his sack, the bloody stump sticking out of the water to be lovingly lingered on by the voyeuristic camera. Only three years earlier the censors got upset at Hitchcock for what their minds incorrectly told them were knife wounds and nudity in the shower scene of *Psycho*. Here Lewis was showing everything Hitch couldn't and wouldn't even before the credits ran, literally dripping the words of the title onto the screen in blood. No wonder nurses dished out vomit bags in theatre lobbies. No wonder *Blood Feast* became the oldest film on the video nasty list compiled by the Director of Public Prosecutions in the UK. No wonder it started a revolution.

Pat Tracey's murder turns out to be the seventh in two weeks. "I don't know what to make of it," says the inept police captain. "We're just working with a homicidal maniac," says inept Det Pete Thornton, who seems somehow surprised that the media are interested in such a thing. They're not the sharpest tools in the shed but that's why we have a full hour of gore time to go. If they could actually detect, this story would have ended before it began. Ramses is no master criminal and clues are continually dangled in vain in front of Thornton's eyes, but he's busy falling for the leading lady, Suzette Fremont.

This romantic subplot isn't remotely believable as he's a decade older and she was about to be *Playboy* Playmate of the Month, but it was real as actors William Kerwin and Connie Mason were married a year later. She promptly retired to be a wife and mother, giving him two children and they remained married until his death in 1989.

Her character is a student of Egyptian culture, even though she's as dumb as a post, so when her mother wants "something unusual", "something totally different" to be served as a surprise at her birthday party, she goes to Fuad Ramses Exotic Catering. This scene is a real gem for Z grade movie nuts and I could just see Ed Wood mouthing the lines in awe. "Have you ever had an Egyptian feast?" Ramses asks slowly as actor Mal Arnold leans for effect and Lewis struggles to keep him in frame. "It has not been served in five thousand years!"

He's trying to be Bela Lugosi, from the staring eyes to the exotic accent which Lewis plays up even more in interviews, but he sounds more like Adrian Paul. He walks with a shuffling limp and he hypnotises Mrs Fremont into submission even though she's sold from moment one anyway. For an exotic caterer he's a pretty good grocer, so maybe he just wants to guarantee a use for all the limbs he's been collecting.

The rest of the film is just as camp but not quite as fun, though I can't resist Ramses shuffling off downstairs to demean himself before the gilt store mannequin dressed up in jewels that he's set up in effigy. She's his "divine and wondrous woman of the pale light", "his lady of the dark moon". She's the goddess Ishtar, who was really a Babylonian deity rather than an Egyptian one, thus rendering the entire script meaningless in a single touch.

The story, thought up by Lewis and Friedman, was scripted by Lewis's second wife Allison, credited as A Louise Downe but better known as Bunny, the star of a number of his and other nudie cuties. As plot was hardly the most important factor in those nudie cuties, it's not surprising to find so many inconsistencies here, so many incoherent motivations and so much that seems destined for an exploitation trailer. Criticising on aesthetic grounds is insane but we can relish in how definitive this is as 'so bad it's good'.

It isn't just one plot hole; everything seems to be wrong, right down to the most remembered scene in the film. This is the tongue scene, where Ramses rips out the tongue of an unwitting victim with his bare hands. It's delightfully gross, but he holds the thing up for us to see and it's huge! In reality it was a lamb's tongue, far too big to even fit into a woman's mouth folded in half, let alone alongside all the strawberry jam that substituted for blood.

My favourite insanity is *Ancient Weird Religious Rites*, the book that links all these Miami cuties together. Det Thornton knows it's a clue. The father of Marcy Franklin, scalped on the beach for her brain, tells him that she was on a book club list run by Fuad Ramses. The killer takes a different body part from each victim. Yet even after conveniently attending a lecture with Suzette all about the blood feast of Ishtar that explains absolutely everything, he just can't figure out the book's significance.

Nobody seems able to figure out anything, even reality, and that includes Bunny the scriptwriter. Every scene seems to contain another leap of logic, so that they stack up to unwieldy levels. The local police force is so overwhelmed by these murders that Det Thornton is a 24 hour cop, but he has time to attend that lecture on Egyptian cults. Oh, and he's the boyfriend of Suzette Fremont, the intended recipient of the blood feast, who wants him to be her date to the party. But she has to ring her mom to come get her afterwards because it's late, even though it's daytime outside and her boyfriend wants to take her home via a smooching spot overlooking the beach. That's where he hears the radio announce that the latest victim survived, because the cops wouldn't call in the lead detective for something like that, right? He gets back to the station so the chief can begin an explanation with the words, "Well, that's it, the whole story."

Just as the characters seem confused by the entire film being a vaguely linked collection of plot conveniences, none of which make any sense whatsoever, so the actors follow suit. I use the term 'actors' loosely here because some of them are truly stunning in their ineptitude.

Worst is Gene Courtier in his only film appearance as Tony, the frustrated boyfriend of the beach victim, Marcy Franklin, who won't put out even though they've been going steady for a year. Just as she might become willing, she's scalped to death and he falls apart. "She wanted to leave," he sobs to the cops. "It's all my fault." He's so emotional he makes Tommy Wiseau look like Marlon Brando as he hysterically repeats, "I can't remember!"

Yet the rest of the cast aren't much better, perhaps as many of them were nudie cutie regulars who simply didn't go home when *Bell, Bare and Beautiful* wrapped so they could begin shooting *Blood Feast* a single day later.

William Kerwin was the most experienced, with credits dating back to *River Goddesses* in 1951, but that was just a nature excursion for five models, hardly high art. He racked up bit parts until Lewis gave him a lead role in 1961's *Living Venus* and they became regular collaborators, Kerwin appearing in everything he made, and even issuing all the warnings on the trailers. He's more like a cheap car salesman but he's by far the best actor in the film.

Connie Mason, his future wife, is as great an actress as you might expect a Playmate of the Month to be. She was better later in 1963 in *Two Thousand Maniacs!* but even there Lewis had to remove about two thirds of her dialogue as she was never able to remember her lines. "I often felt if one took the key out of Connie's back," he told John Waters in an interview, "she'd simply stand in place." She's like a living Barbie doll but she's only there to look like a victim and at that she's capable because her limbs move.

Mal Arnold is a memorable Fuad Ramses, with artificially greyed hair and thick eyebrows. He's no worse a ham than any of the many horror icons who he channelled for the part and his loping run was paid tribute by Peter Jackson, who channelled it himself as the alien Robert in *Bad Taste*. In fact Arnold is surprisingly good, given that this was only his second picture, bookended by simple roles as a nudist in nudie cuties. After five films in four years for Lewis or Kerwin, he only came back for one more, 1990's *Vampire Cop*.

Al Golden plays Dr Flanders, the expert on Ishtar and the blood feast, as sensationally as the headlines of the Daily Chronicle we see early in the film that read, "Teenage Girl Found Slaughtered! Legs Cut Off!" He never acted again. Scott Hall, the police captain, would only return to the screen for *Color Me Blood Red*; Lyn Bolton, a daffy Mrs Fremont, only for a late nudie cutie from the Kerwins, 1970's *Sweet Bird of Aquarius*.

But nobody watched *Blood Feast* for the acting, they watched it for the gore, which is as graphic as you could imagine without ever being realistic. Even the victim who doesn't die at the scene lies in her hospital bed with blood seeping through the bandages that cover her head. Suzette's friend Trudy Sanders is whipped raw so Ramses can collect the blood dripping from her back in a cup. This takes place in his basement, which by this time looks like an abattoir, with corpses and bits of corpses left everywhere. Most of them aren't even recognisable as anything except slabs of bloody meat because Ramses is apparently rather wasteful of his ingredients and rather sloppy at cleaning anything up. We get an illustrative flashback sequence during Dr Flanders's lecture, where a toga clad girl has her heart carved out to be held glistening above her bloody flesh by a high priest, even though the wound is just a mass of gore without a single cut to the skin.

The gore travels well down the years, not in the sense that it's well done but in the sense that it's gloriously exploitative. It has precisely the same effect today as when the film was first released. Modern viewers will surely hate this movie, make no mistake about that, but if you can keep them in front of the screen they'll cringe and shudder and bury their faces in their arms just like they were teenagers at a drive-in in 1963. Unlike most drive-in films, this was one that people watched. Sure, it may have been in disbelief at what they were seeing but they watched anyway, because it was new and groundbreaking and they couldn't get enough, however ineptly it was all done. Their kids grew up with the extremes of the seventies and today's audiences can find worse things on the internet without even trying, so today it's hard to see past the ineptitude.

Those who can are probably filmmakers who owe *Blood Feast* big time.

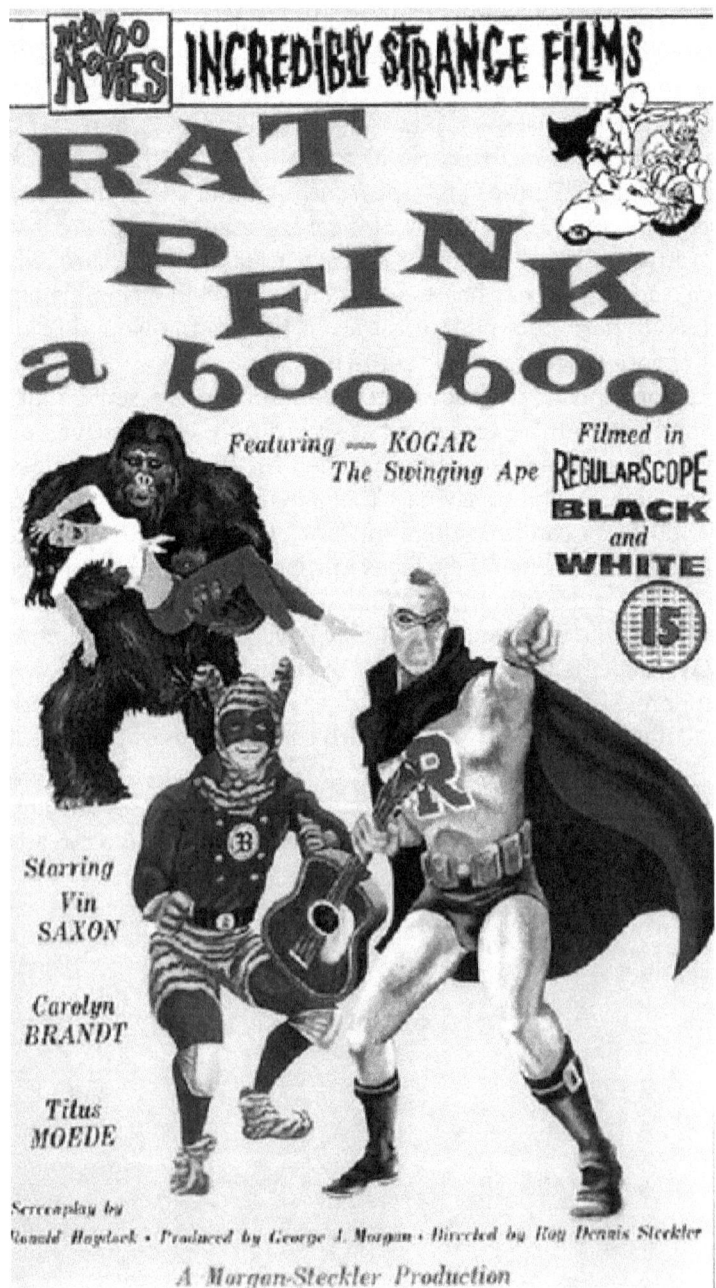

W is for Whimsy:
Rat Pfink a Boo Boo (1966)

Director: Ray Dennis Steckler
Writer: Ron Haydock
Stars: Carolyn Brandt, Vin Saxon, Titus Moede, George Caldwell, Mike Kannon and James Bowie

When you kick off your directorial career at 24 shooting an Arch Hall Jr musical, *Wild Guitar*, you're definitely on the road to cult stardom. When you name your first solo film *The Incredibly Strange Creatures Who Stopped Living and Became Mixed-Up Zombies!!?*, you've arrived, but while that's still Ray Dennis Steckler's most famous picture, it's not his most memorable work. For me, it has to take a back seat to *Rat Pfink a Boo Boo*, a film so amazing that it's going to be impossible to do it justice here.

Put simply, you have to see this film to understand it, because it occupies a space comfortably outside the realm of expectation. It's one of those rare movies that remain unique in the history of cinema, however long it's been since they were made, because nobody would dare to attempt to copy them and wouldn't know how anyway. It takes a special mind to make a film like this. The only thing remotely comparable is *The Monster of Camp Sunshine*.

More than anything else, Steckler is known for two things. Firstly, he never had enough money to make the movies he wanted, so he had to make the movies he could. Secondly, and because of this, he didn't work with scripts.

He's explained in interviews that any time he started a project with a script, the film never got finished because he could never afford to do so. Working without a script means filming whatever seems like a good idea at the time given the funding available. Next week might bring more money, in which case something else can get added. Add a fertile imagination in the editing room and, hey presto, there's a movie. The budget for *Rat Pfink a Boo Boo* ended up under four or five thousand dollars, and that amount didn't stretch so far as the thirty bucks needed to fix the opening credits. Thus *Rat Pfink and Boo Boo* lost a couple of letters and became *Rat Pfink a*

Boo Boo, which is really just icing on the cake given what's in the film.

It's an exercise in growth. Steckler started out with two rolls of film and twenty bucks, not even enough to develop the footage, but it was a beginning and he had energy, passion and abiding confidence that he'd end up with enough to finish the movie. Like any Steckler picture, it didn't have a script, just a set of inspirations. Even the name came from a song, *You is a Rat Pfink*, by Ron Haydock, who had played a state trooper in Steckler's *The Thrill Killers* and was elevated to the lead here as both Lonnie Lord and his alter ego.

Initially it was a straight crime film, taking inspiration from the obscene phone calls Steckler's wife Carolyn Brandt was getting each time he left her apartment. She's the leading lady here but that's not her as the film opens, being chased by the Chain Gang through a succession of blue tinged noirish settings and eventually strangled. It's all surprisingly effective, given that Steckler was handling the cinematography himself.

Steckler isn't in the same class as Roger Corman for providing a cinematic start to half the great names of Hollywood, but a surprising number did go on to greater things. The cinematography on *Incredibly Strange Creatures* was by Joseph V Mascelli, who wrote *The Five Cs of Cinematography* a year later, still a key textbook on the subject. His cameramen on that film were László Kovács and Vilmos Zsigmond, both future greats; Kovács shot *Easy Rider*, *Five Easy Pieces* and *New York, New York*; Szigmond won an Oscar for *Close Encounters of the Third Kind* and was nominated for *The Deer Hunter*, *The River* and *The Black Dahlia*. Even *Rat Pfink a Boo Boo* had sound by Keith Wester, who later racked up no less than six Oscar nods in that department for films like *Black Rain*, *Armageddon* and *The Perfect Storm*. This was his first experience in that realm, though he also edited this film and provided the narration, under the pseudonym of Dean Danger.

In that role, he introduces Lonnie Lord, who sold ten million records last year but carries his guitar around with him everywhere as he just loves to sing and wants to be ready whenever it's called upon. He's Ron Haydock, acting under the name of Vin Saxon, and he promptly gets his chance as the story morphs into a rock video, with him serenading Cee Bee Beaumont, our leading lady.

She's next on the list of the Chain Gang, a trio of young thugs who pick her at random out of the phone book, then annoy her with phone calls and follow her with links of chain to jangle. I think this scene is as long as it is only because Steckler liked shots of his wife's backside walking away from the camera, because we get that for six full minutes. Attempts at suspense are ineffectual, so all we really have is a few capably framed shots and a constant reminder of Carolyn Brandt's butt. I should emphasise that that's hardly a bad thing but it's a full ten percent of the film!

Just when we think the suspense might kick in, that night as the Chain Gang rattles Cee Bee's windows, we switch back to Lonnie Lord singing the film's theme tune while girls jiggle in leopard print bikinis and horror masks.

Like most of this movie, in fact like most of Steckler's movies, this feels like a home video, which it really is. Like many low budget filmmakers, Steckler used sets he had immediately to hand, like his house or his neighbour's house or the park just down the road. He also used his own family as much as he could, casting himself as the lead in many of his films, under the name of Cash Flagg, acting alongside his wife and daughters and whoever else was willing to get in front of the camera.

At least here we're given a segue from this home movie back to the plot, as Cee Bee gets another phone call and drives home frantically, only for her to be kidnapped by the waiting Chain Gang. One valid segue is good for an entire film, right?

Well we're coming up on something that is far better than any segue, one of the most legendary scenes in all of exploitation film history. We're halfway through the film by this point, the picture only running 66 minutes, and we find ourselves stuck in Cee Bee's apartment while Lonnie Lord sings a mopy song and Titus Twimbly, her gardener, recovers from the beating the Chain Gang gave him on her lawn. It feels like the movie has stalled, because *I Stand Alone* doesn't compare well to up tempo songs like *You is a Rat Pfink* or *Big Boss a-Go Go Party* and Titus Moede, who plays Twimbly, looks like nobody less than a retarded Anthony Perkins in dungarees.

Obviously something is needed to seriously shake the film up, and the ransom demand from the Chain Gang just isn't it. They want $50,000 in a black case before dinner. Nah, what we want is what happens next, except you won't believe it unless you've actually seen it.

"Titus," says Lord, "there's only one thing we can do: this is a job for You Know and Who!" Well, we have no idea what he's talking about but Titus perks up and off they go into the closet, only to emerge as the comedy superhero double act of Rat Pfink and Boo Boo. Now, if you didn't see this coming, don't despair, because neither did anyone else, including the people making the movie.

Steckler had merely got bored with his own story and didn't feel like it was going anywhere. Adam West's *Batman* had been a massive hit since it began in January and Steckler was a *Batman* fan from way back, having sneaked out to see one of the serials at a very tender age, probably 1949's *Batman and Robin*. So he got Moede into his Halloween costume, complete with a jester's hat with flashing lights, cobbled together an outfit for Haydock with a ski mask and a cape, slapped an R and a B onto them and in the process turned this movie into something completely different.

I'm convinced I have dreams where I try to fathom just what audiences thought when they first saw this on initial release and had to deal with this scene. Talk about a blatant attempt to grab the attention of necking couples at drive-ins across the country to focus their eyes on the screen instead of each other! It's emphatic and impossible to ignore. The narration goes like this: "Rat Pfink and Boo Boo! Friends to those who have no friends! Enemies of those who make them an enemy! Champions of women and children everywhere! Rat Pfink, mysterious masked nemesis of hoodlums and rackeeters the world over; and Boo Boo, by day a mild mannered gardener, by night the scourge of the underworld! Rat Pfink and Boo Boo! Together they blaze a four fisted campaign against the enemies of truth, justice and the American way of life!" They have only one weakness. What's that, you ask? Bullets. "Now, let's go to fight crime!"

This scene more accurately provides the feel of being transported into the Twilight Zone than any actual episode ever did. Everything that happens from this point on is beyond surreal. They do deliver the case, but it doesn't contain any money; it contains copies of *Variety*, *Screen Trade Illustrated*, some DC *Batman* comics and an issue of *Monster World*, with exclusive first photos of *The Munsters*. I'd take it, but the Chain Gang aren't happy. They even dare to fight Rat Pfink and Boo Boo when they show up, prompting a seemingly endless chase on the Ratcycle, a motorbike with sidecar, upon which Haydock tries desperately to keep his footing during the pursuit. This isn't greenscreen, folks, they just shot at 35mph to abide by the speed limit and to help Haydock to avoid certain death through such a stunt. He often lies down when on the open road, hardly isn't the usual way to build suspense. We're not fearing for Rat Pfink, we're fearing for Haydock!

Now if you felt that the six minutes of Carolyn Brandt's butt early on during this picture was an overlong scene, this chase beats it hands down. We get another six minutes on vehicles as they chase on out into Topanga Canyon, but when the Chain Gang's truck gets stuck in the mud, it all carries on by foot. While Steckler began spoofing Adam West's TV *Batman*, which was a spoof to begin with, this all hearkens back more to the old serial days. We even get a gorilla, one of the staples of low budget exploitation in classic Hollywood. Kogar the Gorilla was an opportunity for Bob Burns to get into a gorilla suit. He's a world renowned archivist and Hollywood prop collector whose basement museum contains such gems as the Time Machine from the George Pal movie and the original King Kong armature, among many others. As Kogar he reappeared in Steckler's *Lemon Grove Kids Meet the Monsters* and a number of fan films and homages to the golden era.

So, just in case you're keeping track, this has run through most genres already. It began as a crime picture, albeit a schizophrenic crime picture that wants to be on MTV. We watch Carolyn Brandt walk for six minutes, but we don't mind too much. Halfway through the film, it turns into a Batman spoof, but promptly forgets about the TV show to become a cliffhanger serial. Now we have a gorilla added to the mix like it's been a Monogram adventure comedy all along. Once we get past that, Steckler hijacks a random parade to celebrate, with Rat Pfink and Boo Boo waving to the crowds as if it was all being held in their honour. What these folks thought of a couple of nutjobs in bizarre costumes, I have no idea, but what we hear isn't real as Steckler shot silently on a Bolex and Keith Wester added all the sound in later. And we finish off as a beach movie.

Yeah, a beach movie. Is there anything that Steckler didn't cram into this 66 minute trip?

So what's the draw of this picture? I don't think anyone's been able to explain it in terms other than *Rat Pfink a Boo Boo*. That's it. It's a home movie, a record of what Steckler and his buddies got up to over a summer. All these folks knew each other and it shows, because even the most overt nastiness is devoid of any real danger, like it's just a bunch of friends messing around. I've seen a lot of low budget films premiéred with cast and crew in attendance but I've never got that feeling myself in real life, even when watching the one movie I've been in. I spent four hours at a location one day doing extra work but was never really part of the project. Yet I feel I was part of the project when I watch this film. I feel like I'm part of the Steckler household, along with him and his wife and his friends. James Bowie, one of the Chain Gang, was his best man. Mary Jo Curtis, the first victim, was Ron Haydock's girlfriend. I was... well I wasn't but I feel like I was.

Ray Dennis Steckler never did get to turn *Batman* into a Broadway musical, but he did get to do unspeakable things to Bob Kane's creation with this film. Unfortunately while Steckler made a lot of movies over four decades, he didn't make any more like this, though to be honest, neither did anyone else. He did make a few other amazing B movies around the same time and anything he put out in the sixties is fascinating.

When the seventies came along he ended up making strange porn movies, often under pseudonyms like Cindy Lou Sutters or Sven Christian. Many had horror themes, like *The Mad Love Life of a Hot Vampire*, *The Sexorcist* or *The Horny Vampire*, but some were as bizarre as roller skating porn flicks like *Sex Rink* and *Plato's Retreat West*. One day I'll see a Steckler movie that was made after I was born, but it's most likely to be the dialogue free *The Hollywood Strangler Meets the Skid Row Slasher*. It'll take something unique to follow this.

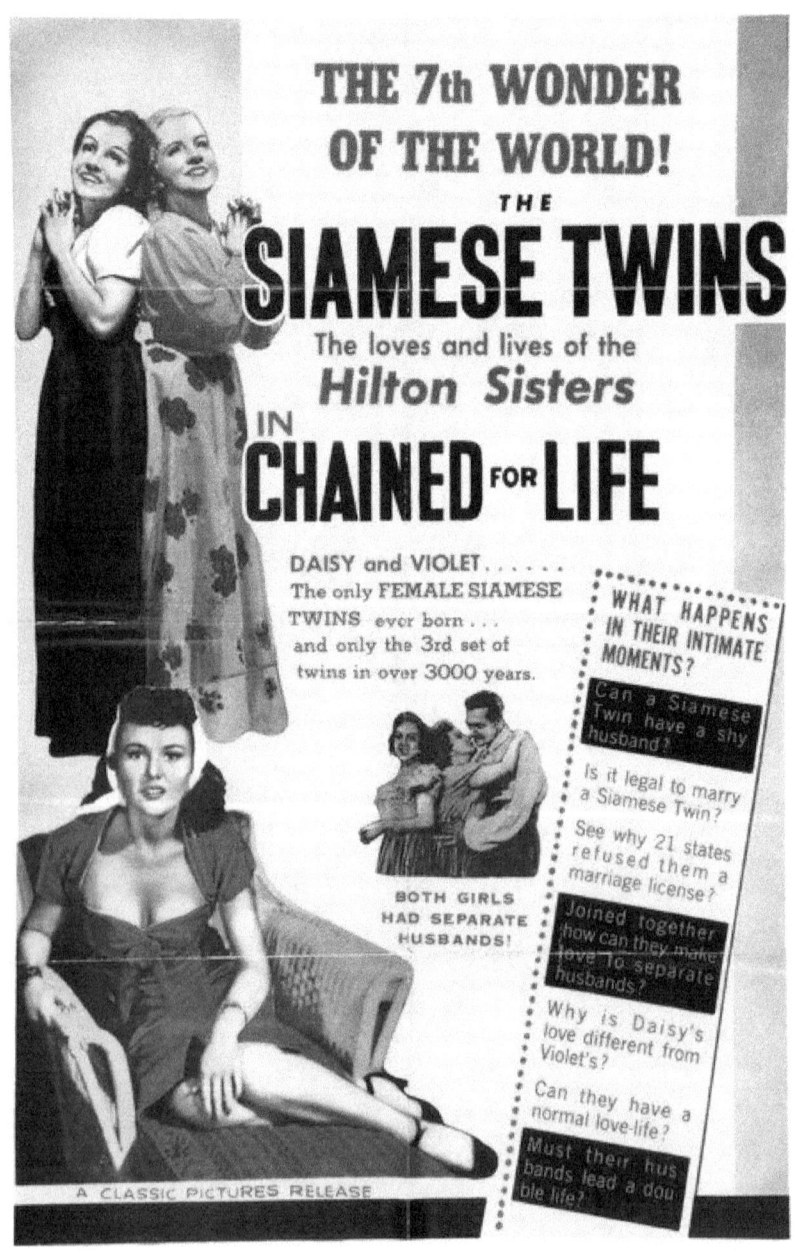

X is for eXploitation:
Chained for Life (1951)

Directors: Harry L Fraser
Writer: Nat Tanchuck
Stars: The Hilton Sisters

Chained for Life really ought to have been a gimme. Phrased as a story full of moral and legal questions centred around a pair of Siamese twins committing murder and matrimony, some are posed on the wild publicity material. "What happens in their intimate moments?" the posters ask. "Is it legal to marry a Siamese twin?" "Can they have a normal love life?"

Having a pair of Siamese twins play a pair of Siamese twins is a dream for any exploitation filmmaker; but the Hilton twins, as Dorothy and Vivian Hamilton, also play themselves. Yes, long before Paris and Nicky there were Daisy and Violet, as unlike the modern Hiltons as could be. By all accounts they were pleasant, intelligent, talented ladies who simply happened to share a circulatory system. They're the Siamese twins from Tod Browning's *Freaks* and they lived amazing lives that are more than worthy of a genuine biopic, but that's utterly not what writer Nat Tanchuck and director Harry L Fraser made here.

It's difficult to truly comprehend how wrong these filmmakers went. Somehow they managed to remove every fascinating snippet, every cult moment, every salacious scene in the Hilton Sisters' lives in favour of all the boring bits in between. *Chained for Life* flopped horribly, even a widespread ban not generating free publicity.

Amazingly, it was banned for its lurid nature, though there isn't a single lurid moment within. This is an exploitation film that feels ashamed to be an exploitation film. It isn't that it doesn't live up to the hype, as exploitation films never aim to, hence the name. It's that there's so much material to exploit and it doesn't attempt to exploit any of it.

There's a scene where the twins sit up in bed to talk about their lives and how a hypothetical separation would change them. If the crew had left the room with the camera quietly capturing it all, it would have been gripping and poignant. Instead an overblown script murders it all. These Siamese twins aren't even allowed to be real, even when playing themselves.

The whole thing unfolds in flashback, from Judge Mitchell's courtroom, where Vivian sits accused of murder. This is an awesome setup; just think about it. One Siamese twin is apparently guilty of cold blooded murder but the other is as innocent as a lamb. If that's the court's judgement, then what happens next? They can't lock up only one twin. They can't fry only one in the electric chair. Blackstone's formulation suggests that it's "better that ten guilty persons escape than that one innocent suffer", but how do you apply that here? Unless both twins are charged with the crime, one intrinsically cannot be guilty. Why even stage a trial if a guilty verdict can't be acted upon? Even if the guilty twin pulled out a gun and shot the judge dead in his own courtroom with the jury and lawyers first hand witnesses to the act, they still couldn't sentence her to any punishment without also condemning an innocent to the same.

There are so many permutations to this that the mind reels, but how many do you think *Chained for Life* decides to explore? That's right. None.

In the minds of the filmmakers, why would anyone care about legal loopholes to organised massacre when we can watch a man ride around a stage backwards on a bicycle for five minutes instead? Sadly, I'm not kidding. There's enough substance to the lives of the Hilton sisters for this to be a rivetting three hour movie but no, we break off for a trick cycling stuntman. We see Whitey Roberts too, who tap dances and juggles, all at the same time, and Tony Lovello, who plays classical tunes such as the *William Tell Overture* at breakneck speed on a button accordion. All of them are mildly amusing but they have as much to do with the story at hand as the stock footage audience. They're in the wrong picture. I can understand the sappy love songs that Daisy and Violet duet on, but even these are poor choices.

The only vaudevillian with any connection to the so called story is Andre Pariseau, a sharpshooter who performs basic feats for us to be underwhelmed by. He's easily the least interesting character on the bill but he looks a little like Jeremy Irons and he thinks he has some Latin charm, so when the sisters' manager decides to set up a publicity marriage, he promptly becomes the man who can.

That manager is Hinkley, sleazy but run of the mill and played in his sleep by Allen Jenkins, one of my favourite Warner Brothers supporting actors from the thirties. He looks tired here, not because he's too old as he had a quarter of a century left in him, not even becoming Officer Dibble in the *Top Cat* cartoons for another decade, but because he knows how bad this material is. He served as able support to Cagney, Robinson and Bogart, but here he was stuck under Mario Laval who never acted again. He must have really needed a payday. I hope it worked out.

Of course, we're supposed to believe that Andre really falls in love with Dorothy, not only to play along with the scam Hinkley sets up but because that's *amore*, and we're also supposed to believe that Dorothy falls for him right back. Now, we may buy that these two actors share the same screen on occasion but we don't buy them sharing anything else, least of all chemistry.

Worse, Vivian has to get upset at her sister for being a sap over him. That doesn't work at all, not just because they're clearly good people who don't want to get upset with anyone, least of all each other, but because they're real Siamese twins. I believe that if Mother Nature attached you to someone else by the butt cheek, from birth to death, so that you even had to share the same toilet bowl, you'd surely get over the whole upset thing really quick too. The Hilton sisters couldn't take time outs. They were stuck with each other, for better or worse, and better was the only realistic option.

By the way, here's where the lurid and sensational story turns out to be a damp squib compared to the truth. In real life Daisy and Violet were socialites, albeit nothing like Paris and Nicky. Violet had an eye for the celebrities, working through musicians and boxers before becoming engaged to Maurice Lambert, a bandleader. The various legal shenanigans that Dorothy and Andre go through in *Chained for Life* are a fictionalised version of what Violet and Maurice got stuck with in real life. Twenty one states refused to issue them a marriage license; some saw it as bigamy, while others refused because Daisy wasn't engaged too. Two years later, long after that relationship was over, the sisters' agent found a way to make it happen, so Violet married a long term friend, Jim Moore, on the 50 yard line of the Cotton Bowl at the Texas Centennial Exposition. Daisy got married a few years later. None of the marriages lasted, but nobody shot anyone.

Where exploitation flicks usually play up the sensational, this one tries to hide it. The Vivian and Andre marriage scam is a combination of Violet and Maurice, Violet and Jim and maybe Daisy and bandleader Jack Lewis or dancer Harold Estep too, but it's boring, the Bijou Theatre stage a cheap substitute for reality. We forget that the twins were sold by their mother to an abusive and corrupt manager, or that they were kept in abject slavery for decades, freed by a lawyer when the truth came out during a divorce case that had them named as co-respondents. We ignore their fortune and fame, their working relationship with Bob Hope and their friendship with Harry Houdini. All we get is Hinkley's successful publicity stunt and a dumb love triangle. Yes, Andre serenades Dorothy over the phone then cosies up with his stage assistant, the supposedly lovely Renée. This is shown to be exotic even though she's plain old Patricia Wright from Spokane, WA and Andre's a cad.

There's such a lack of romance in this film that it's surprising to realise we should be moved. The whole relationship starts as an angle, a fraud to generate publicity, but fails to heat up from there. I blinked when Andre proposed, so had to rewind to work out what he'd done. "I love you. Will you marry me," he asks her, at a restaurant table, almost as an aside while we're not paying attention. Why does she accept? "I'm not a machine," she tells her twin. "I'm a woman. I want to live like one."

Yes, we run through all the standard clichés. "How much can love demand from us?" the sisters ask each other as we cringe into our seats. There's even a surreal dream sequence where Dorothy pretends she isn't a Siamese twin any more by magically turning into someone who only dances in the distance because she's six inches taller and doesn't look remotely like her. For the close ups, she stands behind a tree wondering why there isn't an effects budget.

At least we're going to get a wedding night, right? We get a wedding, on stage at the Bijou with a host of uncomfortable looking vaudevillians and audience members, so surely we'll get a wedding night. Well, no. We get a fade to black and Andre's gone. He couldn't do it after all. It's all over. Why did he do it, the vaudevillians wonder. "I'll tell you why: because he never loved her," quips Renée, as if that's an Oscar winning line. Dorothy's heart is broken but Andre and Renée stay on the same bill to molest each other in the wings, because the show must go on. Why it has to go on with the twins centre stage singing *Never Say You'll Fall in Love*, I really don't know, as that's just tacky, but I didn't write the script.

It's cruel and unusual punishment and the only good thing that it brings is a stunning memory of the twins' last film, made two full decades earlier: *Freaks*, the most outlandish picture that classic Hollywood ever released. Anyone who's seen that film knows what happens when normal folks disrespect the freaks: they mount their vengeance in truly spectacular style. One of my favourite movies of all time, it's a joy to watch and it's everything this one isn't.

The Hilton sisters are the only commonality between the two pictures but maybe my fond memories of *Freaks* are the reason why there seems to be one well framed shot in *Chained for Life*. Andre has an intriguing trick, you see, where he can shoot a rifle at an organ and make it play, even though he has a rhythm and the organ doesn't. The twins watch on from the wings as we focus on his prophetic words. "Accidents can happen," he threatened Renée before the show; "Don't forget I use live bullets." It's no accident when Vivian shoots him dead with his gun, but she appears to stand on the other side of a stage flat to her sister, framed head on, their hair colour making them seem like yin and yang. It's a good shot, in both senses.

It took seventy minutes for a good shot and we don't get another one, so if you must watch this for historical value, do yourself a real favour and quit at this point. Don't go back to the courtroom, where everything is even stagier than it was on the stage. There are no tap dancing jugglers or trick cyclists in court to distract you with a moment's entertainment, so you have to sit through all the inanity as you close in on what may be the worst ending in cinematic history.

I hate spoilers but I'm going to give you this one, in the vain hope that you don't have to be slapped in the face with it after eighty minutes of torture. You see, everything thus far has built up to this moment, this moral dilemma. The lawyers are all idiots but they don't matter. Only the judge matters and how he will rule in this unique case. It's what it's all about. And how does he rule? He doesn't. He cops out at the very last minute and asks you to come up with a ruling instead!

In all the films I've ever seen, I can't remember another ending that annoyed me like this one. It feels as if the filmmakers, through the proxy of actor Norval Mitchell, look directly at us through the fourth wall and say, "Hey viewer, you watched our movie. You stayed through the bad acting and the bad writing, the clichéd dialogue and the ponderous narrative. You didn't leave when we mangled the careers of the lovely Hilton twins into this unholy mess of a picture. In gratitude, we should give you our answer to the key moral question that we posed. Not the answer, mind you, just our answer, how we saw it. But no. We can't be bothered. You work it out. It's your problem. Stay up all night if you want. This entire picture is a waste of your time. It's one long 81 minute question that we won't answer because you suck and we hate you. Have a nice day."

In this, it's perhaps the purest exploitation film of all. It took my money and gave me nothing in return.

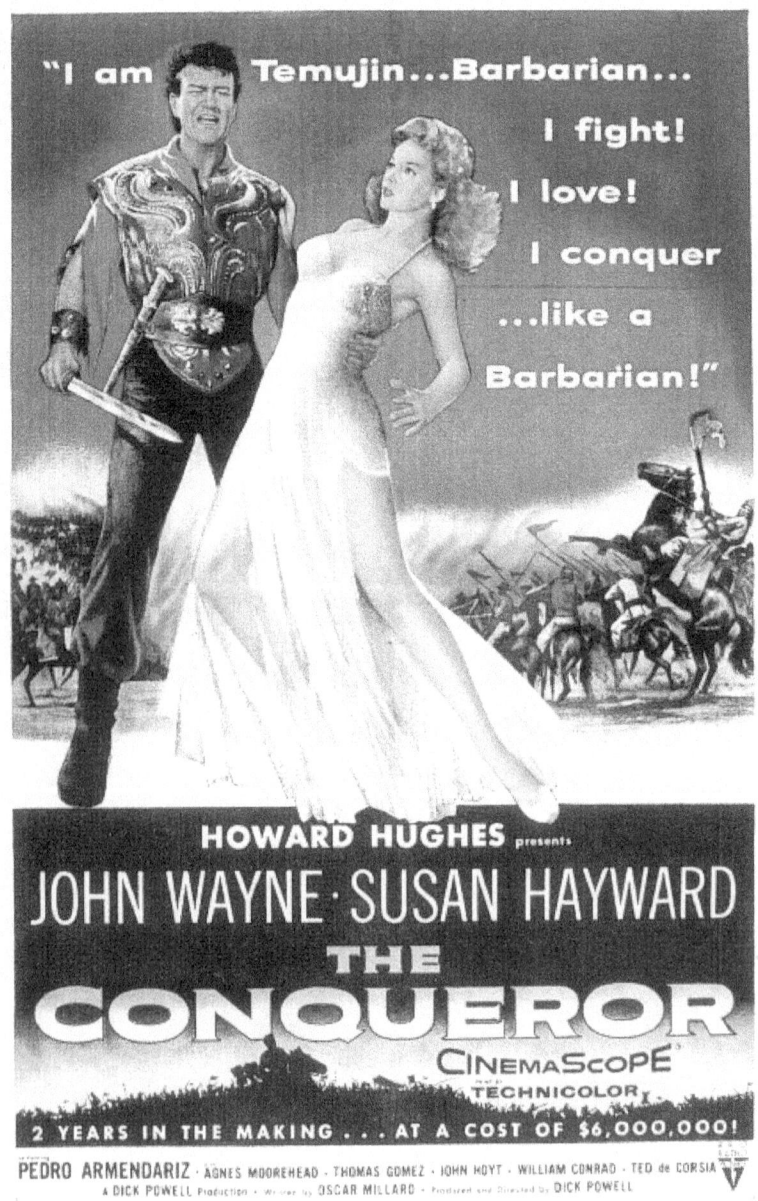

Y is for Yes:
The Conqueror (1954)

Director: Dick Powell
Writer: Oscar Millard
Stars: John Wayne and Susan Hayward

Howard Hughes had a knack for making money so strong that it could almost be called a Midas touch, but occasionally even he lost it.

The Conqueror was a rare financial flop for him, though it did tie Rebel without a Cause for the 11th place in box office rentals in 1956, earning $4.5m. The catch is that it cost $6m to make and, apparently feeling guilty over some of the decisions made during production that may have cost the lives of many of his cast and crew, he shelled out $12m more to buy back every print of the film. After initial release, nobody saw The Conqueror except Howard Hughes himself until 1974, when he allowed it to be broadcast on television. Reportedly he watched it a lot, screening it and either Jet Pilot or Ice Station Zebra continuously during later reclusive years, in which he may well have suffered from allodynia, pain from being touched, so distracted himself by stripping naked and watching movies continually.

Virtually everything associated with The Conqueror was an unmitigated disaster, but most disastrous was the choice to shoot on location in the Escalante Desert near St George, UT, downwind from the Nevada Test Site where the government had conducted Operation Upshot-Knothole in 1953, only a year earlier.

There were other problems too: Susan Hayward's black panther attacked her, Pedro Armendáriz's horse threw him, breaking his jaw, a flash flood nearly wiped out production and sweltering 120° heat made the fur costumes unbearable.

Yet these fade into insignificance compared to the the acutely radioactive sand of Snow Canyon, into which clouds of fallout from eleven above ground nuclear tests in Nevada had funnelled, exposing the filmmakers for thirteen full weeks. You might think that this situation couldn't have been made any worse, but Hughes shipped sixty tons of this radioactive Utah dirt back to Hollywood to give retakes authenticity.

It's often been stated that Hughes simply accepted the government's assurances to the locals in St George that there was no danger to public health and that later on he felt "guilty as Hell" that he had risked the lives of his cast and crew for a movie. However, Charles Higham's biography of Hughes highlights that this isn't fair.

He was running RKO Pictures in 1953, as it produced *Split Second* that focused on the dangers of radiation in Nevada. That was actor Dick Powell's directorial debut, which he followed up with this. Hughes contracted to the government and the military, so uneasy with their ongoing testing that he delayed building any factories in Nevada. He was also notoriously germophobic, using tissues when picking up objects and requiring others to remove dust from their clothes. Tellingly, he never went to St George, which perhaps he only chose for being a Mormon town; he had long hired only Mormon aides to be sure they didn't drink.

The production numbered 220 cast and crew on location. By 1981, 91 of them had contracted a form of cancer and 46 were already dead of the disease, including many of the key players: John Wayne, Susan Hayward and Agnes Moorehead all died of cancer in the seventies, director Dick Powell in 1963 and Pedro Armendáriz that same year, by shooting himself in the heart to bypass suffering from terminal cancer. Half the residents of St George had contracted the disease by this time, and eventually, over half the cast and crew would too. While it has never conclusively been proved that the tests were a factor in these deaths and many victims smoked heavily, including the Duke, who survived lung cancer in 1964 before succumbing to stomach cancer in 1979, it's still likely, given a statistical anomaly of instances over three times higher than would usually be expected and a wide variance in these instances, not restricted to lung cancer in the slightest.

Today, we don't look back at *The Conqueror* and see radioactive fallout, we look back at one of the most insane casting choices Hollywood ever made. There had been others, not least a trio of roles for Katharine Hepburn, whose impeccable Bryn Mawr accent inexplicably voiced backwoods girl Trigger Hicks in *Spitfire*, Mary,

Queen of Scots in *Mary of Scotland* and, worst of all, Chinese peasant girl Jade Tan in *Dragon Seed*.

Yet John Wayne is perhaps the most iconic American film star of all time, forever associated with rugged, hardworking, heroic types. Here he's tasked with playing Temujin, later known as Genghis Khan, which is as utterly ludicrous as it sounds. In later years he stated that the moral of the film was "not to make an ass of yourself trying to play parts you're not suited for." This is the most ridiculous part he ever played, eclipsing his brief performance as Longinus in *The Greatest Story Ever Told*, drawling, "Truly, this man was the son of God."

The reason the Duke took the part to begin with is the stuff of legend. Studio releases suggest he demanded the part, having seen the script lying around somewhere. According to the Medveds' book, *The Hollywood Hall of Shame*, this took place in the office of Dick Powell, who had already been assigned to shoot Wayne's third and last RKO picture. They were discussing script choices, when Powell was called away for a few minutes. On his return, he found Wayne engrossed in the script for *The Conqueror* and insisting that the part be his. Powell attempted to dissuade him in vain, later explaining, "Who am I to turn down John Wayne?" Some reports suggest that Powell intended to discard the script, others that he already had and the Duke had retrieved it from the bin. Perhaps he seriously felt it was a good choice for him to stretch his acting muscles, or maybe he just wanted to make a movie, perennial RKO delays affecting his work for other studios.

To me, it's an iconic story that explains well how such an awful script could make it to production. A leading man since 1930, Wayne was arguably at the peak of his powers in the 1950s. With recent successes like *Fort Apache*, *Red River* and *She Wore a Yellow Ribbon* under his belt, he kicked off the decade with *Rio Grande* for his favourite director, John Ford. His best non-western, *The Quiet Man*, came in 1952, and one of his personal favourites, *Hondo*, in 1953. His most acclaimed film, *The Searchers*, was released in 1956, so that year saw both his best and worst movies. No wonder Wayne would become the industry's biggest star, topping Quigley's list of all time money makers. It's no stretch to see that a simple 'yes' from him might be enough to turn a discarded screenplay into a six million dollar picture and an emphatic 'yes' might guarantee it. Certainly, he was serious about the rôle once it was his, going on a crash diet that included Dexedrine four times a day.

While John Wayne's 'yes' to play Genghis Khan appears to have been a personal choice, the 'yes' from his leading lady took a lot more persuasion. Howard Hughes saw Susan Hayward as perfect for the part of Bortai, the fiery Tartar princess taken forcibly by Temujin but who gives herself to him willingly in the end. After all, she wasn't just a talented actress, Oscar nominated in 1947 for her role in *Smash-Up, the Story of a Woman*, she was also a fiery character in real life, something Hughes knew well as he was having an affair with her at the time.

He constructed this film around her as much as around John Wayne, however much she hated it. He literally wouldn't take 'no' for an answer, even offering Darryl F Zanuck, who owned her contract, a million dollars under the table to release her for this film. Zanuck threatened to suspend her and her rising divorce costs forced her to accept. Still, she hated the script, the costumes, the heat, everything about the film.

It's easy to see why. It's unintentionally hilarious from moment one, looking utterly like a western in every way except for the props and costumes. It opens with Temujin, with slanted eyes, a hint at a moustache and a falcon on his arm, riding down with his men to discover why Chief Targutai is crossing his land and discovering Bortai, the chief's haughty third wife to be. "I feel this Tartar woman is for me," he tells his Mexican sidekick. "My blood says take her!"

Take her he does, in a raid that sparks war between Mongols, Tartars, Merkits, Karkaits and whatever other races show up in the form of local Navajo indians who didn't even wear make up to hide their ethnic origins. Bizarrely, much care was made to construct twelfth century villages from ancient drawings, but nothing else looks remotely authentic. Even the desert, described in the opening text as "harsh and arid" is remarkably green, the Escalante a poor casting choice for the Gobi.

Admittedly, some actors fare better than others. The ever-reliable Agnes Moorehead is capable as Hunlun, Temujin's mother, her only failure the fact that she speaks in English like everyone else. Lee van Cleef is prominent in the background, always doing something without ever doing much. If anyone's needed to fetch a fur, deliver a present or just ride a horse out of frame, it's him, but he gets maybe one word in the entire film. Relying on his looks, which served him well for many ethnicities, works fine. The great Wang Khan's shaman is played by John Hoyt, a western staple, especially on television, but he goes all out, like Basil Rathbone playing Fu Manchu, and in doing so finds a slot in the long line of surprising white actors who aren't entirely terrible in yellowface make up, such as Peter Lorre and Boris Karloff. These are rare exceptions, as most cast members fail to treat this as anything but just another western, which in most regards it is.

It's often said that Kurosawa's films, which he freely acknowledged had roots in John Ford's, were Japanese westerns or easterns, if you will. At least he adapted Ford's techniques to fit essentially Japanese settings, populating them with samurai and historical authenticity. *The Conqueror* ought to feel like such an eastern but it doesn't.

It feels irrevocably like a western, somewhat like a play put on during a down moment on a cattle drive. If *Buffy the Vampire Slayer* can go musical, then the cast of *Red River* can stage a biopic of Genghis Khan just for fun, right? Hey, I could be the great conqueror, says the Duke. My frequent Mexican co-star could play my brother and the red haired Irish lass over there could be my bride. Maybe in an alternate universe where the Nazis won the war and occupied the US, the cast of a Paramount western are thrown into a POW camp and bide their time with frivolities like this. Think the play in *Grand Illusion* turned on its head.

It looks like a western in eastern clothes, guns swapped for swords, stetsons swapped for ornate eastern headgear, horses swapped for, well, horses. If props and costumes were swapped back, only the dancing girls in Wang Khan's palace would feel out of place in a western. The woman of Samarkand doesn't dance like a saloon girl in her outfit of Christmas tinsel, protected from the Breen Office by a flesh coloured bodysuit underneath.

It sounds like a western too, Victor Young's score much better than what he gave Hughes for *The Outlaw*, but just as inappropriate, without even of a hint of eastern flavour. The language Oscar

Millard puts into the characters' mouths is Elizabethan. Kurosawa adapted Shakespeare to the east; he adapted the east to Shakespeare. "While I have fingers to grasp a sword, and eyes to see your cowardly faces, your treacherous heads will not be safe on your shoulders," pronounces the Duke, "for I am Temujin, the Conqueror."

It's all about as authentic as *Carry On... Up the Khyber*, but without tapping into any underlying truth. Like *The Outlaw*, its only success lay in being sumptuous to the eyes, the cinematography from Joseph LaShelle, an Oscar winner for *Laura*, being accomplished.

None of this mattered to Howard Hughes, of course, whose many action packed but nonsensical pictures suggest that he's the classic equivalent of Michael Bay. Maybe he didn't screen it over and over for decades out of guilt. Perhaps, as Higham suggests, he identified with the conqueror, having dated most of the leading ladies of the golden age, not least his own fiery princess, Susan Hayward, who he could forcibly take over and over again by simply rescreening the movie. In a way he already had, by forcing her to say 'yes' to the part.

The Conqueror would surely have been horrible in any form, but its legendary badness is mostly due to John Wayne. The 'yes' that he volunteered was its death blow.

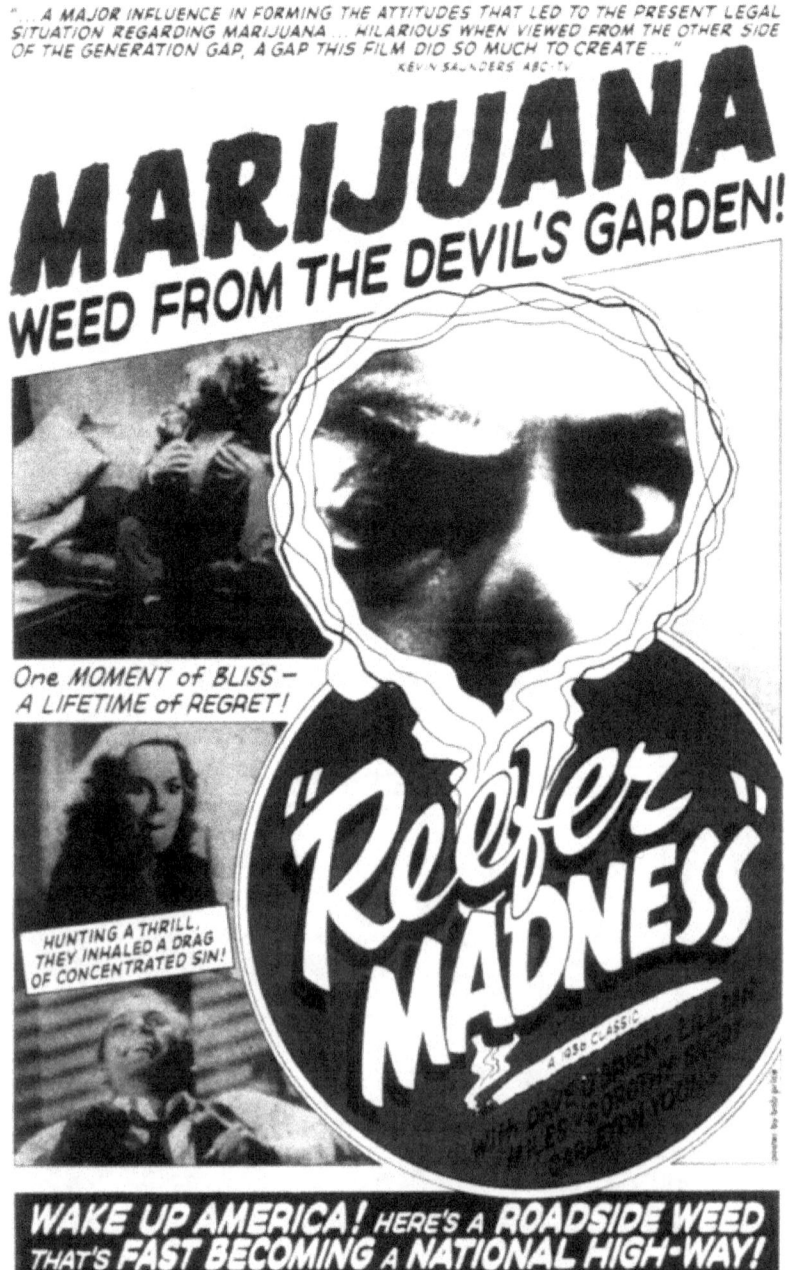

Z is for Zeal:
Reefer Madness (1936)

Director: Louis J Gasnier
Writer: Arthur Hoerl
Stars: Dorothy Short and Kenneth Craig

It isn't clear who really made *Tell Your Children*, which found fame decades after its 1936 release under the title *Reefer Madness*, but I'd love to find out. Every review seems to highlight the irony that a film financed as a cautionary tale by a concerned church group found its audience decades later in the very marijuana smoking youth culture that it railed against. The suggestion is that this church group aimed to show the film to parents, possibly for free, as a serious attempt to curb the use of marijuana in children.

Yet, surprisingly, even the name of the church group which was able to raise the $100,000 budget, slight by major studio standards but hardly a small amount, proves elusive. In fact, the more I search, the more the whole church group story seems like a front, or at least a misleading truth, and a whole swathe of sinister possibilities come to light, none of which can be verified but which are nonetheless well within the bounds of possibility.

There were many such cautionary tales shot in the thirties and into the forties, warning against what seems like every possible moral infraction known: pregnancy, venereal disease, prostitution, you name it, but especially drugs, and there are reasons behind that prominence that don't tie to either filmmaking or narcotics.

Attacks on marijuana grew in the twenties out of racism, initially against migrant Mexican workers who brought it north with them and then against the black jazz musicians who made it cool. These led to some states banning what was known as 'Indian hemp' but at the International Opium Convention in 1925 the US supported regulation instead.

The real war on marijuana wasn't really a war on marijuana at all but a war on hemp, the plant from which marijuana happens to be derived. Hemp had been used to make many substances from rope to oil, cloth to paper, and improving processing technology began to threaten established industries.

The problem was that these industries had serious clout. William Randolph Hearst, who owned the largest newspaper chain in the country, had major investments in the timber industry to produce the paper he needed. Companies like DuPont produced chemicals used for paper processing and in the cotton industry. Both Hearst and DuPont, among others, were backed by the Mellon Bank, owned by Andrew Mellon, who served as US Secretary of the Treasury from 1921 to 1932.

It was Mellon who appointed his niece's husband, Harry J Anslinger, to be head of the Federal Bureau of Narcotics in 1930, a position he held for 32 years. Starting in 1934, he fought hard against hemp, writing the Marihuana Tax Act of 1937 which taxed hemp production and financing propaganda films, 'the more fearful the better'. Interviewed by drug historian David Musto in 1972, Anslinger expressed surprise at his failure to stop illegal drug use through these means.

It seems clear that Anslinger helped with production of *Tell Your Children*, though there is no proof he actually funded it. Thelma White, who plays Mae Coleman, was contracted to RKO Pictures at the time and was required to appear in the film, for which she was paid by RKO. This wasn't an RKO picture though, being produced by George A Hirliman for his own G&H Productions. He was an indie producer who worked with many distributors, though at least one of his other 1936 films, *Daniel Boone*, was also distributed through RKO.

However much RKO was involved, what's clear is that *Tell Your Children* flopped badly and it was quickly purchased by Dwain Esper, exploitation filmmaker who had already directed cautionary tales of his own such as *Narcotic* and *Marihuana*. He recut and redistributed it under its most famous title, *Reefer Madness*. Other releases saw it retitled again and again, to *Dope Addict*, *Doped Youth*, *Love Madness* and *The Burning Question*.

Its potential eventually extinguished, it languished forgotten and drifted into the public domain, only to begin its current renaissance in 1971, when Keith Stroup, who had founded NORML, the National Organisation for Reform of Marijuana Laws, discovered the film in the archives of the Library of Congress, bought a print and began to exhibit it afresh at pro-pot rallies and college campuses across the country. Its success was immediate, as every American college student in the seventies was stoned all the time. I know that because I saw *That '70s Show*.

Finally the film had found its audience, albeit the precise opposite of the one originally aimed for. Beyond that base irony, legend suggests that it improves in quality the more stoned you are, mostly through unintentional comedy. To be truly entertained, you must be so high that every wild inaccuracy serves to build a parody of the Man, hurling clearly ineffectual propaganda.

Unfortunately because I didn't watch it while stoned, and in fact have never smoked anything in my entire life, legal or otherwise, I'm obviously missing out on a good portion of the hilarity that *Reefer Madness* has brought to countless college students and other lowlife ne'erdowells. To me, it becomes merely another bad movie, but perhaps the message that screams out at me loudest is that perhaps I should start smoking this stuff just to be able to keep up with the film. The story unfolds so quickly that I can hardly keep up with the constant introduction of new characters and maintain my judgement of who I'm actually supposed to be watching, let alone all the sensational headlines spattered at the screen like a hail of machine gun bullets. If only I'd got high on reefer first, time could have slowed down and this could have morphed into a ten hour David Lean epic, merely one as funny as anything Mel Brooks could have conjured up.

The opening text begins the diatribe, describing "dread marihuana" as "an unspeakable scourge, the Real Public Enemy Number One!" Why? Well, I should quote verbatim: "Its first effect is sudden violent, uncontrollable laughter; then come dangerous hallucinations – space expands – time slows down, almost stands still... fixed ideas come next, conjuring up monstrous extravagances – followed by emotional disturbances, the total inability to direct thoughts, the loss of all power to resist physical emotions... leading finally to acts of shocking violence... ending often in incurable insanity."

Thank the Lord for the authorities we see taking action on the front pages! The police are waging war, the feds are aiding them and after dope peddlers are caught in a high school, school-parent organizations are joining the fight. High school principal Dr Alfred Carroll speaks to his, with a subject of *Tell Your Children*, to explain how serious it's all become.

It can hardly come as a surprise that his first words are "Must be stopped!" He's aiming to lay the foundation for a nationwide campaign to demand compulsory education on narcotics, as it's "only through enlightenment that this scourge can be wiped out." This scourge, of course, is marijuana, because the letter he reads from an anonymous member of the Narcotics Bureau explains that it's "more vicious, more deadly" than all those other soul-destroying drugs like opium, morphine and heroin.

You don't believe it? Well, in case you think he's exaggerating, he proves it conclusively by introducing us to Mae Coleman and the den of iniquity she ran in his very city. As we'll soon find, even a single puff of her "dread marihuana" can turn any decent Godfearing all-American child into a cackling, twitching, murderous sex fiend. They'll rape! They'll murder! They'll drive over 40mph! Of course it must be stopped! Won't someone please think of the children!

And so the hour long dramatisation that serves as the core of the film begins. Mae Coleman and Jack Perry are the focal point of this gang of drug dealers. They're depraved enough to live in sin but still obey the edicts of the Production Code and sleep in separate beds. Mae is a shameless hussy who dares to dress herself in her own bedroom while we watch, but she does have a heart so she doesn't like that her boyfriend sells drugs to schoolkids instead of just consenting adults like she does. Jack is like the supporting characters Humphrey Bogart got landed with around this time at Warner Brothers before they worked out what he could do, but actor Carleton Young doesn't have a hint of his charisma. We don't know what he thought of the film but Thelma White, who played Mae, told the *Los Angeles Times* that "I hide my head when I think about it." She added that, "I'm ashamed to say that it's the only one of my films that's become a classic."

While there is a boss, who is never named, his gang is a distributed network of young ladies and gentlemen, such as Mae and Jack, who entice innocents up to their apartments to party on down and get hooked. Jack is the real fiend of our story because this is 1936 and under the Hays Code women had to be kept in the kitchen or at least be decently victimised. He invites that nice Bill Harper boy, who goes to Dr Carroll's school, up to the apartment so that our real cautionary tale can begin. You see, Bill has a girl, Mary Lane, a girl who's as gosh darned nice as he is, and Jack doesn't realise that they're both giddy enough already without needing to smoke some evil weed and that they're already doomed to tragic deaths. We know this because during the token soppy scene at Mary's house, he shows her a copy of *Romeo and Juliet* and explains that he thinks of her while he studies it. Romantic suicide pact, anyone?

As you can imagine, this is the beginning of the end for a bunch of characters. First up is Jimmy, Bill's friend and Mary's kid brother. Jack has him drive over to the boss's place to pick up reefer and gives him a joint while he waits. "Let's go, Jack! I'm red hot!" he cries and speeds off like he's Steve McQueen, reaching a scarily excessive 45mph and knocking over a pedestrian. Bill himself starts an affair with Blanche, one of Jack's dealers, only to leave her bed to find another of them, Ralph, trying to rape Mary. He hallucinates that she's giving herself to him and attacks him, in a scuffle that leads to Mary's accidental death and his trial for her murder. Ralph himself becomes so whacked out that he beats Jack to death with a poker while Blanche giggles maniacally. Ralph is arrested and locked up for life in an asylum for the criminally insane. Tormented by her sins, Blanche confesses to the cops, then throws herself out of a window to her death.

What makes this film special isn't the overblown melodrama that follows Bill Harper's seduction into vice from the point of view of high school principals, federal agents, cops, judges and juries, as well as drug lords, gang members, addicts and foolish young Americans, though it's rare for a picture to run the gamut that widely. It's the degree of abandon by which it all unfolds.

We're supposed to feel warned by Jimmy's mad audition for *Death Race 2000*, Bill's hallucinations of Mary stripping for Ralph, Blanche's suicide leap and especially Ralph's attempts to outdo Dwight Frye at his most manic, but of course we just laugh instead. The funniest is surely when Blanche plays the piano to appease Ralph and he launches into a mantra of "Play it faster! Faster!" Even

I'm aware of how all of this is hilariously unrealistic and I've never watched it stoned. It's hardly difficult to imagine stoners watching this when high and chanting that mantra back at the screen.

What's difficult is to imagine today what impact this film might have had in 1936. Did what little audience *Tell the Children* got take Dr Carroll seriously and tell their children? Did they know that little about drugs in the decades before the US government pronounced their war on them?

Were the names involved recognisable? French director Louis J Gasnier was closing in on the end of his career, having discovered Max Linder, the chief inspiration for Charlie Chaplin, and built up Pathé as a film production company with highly popular serials including the most famous of them all, *The Perils of Pauline*, in 1914. Scriptwriter Arthur Hoerl had almost a hundred movies behind him. The actors were relatively new, but some went on to film careers. Dorothy Short, who plays Mary, did fairly well in B movies, though her legacy stems from this film and the fact that she married Dave O'Brien the same year, even though he played Ralph, her lunatic would-be rapist in it.

To us, it's impossible to look past the legacy the film has had, sparked by its rediscovery in the seventies and the genesis of its cult following on college campuses. Nowadays, the film is readily available from many companies and it's free to view online, where it continues to be popular. It spawned a musical comedy version off-Broadway in 2001, which itself became a movie in 2005. 20th Century Fox released a colorised version in 2004 which enhances the unintentional humour with very deliberate effects, each character's smoke shown in a different colour to represent their mood and level of addiction.

Nobody today could possibly take it seriously, even before factoring in that the War on Drugs is faltering, as states begin to legalise marijuana and the internet gives easy access to much more realistic information. The unfettered zeal *Reefer Madness* exudes can only get funnier as new audiences wonder why it, and films like it, were ever made.

Hopefully this book will provide a few answers.

Bibliography

While movie reviews are inherently based on personal opinion, there's also a factual side that has to be covered by research.

I tracked down details about these films from many sources. IMDb and Wikipedia are always useful but never absolute. I found some verification directly from the filmmakers or their relatives, more from commentary tracks on DVDs and a host of previously published articles and interviews in print and online, along with a film documentary.

In addition to sources cited within the reviews themselves, the following sources were especially useful in writing this book:

Brian Albright - liner notes for BCI's DVD box set *Drive-In Cult Classics Vol 2*

Mark Patrick Carducci - *Flying Saucers Over Hollywood: The Plan 9 Companion* (documentary film)

Paul Holbrook - *Making Child Bride* in *FilmFax Plus* (#124; Summer 2010)

Paul & Donna Parla - *Terror at Half Day: A Walk Down Randolph Street* in *Scary Monsters Magazine* (#74; April 2010)

Dalton Ross - *The Worst Movie Ever Made* in *Entertainment Weekly* (#824; 10th June, 2005)

Ed Tucker - *Velveeta Las Vegas! Ed Tucker Interiews Cult Movie Legend Ted V Mikels* at Crazed Fanboy (website)

Tom Weaver - *Return to Yucca Flats: Anthony Cardoza's Tor of the Desert* at The Astounding B Monster Archive (website)

About Hal C F Astell

While he still has a day job, Hal C F Astell is a teacher by blood and a writer by inclination, which gradually morphed him into a movie reviewer. He writes primarily for Apocalypse Later, his movie review site, but also for others who ask nicely.

Born and raised in the rain of England, he's still learning about the word 'heat' after nine years in Phoenix, AZ, where he lives with his better half, Dee, in a house full of assorted critters.

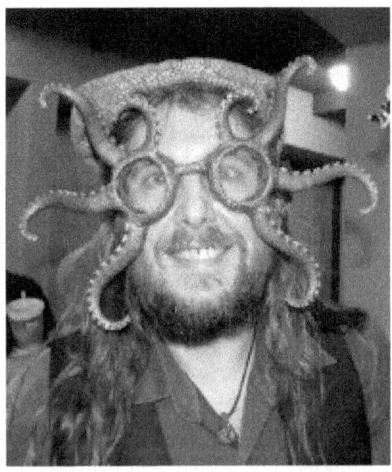

Photo by Dee Astell

Just in case you care, his favourite movie is Peter Jackson's *Bad Taste*, his favourite actor is Warren William and he thinks Carl Theodor Dreyer's *The Passion of Joan of Arc* is the best movie ever made. He's always happy to talk your ears off about the joys of precodes, fifties B pictures or Asian horror movies.

He's usually easy to find at film festivals, conventions and events because he's likely to be the only one in a kilt. He's friendly and doesn't bite unless asked.

About Apocalypse Later

Initially, Hal C F Astell wrote movie reviews for his own reference because he could never remember who the one good actor was in otherwise forgettable entries in long crime series from the forties. After a while, they became substantial enough for a dedicated blog.

As he was reviewing his way through each movie in the IMDb Top 250 list at the time for a project titled Apocalypse Later, that name promptly stuck. Originally it was just a joke with the punchline of reviewing *Apocalypse Now* last, but hey, there are worse names.

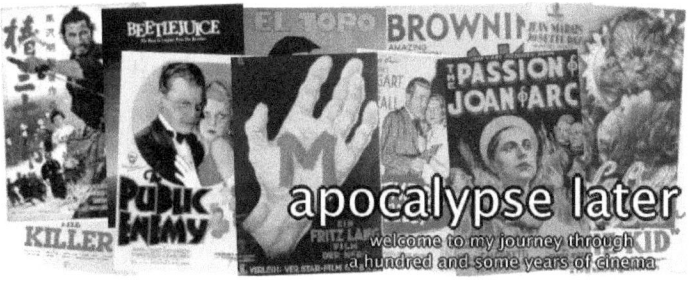

Over time, it became something of an anomaly, a movie review site full of reviews of movies most reviewers don't review. The focus is on silent films, classic films, foreign films, indie films, short films, microbudget films, obscure films, genre films, festival films... pretty much everything except modern mainstream films. It's also one of the rare sites reviewing new horror movies that doesn't kill your eyes with white text on a black background.

Think of it this way... if you want to read about *Frankenweenie*, the $39m Tim Burton animated feature from 2012, you can go to any one of ten thousand sites or even your local paper, but if you want to read about the original *Frankenweenie*, the black and white short film Burton made for Disney in 1984, you'll find that Apocalypse Later is one of the few that'll help you out. If you're interested in the unreleased movies Burton made with a bunch of colleagues at Disney who all needed to blow off steam, then there might just be somewhere other than Apocalypse Later but I wouldn't count on it. If there are any, they'll probably be good reads too.

www.ingramcontent.com/pod-product-compliance
Lightning Source LLC
Chambersburg PA
CBHW060838170526
45158CB00001B/180